Women in the Streets

Women in the Streets

ESSAYS ON SEX AND POWER

IN RENAISSANCE ITALY

Samuel K. Cohn Jr.

THE JOHNS HOPKINS UNIVERSITY PRESS   *Baltimore and London*

© 1996 The Johns Hopkins University Press
All rights reserved. Published 1996
Printed in the United States of America on acid-free paper

05 04 03 02 01 00 99 98 97 96   5 4 3 2 1

The Johns Hopkins University Press
2715 North Charles Street
Baltimore, Maryland 21218-4319
The Johns Hopkins Press Ltd., London

Library of Congress Cataloging-in-Publication Data will be found
at the end of this book.

A catalog record for this book is available from the British Library.

ISBN 0-8018-5308-7
ISBN 0-8018-5309-5 (pbk.)

To G. A. W.

Contents

List of Figures and Tables
ix

Acknowledgments
xi

*1. The Social History of Women
in the Renaissance*
I

*2. Women in the Streets,
Women in the Courts, in Early
Renaissance Florence*
16

*3. Last Wills: Family, Women, and the
Black Death in Central Italy*
39

*4. Women and the Counter Reformation
in Siena: Authority and Property
in the Family*
57

*5. Nuns and Dowry Funds: Women's
Choices in the Renaissance*
76

*6. Sex and Violence on the Periphery:
The Territorial State in Early
Renaissance Florence*
98

CONTENTS

7. Prosperity in the Countryside:
The Price Women Paid
137

Notes
167

Bibliography
217

Index
241

Figures and Tables

Map

Florentine Contado, Sample Villages   139

Figures

5.1   Bequests to Nuns: Individuals and Convents   82

5.2   Six Cities: Bequests to Nuns, Individuals and Convents   82

5.3   Values of Bequests to Nuns: Individuals and Convents   83

5.4   Bequests for Dowry Funds   89

6.1   Political and Sex Crimes: Sentences per Annum   126

6.2   Sex and Rebellion: Sentences per Annum   127

6.3   Sex and Politics: Percentages of Sentences   128

7.1   Household Wealth, 1371–1460: Animals and Land   140

7.2   Household Wealth, 1371–1460: Ratio of Mountains to Plains   141

7.3   Tax Rates on Wealth: Propertied Peasants   142

7.4   Peasant Migration   143

7.5   Population: Six Villages, Households   144

7.6   Population: Six Villages, Individuals   145

7.7   Sex Ratios, Infants: Plains   154

7.8   Sex Ratios, Infants: Plains and Mountains   155

7.9   Sex Ratios, Plains and Mountains: Infants   157

7.10   Sex Ratios: Adults Between 14 and 70   161

7.11   Sex Ratios: Elderly, Sixty and Older   163

Tables

2.1   Female Crime and Prosecution, 1344–1466   26

2.2   Female Crime: Plaintiffs and Defendants, 1344–1466   33

4.1   Piety by Gender, 1451–1800   62

5.1   Pious Bequests, by Sex, 1200–1425   79

5.2   Pious and Nonpious Bequests by Sex, 1200–1425   91

7.1   Population: Plains and Mountains, 1365–1460   144

7.2   Males and Females, Total Population, 1371–1460   152

7.3   Males and Females, by Age Group, 1371–1460   153

Acknowledgments

I am grateful to Albertina Vittoria and Alberto Merola for their encouragement over the past fifteen years and to *Studi Storici* for permission to translate and publish three of my essays for this volume. The essays are "Donne in piazza e donne in tribunale a Firenze nel rinascimento" (1981), 20:515–33; "Donne e controriforma a Siena: autorità e proprietà nella famiglia" (1991), 30:203–24; and "Le ultime volontà: famiglia, donne e peste nera nell'Italia centrale" (1991), 32:859–75. The first of these, "Women in the Streets, Women in the Courts," has been rewritten and expanded with new materials and reflections, while the other two have been only slightly retouched to include the notes and passages introduced in the versions of these essays included in my books *Death and Property in Siena, 1205–1800*, and *The Cult of Remembrance and the Black Death*. The other four essays in this volume are new.

I wish to thank the librarians and archivists at the Archivio di stato of Arezzo, Florence, Perugia, Pisa, and Siena; Archivio arcivescovile di Siena; L'Archivio della fraternità dei laici di Arezzo; Sacro convento di Assisi; Villa I Tatti, Florence; the Biblioteca comunale, Assisi; Archivio capitolare di Assisi; Archivio di San Pietro, Perugia; Biblioteca comunale, Siena; Istituto storico italiano per il medio evo, Rome; Biblioteca per la storia moderna e contemporanea, Rome; the British Library, London; the Warburg Library, London; and the Institute for Historical Research, London. Of the many friendly and efficient members of these institutions, I wish to single out Dottoressa Raffaella Zaccaria, Carla Zirilli, Amanda George, and the late *direttrice* of the Archivio di stato, Siena, Sonia Fineschi.

Finally, I wish to thank all those who struggled through early versions of these chapters: Trevor Dean, Kate Lowe, Marino Berengo, Lauro Martines, Sara Grieco Matthews, Chris Black, and especially Rudolph Binion, Christiane Klapisch-Zuber, and Genevieve Warwick, who went over this manuscript with more care and patience than they would wish to remember. The essays are dedicated to G. A. W., whose idea it was to publish them.

1. The Social History of Women in the Renaissance

These seven essays on women, sex, violence, and piety in Renaissance Italy draw on a large array of archival documentation and are bound together by a common theme and set of methods. All of them bespeak the darker side of the Renaissance and, in particular, the decline in Italian women's status from the late fourteenth century until the Counter-Reformation visitations of the 1570s. In this sense, these essays run directly counter to Jacob Burckhardt's claim for Renaissance Italy, "that women stood on a footing of perfect equality with men."[1]

Chapter 2, "Women in the Streets, Women in the Courts, in Early Renaissance Florence," shows that the latitude that women possessed for redressing their grievances shrank radically in the fifteenth century in at least two arenas: the streets, where they had used their own hands and curses to resolve conflict, and the criminal law courts of the city. Further, chapter 3, "Last Wills: Family, Women, and the Black Death in Central Italy," shows that Florence, which from Giorgio Vasari to Hans Baron has been seen as the capital of the Renaissance, was the worst place to have been born a woman, at least within central Italy and at least as far as women's control over property was concerned.[2]

In contrast not only with Burckhardt but also with more recent historians who cast the Counter Reformation as one of the great moments of Western misogyny, chapter 4, "Women and the Counter Reformation in Siena: Authority and Property in the Family," argues the opposite.[3] It shows an easing of the constraints imposed on women of all social ranks by the laws and customs of property descent established during the Renaissance. These Renaissance customs impressed on men and women alike the need to pass the bulk of their property down male bloodlines, thus forging a system of charity, piety, and salvation that came to worship male ancestors and the survival of the masculine line over the eternal health of the soul. The Counter Reformation, by what appears to have been an unintended alliance between women and the church, broke this hold over piety. As new forms of piety and charity began to emerge soon after the apostolic visitations of 1575, last wills and testaments show women at the forefront of new Counter Reformation forms of faith, sponsoring new charitable organizations that largely served the physical and spiritual needs of women. Both as donors and as recipients, women were at the forefront of the Counter Reformation.

Chapter 5, "Nuns and Dowry Funds: Women's Choices in the Renaissance," welds together the two chronological ends of these studies—the late Middle Ages and the Counter-Reformation. An analysis of testamentary acts shows married women championing the cloistered life long after such support had declined in men's wills. Women, moreover, resisted the new forms of Renaissance piety that came to fruition after the second strike of pestilence in 1362–63. Most important, they shunned dowry funds for selected nubile girls as a part of their charitable legacies. This chapter seeks to understand why women across Tuscany and Umbria were slow to adopt the new Renaissance forms of piety and religious ideology, in contrast to two centuries later, when they were the first to initiate new Counter-Reformation charities.

Chapter 6, "Sex and Violence on the Periphery: The Territorial State in Early Renaissance Florence," and chapter 7, "Prosperity in the Countryside: The Price Women Paid," take us from the cities to the countryside to expose "Renaissance civilization" to other vistas. The first of these shows the Renaissance state's brutality in its efforts to "civilize" its newly incorporated districts and argues that women and sex, so often shoved aside to the "private" sphere, were not divorced from questions of high politics and the growth of Florence's territorial state.[4] The last essay sheds light on the countryside's forms of family limitation—female infanticide, child abandonment, and the outmigration of older widows—as the price women paid for fifteenth-century prosperity, especially in the mountain hamlets on the borders of the Florentine territorial state.

In method and approach, these essays run counter to recent trends in women's historiography, especially as far as the Renaissance is concerned. Throughout, they use quantitative methods and ask repeatedly, from different angles, how woman's social status changed over the long period from the thirteenth to seventeenth centuries. In so doing, they use, criticize, and attempt to extend the approach of the new narrative history.[5] Chapter 2 begins with a remarkable story—a criminal case—of a socially undistinguished woman from the working-class parish of Sant'Ambrogio. Initially, she is indicted for slandering and perhaps assaulting a man from a nearby neighborhood, but midstream the court scribe changes the charge to blasphemy when the accused asserts her equality with, and even superiority over, men. This case is not left to speak for itself in microhistorical fashion but is interpreted through a statistical analysis of hundreds of unremarkable cases involving women from the mid-fourteenth through the fifteenth centuries. It finds that this woman's act was not an isolated event, at least in the insurrectionary mid- and late-fourteenth century. But, by the mid-fifteenth century, as far as the court blotters reveal, urban women had largely vanished from the streets in their efforts to resolve conflict directly with other men and women. The essay then interprets what the criminal data may have meant for laboring and artisan women more generally.

Chapter 6 also mingles remarkable stories of sex, violence, and revolution with changes in criminal statistics, not so much to derive conclusions about criminal behavior as to chart the Florentine courts' strategies to control and discipline their newly acquired territories. In the fashion of microhistory, these cases are offered to reveal the uses of violence, the importance of pictorial symbols, and the conflict over authority.[6] The latter could extend to the struggle between Florence and its adversaries over key words, matters that cannot be readily drawn with charts or demonstrated by chi-square tests. At the same time, however, chapter 6 attempts to expose the pitfalls of the microhistorical approach (which now dominates the study of criminal records). By placing the extraordinary in a systematic treatment of the ordinary, it shows how a good story or a set of unusual court cases do not always exemplify Edoardo Grendi's now famous oxymoron, the "eccezionale normale," but instead can easily lead to distorted visions of the past.[7] Through reading the remarkable within the context of the statistical, this essay draws new hypotheses about the growth of Renaissance territorial states, political acculturation, and the control of sexual mores.

Finally, these essays look at populations as a whole and not at elites, as has been, with few exceptions, the tendency of women's Renaissance history since the 1970s. The social bias of these essays, if any, runs in the opposite direction, stressing the worlds of workers, peasants, and commoners, especially in chapters 2, 6, and 7. To understand the intellectual context from which these essays derive, I sketch below achievements in women's history of the Renaissance made over the past two decades, largely in the fields of social and economic history.

The Question of Women's Status in the Renaissance

Joan Gadol Kelly's question, Did Women have a Renaissance? inspired historians to examine the position of women in Renaissance society at a new level of intensity.[8] It is not, however, as though women have been totally neglected as a subject in Renaissance historiography, as some women historians claim.[9] Indeed, Kelly's essay was written in vehement reaction to the prevailing interpretation of women in the Renaissance proposed in that most seminal of Renaissance studies, Burckhardt, *Civilization of the Renaissance in Italy*.[10]

Despite sharp criticism, Burckhardt's work continues to define the terrain of Renaissance historiography. Historians such as Richard Goldthwaite have reinvigorated the Burckhardtian position with new methods and new documents, lending credence to one of Burckhardt's most spectacular claims: female emancipation in the Renaissance.[11] Even historians such as Diane Owen Hughes and David Herlihy, who have argued vigorously that the late Middle Ages and the Renaissance saw a decline in women's status, have nonetheless found realms of women's activity and ideology that express Burckhardt's "defining feature of Renaissance culture"— individuality: for Hughes, women's self-fashioning in dress; for Herlihy, the charisma of women saints.[12]

Joan Kelly's essay came at a time when work on the Renaissance family was reaching a crescendo. Throughout the 1970s, David Herlihy and Christiane Klapisch-Zuber, Francis W. and Dale V. Kent, Anthony Molho and Julius Kirshner were drawing conclusions about the family in sharp contrast with those of Richard Goldthwaite.[13] Yet these conclusions bear less directly on the position of women than on questions of family structure, social mobility, and to what extent the Renaissance (or more precisely, Renaissance Florence) was a "traditional" or a "modern" society. Three years before the appearance of Kelly's essay, Lauro Martines beseeched Renaissance historians of the family to "bring the evidence to bear on women's perceptions."[14]

Joan Kelly came to the Renaissance from the side of high intellectual history. Her previous work had concentrated on Leon Battista Alberti, and the answers she gave to her seminal question came exclusively from tracts of high culture—Alberti, Castiglione, and traditions of courtly love poetry. Instead of wage series or laws and customs regarding changes in women's rights to their dowries, her comparisons juxtaposed the lives of Eleanor of Aquitaine and the women of Castiglione's *The Courtier*.[15] The question about Renaissance women quickly became a question about the Renaissance lady, Kelly claiming that the Renaissance lady, unlike her counterpart in the more liberating twelfth-century chanson de geste tradition, was "not desired, not loved for herself."[16]

Yet, despite her methods and materials, which hardly differed from those employed by Burckhardt more than a century earlier, the opening hypothesis of her essay begged for new research of a sociological character: "women as a group . . . experienced a contraction of social and personal options that men of their classes either did not, as was the case with the bourgeoisie, or did not experience as markedly, as was the case with the nobility."[17] Furthermore, her opening question, "How to establish, let alone measure, loss or gain with respect to the liberty of women," pointed more in the direction of the social sciences, even quantitative methods, than in the direction her argument followed.[18] Instead of social or economic realities—questions of power over property, control over the dowry, wages, and the composition of professions—Kelly's essay focused on how women are represented by male authors.

Had Kelly's essay appeared a decade earlier, subsequent scholarship in Renaissance women's history might have developed differently, at least in the United States. Historians might have directed their archival research more along the lines of social history, even quantitative history.[19] Yet, along with the general surge of interest in women's history in all periods, Kelly's essay came at a moment when historiographical fashion was changing. To use Lawrence Stone's terms, history writing in Europe as well as in the United States was turning away from "the big why questions" lodged in social science theory and supported by large data sets that cut through social classes.[20] Instead, historians and their public were discovering once again the charms and power of storytelling—but now informed by ethnography and an analysis scaled down to the individual or the local village level. Stone called it the revival of narrative. Italian historians centered largely in the journal *Quaderni Storici* call it "microstoria."[21]

Measurement was out and representation was in. Individual case studies drawn from legal briefs (*consilia*) or well-told stories, usually derived from criminal or inquisitional church records, suddenly acquired greater credibility among historical audiences than wage series or ratios of criminal indictments, which aroused news levels of skepticism.[22] In the hands of skilled historians, these microhistories enlivened a field that by the late 1970s may well have been overloaded by local and regional histories and family reconstitutions, whose theses were fast reaching points of diminishing returns. Certainly, undergraduates and academic publishing houses appreciated the breath of fresh air.

Women and Work

Yet the important strides in woman's history over the past decade, valuable as they are, largely skirt the questions of changes in economic and social position implied by Kelly's question, Did Women have a Renaissance? Questions of iconography, representation, and intellectual history (in most cases, how men have seen women) are certainly not irrelevant to this question and have spawned important and insightful contributions over the past decade.[23] Similarly, historians, principally in Italy, have explored changes in the power of women in cloistered life and as saints (a literature to which I pay closer attention in chapter 5).[24] Most important, Gabriella Zarri has charted the strides women made as writers and intellectuals during the fifteenth through eighteenth centuries, both inside and outside the cloistered life.[25] Further, she has shown that humanist tracts praising illustrative women increased in number through the fifteenth and sixteenth centuries and that they enumerated increasing numbers of contemporary heroines.[26] Finally, she has exposed the power of *sante vive* as charismatic prophetesses to rulers in courtly circles, such as that of the Ercole in Mantua, and especially during the troubled times of the late fifteenth and sixteenth centuries.[27]

However, answers to Kelly's question must turn in the first instance on social and economic history to analyze the multifaceted problem of changes in status and power.[28] To be sure, historians such as Richard Trexler, Judith Brown, Diane Owen Hughes, Isabelle Chabot, David Herlihy, and most important, Christiane Klapisch-Zuber have continued to view Renaissance women and changes in their representation within the context of social and economic history. Richard Trexler's pioneering studies on infanticide, nuns, old age homes, and prostitutes sketched aspects of the social worlds of Renaissance women in Florence that contrast markedly with the optimistic views held by Burckhardt and others.[29] From the perspective of women's occupations, David Herlihy was the first to chart a steady decline in women's place in the late medieval work force, from the thirteenth through the fifteenth centuries.[30]

Isabelle Chabot has focused more specifically on Florence after the Black Death, showing from the tax records that this change was not simply the result of overpopulation, which began to mount in the thirteenth century and which brought men and women into fiercer competition for positions in the same professions.[31] From her comparisons between the earliest surviving tax surveys (*estimi*) for the entire city of Florence (the Estimo del Sega of 1352 and 1355) with the *catasto* of 1427, she shows that it was after the Black Death, with labor scarcity caused by repeated attacks of plague, that women's participation in the work force dropped, perhaps even more sharply than in the earlier period of labor plenty. Franco Franceschi has corroborated this view from other sources, showing a shift in the hiring of weavers, away from women of the city and the surrounding countryside in favor of long-distance male migrants from the low countries and Germany.[32] These conclusions are further supported by other sources, such as baptismal records and notarial registers, which show the increasing importance of German workers in Florence especially through the second half of the fifteenth century.[33]

Finally, labor shortages alone fail to explain women's participation in the work force, when the Italian case is compared with labor markets across the Alps. In this respect, England appears to have been the mirror opposite of Florence, the post–Black Death epoch being a period of expansion and improvement in women's positions in the work force. According to P. J. P. Goldberg, "it was not until the economic expansion of the later fourteenth century that women moved beyond the most traditional female tasks, such as spinning and laundering, and outside the market-place."[34]

Looking back from seventeenth-century censuses of workers in the wool and silk industries, Judith Brown has confirmed the picture of declining participation by women in the Florentine work force during the fourteenth and fifteenth centuries.[35] Yet she seeks to disprove the Kelly thesis by redefining the Renaissance's chronology as the late sixteenth and seventeenth centuries. For the mid-fourteenth through the sixteenth centuries, her argument instead supports Kelly's: by comparison with the early seventeenth century (the full bloom of the Counter Reformation), women rarely worked outside the home. Her conclusions are further brought into question by the character of those occupations that women began to assume in increasing numbers during the seventeenth century. The rich array of women's occupations found in early fourteenth-century tax records do not reappear.[36] Instead, the new occupations filled by women and children in the seventeenth-century cloth industry of Florence were at the bottom of the occupational scale. As is often the case, women replaced men when a technological shift allowed them to be paid less than men had been paid.[37]

In terms of real wages, housing, and meals, did these new occupations mark an improvement in living standards for Florentine women over those of female domestic servants in the fifteenth century?[38] As Daniela Lombardi and Flores Reggiani have shown, domestic servitude, even if it had declined since its golden age in the fifteenth century, was still more prestigious for young women in seventeenth-century Italy than were jobs in the textile industries.[39] Why did men leave in droves professions in the textile industries during the late sixteenth and seventeenth centuries? What were the differentials in pay between men and women from the Renaissance through the seventeenth century? These are questions that Brown's seminal essay does not answer but that should have been sparked by her courageous claims.

The Dowry, Law, and Lineage

Over the past decade economic histories of the Renaissance have taken a backseat to other avenues of inquiry, even within the broad framework of social history. Much attention has been devoted recently to women's most important economic resource, the dowry, but that attention has come less from an economic perspective than from legal and anthropological concerns. Foremost among these historians for late medieval and Renaissance Florence are Julius Kirshner and Anthony Molho.[40] In a series of articles drawing on communal statutes and legal *consilia*, principally for Florence, Kirshner has shown the decline in women's control over their dowries and extradotal properties in the fourteenth and fifteenth centuries.[41] But against the legal historian of women, Manilo Bellomo,[42] Kirshner has argued that women in Renaissance Florence could find legal remedies to their economic problems within the context of Roman law—that wives could reclaim their dowries and other goods from insolvent husbands during marriage. He concludes: "In practice as well as in theory, wives were not merely passive victims incapable of preventing the loss of their dowries."[43]

Similarly, Thomas Kuehn sees in practice a brighter side to what he calls patriliny, as far as women were concerned, than might first strike the eye from a reading of legal statutes in the abstract. Although he has argued that Lombard law requiring women to be represented in legal contracts by a male protector, or *mundualdus*, persisted longer in Florence than elsewhere in Tuscany, he insists that this requirement made little difference to a woman's power to draft contracts.[44] And in "Some Ambiguities of Female Inheritance Ideology in the Renaissance," he concludes that "clearly a statute like *Qualiter mulier* in Florence did not remove all female inheritance rights. It limited and postponed them. . . . When there were no surviving sons or brothers, women could inherit."[45] Along with Kirshner and Kuehn, other historians such as Sharon Strocchia and Elaine Rosenthal have investigated the ways in which women found possibilities for power and room for maneuver within the structures of patrilineal descent in matters as diverse as property contracts and funerals.[46] But the questions remain whether these possibilities were becoming more or less constricted in the Renaissance and whether women in different social classes had greater or fewer possibilities for the disposition of their property in Florence as compared with other Italian city-states.

Finally, in an exemplary statistical analysis of the Monte delle doti archives, Anthony Molho has argued forcefully that Florentine elites married among themselves as tightly as any aristocratic elite in early modern Europe. Yet his work comments little on possible changes in the status of women, even elite women, except in challenging the claims of Klapisch-Zuber and Herlihy that women married downward in fifteenth-century Florence.[47]

Beyond Florence, Stanley Chojnacki and Diane Owen Hughes have mined archival records and published legal sources in order to reconstruct marriage patterns, to trace the growth of male lineage systems of property, and to investigate women's power and importance within these social structures. While Chojnacki concentrates on samples of patriciate women from fifteenth-century Venice, Hughes's comparison of women's property rights between magnate and artisan families in Genoa stretches over the long period between the thirteenth and the sixteenth centuries. Her research, moreover, is almost unique in investigating marriage patterns, dowry systems, and the changing status of women across the social spectrum of a late medieval urban society.[48] These historians' views of the changing status and strength of patrician women in these two maritime centers diverge radically, but it is not clear whether the differences in their findings result from the social structures and politics of these two city-states or from the authors' sources and interpretations of them.

For the late Middle ages, Hughes finds that urban life strengthened kinship bonds for magnates, while it weakened them for artisans. Among urban elites, a revival of the Roman dowry replaced the reverse dowry common to Lombard law and custom. Daughters of the aristocracy were effectively disinherited, and husbands, instead of endowing their wives through the countergift of the *morgengabe,* concentrated on funding the dowries of their own descent group.[49]

These changes in dowry custom, moreover, spilled beyond the confines of property rights, constraining liberties, from commerce to motherhood, for women in magnate families. In contrast to Genoa in the period of its early commercial rise, Hughes finds not one aristocratic wife who acted as her husband's business agent by the fourteenth century.[50] Moreover, wives of the aristocracy almost never made contracts without the counsel of their kinsmen.[51] By the late fourteenth century and increasingly so after the formation of the Genoese joint family residences called *alberghi,* lineage identity curtailed the aristocratic woman's choice of husband and even weakened the mother's position as "a full, natural parent."[52] After her husband's demise she was surrounded by his kinsmen and, unlike in Florence, did not return to her lineage. According to Hughes, aristocratic women came of age only at widowhood; only then might they begin to participate in the commercial world.[53]

By contrast, the daughters of artisans in Genoa married later and had greater freedom of marriage than the aristocracy; for artisans "the central blood tie was the marriage bond" and not the ancestral bonds of the male line.[54] Unlike the marriages of the aristocracy, the return gift (*antefactum*) of artisan husbands composed more than half the value of the dowry in 70 percent of the marriages sampled by Hughes for the thirteenth and fourteenth centuries, despite its limitation to half the dowry by a twelfth-century Genoese statute.

Stanley Chojnacki concentrates on that other powerful seafaring city-state of northern Italy, Venice, whose "serene" political stability is often contrasted with Genoa's factional strife. He is the one historian of the past decade to offer a consistent and coherent picture of women in the Renaissance more in keeping with that of Burckhardt and Goldthwaite, a view of the increasing power and importance of women, at least of patrician women.[55] Yet, in terms of the penetration of the Roman dowry, the importance of property descent down the male line, and the rise in dowry prices through the fifteenth century, the Venetian patriciate appears little different from Genoese magnates or, for that matter, elites studied in other Renaissance city-states.

In a series of essays that rely on both quantitative and anthropological analyses of last wills and testaments, dowry contracts, sumptuary legislation, registers of nobility, and marriage law, Chojnacki stresses the other side of male-dominated lineages: the importance of women in structuring elite social and political networks and the power of women within them.[56] According to Chojnacki, the "weaker sex" had an advantage in civil law cases that protected women's property, since out of concern for the lineage men protected the property interests of women.[57] In addition, the inflation of dowries from the late fourteenth through the fifteenth centuries meant that women exercised greater economic leverage and, by outliving their husbands, enjoyed increasing economic discretion over their husbands' property as the Renaissance advanced.[58]

In Venice (in contrast to fifteenth-century Florence, where dowries for the elite also began to increase, at least by midcentury), the increasing sizes of dowry-trousseau (*corredo*) packages caused women to marry upward, not downward.[59] According to Chojnacki, "the fifteenth-century patriciate's avid attention to patrilineal descent . . . was only one aspect of a denser, more intricate kinship system"; a young man of the patriciate depended on "a bilateral socialization that gave him a heritage of gratitude and loyalty to both his patrilineal and his matrilineal kinsmen."[60] Chojnacki finally suggests that Venice may have been distinctive among Renaissance Italian city-states, given the patriciate's "unusual degree of interclass cooperation and collective political discipline," which depended on the power of these patrician women and their competing family solidarities.[61] These ties, Chojnacki suggests, were the inner strength and possibly the inner secret of Venice's distinctive long-term political and social stability.

But unfortunately, like so much current Renaissance historiography, Chojnacki's essays do not venture beyond the single city-state into comparative history. We simply do not know whether or not other patriciates of fifteenth-century Italy also characterized by strong male lineage descent and rising dowries (which at this point in research seem ubiquitous for fifteenth-and sixteenth-century Italy) similarly possessed "dense and complex networks of associations" or "an overlapping system of horizontal ties that complemented the vertical ties of lineage."[62] Moreover, his conclusion—that "the role of women in re-enforcing this cross-lineage association, by means of their wealth and their flexible and unprejudiced social orientation, constituted their most significant function in early Renaissance Venice society"[63]—does not appear to distinguish Venetian patrician women from elite women elsewhere in northern Italy—not even in faction-ridden, male-dominated Genoa, where the political consequences for the city's stability and the social consequences for elite women appear to have been so different.

Studies of Renaissance women cry out for comparative analysis. Given their sharp differences combined with some underlying structural similarities, Venice and Genoa might prove a propitious place to begin. In addition, comparative research might go beyond the simple comparison of two or more city-states. Anglophone historians might profit from the essays of Gabriella Zarri, by exposing her analysis to comparative research. Did women of the nobility or even of other social strata fare better in Italian court societies than in republics? Did the strides in women's intellectual development in convents and the charismatic importance of prophetesses in princely courts parallel women's power more generally on the more humdrum levels of family life, access to occupations, property law, and the dowry? Or was it only these privileged few who were allowed to flourish? At the same time, were the avenues to power and prestige for the mass of other women narrowing?[64]

Christiane Klapisch-Zuber and Women in the Renaissance

The most sustained analysis of Renaissance women comes from Florence and now centers predominantly on the work of Christiane Klapisch-Zuber. More than any other scholar, she has studied the complexities of women's property and power in the Renaissance, interweaving analyses that combine the symbolic with the sociological. Two of her most cited essays, "The 'Cruel Mother'" and "The Griselda Complex," draw out the contradictions between fifteenth-century dowry systems and the ideals of patriarchy.[65] From reconstructions of large numbers of private diaries (*ricordanze*), which, like the sources utilized by Chojnacki, concentrate largely on the patriciate, Klapisch-Zuber illustrates that a married woman at the time of widowhood was stripped of satisfactory options. If she claimed her dowry and remarried, she was forced to abandon her children, provoking bitter memories and resentment on the part of sons such as Giovanni di Pagolo Morelli, who bemoaned his mother's cruel abandonment of him. Yet if she remained chaste and celibate, and stayed with her children, she risked violating the lineage strategies of her own blood kin, who, to use Klapisch-Zuber's words, forced her to become a "pawn," demanding that she "come out" of her dead husband's family and create, through remarriage, "a new circle of affines": "The image of the mother loyal to her children countered that of the sister or the daughter faithful to her blood relatives."[66]

Klapisch-Zuber's reconstruction of Boccaccio's story of Griselda, told through the *ricordanze* and letters of the Parenti and Strozzi families, exposes layers of marital ritual that cannot be perceived through the usual sources of notarial contracts and communal statutes. Unlike Chojnacki's claims for Venice and Giulia Calvi's for late sixteenth-century Florence, Klapisch-Zuber argues that the dowry system of fifteenth-century Florence was not bilateral but robbed women of their inheritances.[67]

Moreover, the multiple and complex layers of gifts and countergifts, rings and trousseaus and the mammoth expenditures on clothing and jewels that elite fifteenth-century patrician marriages demanded were not perfectly reciprocal but struck deep lineage imbalances, which, as in Boccaccio's story, could leave the newlywed bride literally stripped of all her possessions. Unlike the *antefactum* or the *donatio propter nuptias*, the husband's expenditure on the wedding—and in particular on his wife's jewelry and clothing—could amount to as much as a third of the dowry, but it was not the usual countergift of the Middle Ages. Instead, the husband remained "the virtual proprietor of the finery."[68] Similarly, the complex exchange of rings, which in the case of Giovenco di Giuliano Medici's accounts amounted to thirty between 1448 to 1492, was a man's game; the wife's kin did not participate in the offering of gifts, whose purpose was to integrate the young bride into the husband's lineage.[69] In the analysis of marriage ritual, Klapisch-Zuber is one of the few to add to her Florentine research a comparative dimension, showing the "limits of Florentine interlineage solidarity" in comparison to the Roman.[70]

Klapisch-Zuber's "The Name 'Remade'" goes beyond the marriage ritual to elaborate further the theme of lineage imbalance and the patrician woman's exclusion from the Florentine system of filiation and inheritance. Children's names came predominantly from the paternal side, forming "a sort of family patrimony," and reflected an ancestor worship in which babies were "reincarnations" spanning "the interests among the living and the group of their dead."[71]

Klapisch-Zuber's exhaustive treatment of surviving family diaries concentrates on the milieu that in large part produced them—the Florentine patriciate, but from these rich deposits of everyday life she extends her analysis to both the countryside and the servant class.[72] The lives of domestic servants are possibly among the few bright moments of social change for women in Renaissance Florence, as salaries and even working conditions improved for this stratum of women (largely recruited from the countryside). Yet Klapisch-Zuber also shows a darker side to servant life, such as when young girls entered into long-term contracts for domestic servitude in patrician homes with the promise of a dowry at the end of their contracts. Often, these dowries were never delivered.[73] Futhermore, the contracts of wet nurses, the best paid of all servants, forced country women to abandon their own babies to nourish those of the Florentine patriciate.[74]

The farming out of infants to wet nurses in the countryside also had negative psychological consequences for women of the urban elite, as Klapisch-Zuber deftly illustrates in her essay on dolls. These plaster and papier-maché figures of the baby Jesus were not the playthings of infants and young girls but were for cuddling by young mothers and nuns, to compensate for the absence of their own infant children—in the case of nuns because of their monastic vows, in the case of patrician mothers because of the farming out of their babies immediately after birth to wet nurses in the countryside.[75] Further, in the realm of women's rituals, Klapisch-Zuber shows that the iconography of marriage chests (*cassoni*) and painted trays presented to new mothers (*deschi da parto*) celebrated "amorous loyalty, female fertility, and the desires for the continuity of the family line but never the relationship of the mother with her child."[76]

As Klapisch-Zuber states in her preface to the English collection of her essays, her materials reflect "the gradual drift" of her interests and approach, since her collaborative work on the *catasto* of 1427 with David Herlihy, away from "figures and graphs" and toward "the symbolic."[77] And in her introduction to volume 2 of *A History of Women in the West*, she points out that "economic and social history are perhaps the areas least affected by the outpouring of recent research" on women in the Middle Ages.[78]

This collection of my essays on women takes a tack counter to the trends of the 1980s; they are quantitative and sociological in orientation and address problems comparatively, over time and space, and focus on those social classes largely missing from the recent historiography of Renaissance women—artisans, laborers, and peasants. Florence, the city-state that has spawned so many generalizations about Renaissance women, is also, here, the center of the investigation. Yet my forays into a comparative analysis of neighboring territories show how perilous such generalizations from Florence can be. Not only was this city and its territory atypical, it may well have been one of the worst places to have been born a women in the Italian Renaissance.

From archival research and the use of quantitative methods, these essays uncover a multifaceted view of women's social worlds not seen from the letters of patrician ladies or the prescriptive judgments of a Renaissance moralist, whether he be the Trecento merchant Paolo da Certaldo or the Quattrocento friar San Bernardino da Siena. Within the larger historical contexts of the Black Death, the growth of territorial states, and the Counter Reformation, these essays chart societal changes in law, the structure and accessibility of the criminal courts to women, and the customs and mentalities that shaped women's lot, from infanticide to the control of sexual mores in the territorial state. At the same time, women are the protagonists of these essays, whether the issue is the resolution of conflict in the streets of Florence, their power over their dowries, or their charity and beliefs, from support of other women to the salvation of their own souls.

These essays are presented with the hope of raising new questions and of inspiring new archival research on women's status across broad stretches of Renaissance life, in terms of both social class and geography. Further, they are presented in the spirit announced by the general editors of *A History of Women in the West*, Georges Duby and Michelle Perrot: "Our history is "feminist" in that its outlook is egalitarian; its intention is to be open to the variety of interpretations. . . . Ours is a plural history: a history of *women* as seen from many different points of view."[79]

2. *Women in the Streets, Women in the Courts, in Early Renaissance Florence*

On 18 June 1375, the *podestà* of Florence accused Filippa, the daughter of Matteo, who resided in the artisan parish of Sant'Ambrogio, of having slandered Piero di Cianchino, who lived in the nearby parish of San Simone.[1] According to the court's record, Filippa had called Piero "Filth, traitor, thief." The court did not make clear the reasons for her outrage, but Piero responded, "If you were a man, instead of a woman, you would not be able to say these words to me." With this challenge, Filippa then threatened: "I am a woman, and I will shame you all the same." At this point, the notary interrupted the record and transformed what had begun as a simple case of slander into one of blasphemy. After several words concerning Christ and "His Mother, the ever-virginal Mary," placing God and Piero's own mother on the same plane as being equally responsible for bringing the wretch Piero into the world, Filippa then proclaimed: "What a feast God and the mother who brought you into this world would have, had they given me the heart to have more men [like you] to kill than you could have over to dinner." Without explanation, the court of the *podestà* absolved Filippa of all the charges.[2]

Though possibly from a different social class and certainly with a different tone, the confidence and assertiveness of this Filippa is not far removed from that of another Tuscan Trecento Filippa, a fictive one from the *Decameron,* day 6, story 7. Charged to be burnt because of adultery, Boccaccio's Filippa, "senza sbigottire punto," pleaded her case before the *podestà* of Prato, asserting the equality of men and women before the law,

16

and similarly won her case, even to the extent of changing adultery law in Prato: "However, as I am sure you will know, every man and woman should be equal before the law, and laws must have the consent of those who are affected by them. These conditions are not fulfilled in the present instance, because this law only applies to us poor women."[3] Yet the real-life Filippa went beyond the cool and collected logic of Boccaccio's smart adultress. The last curse of the Filippa from the streets of Florence sounds strange.[4] Was it a non sequitur, that she would kill more men "than you could have over to dinner"? Can we hypothesize that the dinner table, even for artisans and laborers in late Trecento Florence, was a strictly masculine affair, as in some contemporary African societies or as in early modern Corsica and Languedoc?[5]

From this case, and from Filippa's bizarre threat, one thing is certain: a woman not of the aristocracy or the merchant class, but rather identified only by a patronymic and from an artisan parish of Florence, proudly declared herself to be a woman and as a woman completely capable of confronting publicly a man in the streets of Florence. At the end of the notary's concise account, this woman's initial assertiveness takes on violent antimasculine tones. What do we make of this incident? Was it simply an isolated case of a crazy woman or can it be placed in the larger context of thousands of criminal cases that survive in the Florentine archives from the end of the Middle Ages and the beginning of the Renaissance?

Two facts are worth noting from this episode: one is Filippa's alleged comportment, her self-confidence as a woman, and her declaration of equality, even superiority, with respect to men; the other is the outcome of the case, the fact that it came to trial and was adjudicated in her favor. The man, Piero, lost his case against a woman from the lower classes. This essay examines the possibilities for women of redressing their grievances and defending themselves both in the streets and in the criminal courts of early Renaissance Florence.[6]

At first glance, the self-confidence of Filippa and her victorious defense in the court of the *podestà* might appear only to confirm (or even to expand to the lower classes) one of Jacob Burckhardt's theses, asserted more than a hundred and thirty years ago—the equality of the sexes in Renaissance civilization: "To understand the higher forms of social intercourse at this period, we must keep before our minds the fact that women stood on a footing of perfect equality with men. . . . There was no question of 'women's rights' or female emancipation, simply because the thing itself was a matter of course."[7]

But even without taking into consideration new data, Burckhardt's thesis on the position of women in the Renaissance raises at least three problems. First, one needs to discuss the periodization of his "Renaissance civilization." When did the Renaissance begin and end? Was the period 1300–ca. 1525 (according to Burckhardt's literary sources) a monolithic period without sharp cleavages or developments in the status of women? Second, there arises the problem of Burckhardt's own frame of reference, the values and norms of high-bourgeois culture in nineteenth-century Switzerland. His personal views on women might be read between the lines by examining the section of *The Civilization of the Renaissance* that immediately follows his proclamation of the equality of the sexes in Renaissance Italy. The principal source for this section, entitled "Domestic Life," is book 3 of Alberti's *Books on the Family*, "Economicus." Here, Burckhardt examines intergenerational male relations and the "praise of country life."[8] But even a passing reading of Alberti's book 3 shows that its principal theme concerns, instead, the relationship between husbands and wives, and the book's lesson to future generations of Alberti clearly proclaims the inferiority of women. The nephew, Leonardo, recapitulates what he has learned from the Alberti patriarch, Giannozzo:

> The character of men is stronger than that of women and can bear the attacks of enemies better, can stand strain longer, is more constant under stress. Therefore men have the freedom to travel with honor in foreign lands, acquiring and gathering the goods of fortune. Women, on the other hand, are almost all timid by nature, soft, slow, and therefore more useful when they sit still and watch over our things. It is as though nature thus provided for our well-being, arranging for men to bring things home and for women to guard them. The woman, as she remains locked up at home, should watch over our things by staying at her post, by diligent care and watchfulness.[9]

The paterfamilias, Giannozzo degli Alberti, then examines more closely the question of the position of women, who ought to know that their place is in the home and not in the streets of Florence. Here, although with a difference in exposition, the ideology of the patrician Alberti approximates that of the artisan Piero di Cianchino's warning to his adversary, Filippa, fifty years earlier. The old patriarch, Giannozzo, tells his nephew how he had tenderly instructed his wife in the first days of their marriage:

> Now, there are only two ways of dealing with enemies, my dear. One is to defeat them in open fight; the other is flight, if one is weak. Men ought if possible to fight and win, but women have no alternative but flight for their safety. Flee, therefore, and do not let your eye rest on any enemy of ours. Call only him a friend whom I honor when he is present and praise when he is absent.[10]

Finally, the possible parallels and differences between an Alberti and the antagonist Piero leads to the third question about Burckhardt's thesis: Can we talk about equality of the sexes and female emancipation (even among the elites) from examining only texts written by patricians exclusively for the conduct of aristocratic women? Burckhardt's evidence regards the education of women only from the highest echelons of Renaissance society, indeed mostly not even from republics such as Florence but from courtly societies: the "individuality" of the wives of *condottieri* and the courtly conversation of ladies such as Isabella Gonzaga.[11]

Other scholars relying largely on literary evidence and the letters of elite women have been no less rash than Burckhardt in generalizing their readings of late medieval and Renaissance literature to embrace the condition and behavior of all women of the Renaissance. For example, at the turn of the century Isidoro del Lungo claimed that Dante's idealization of Beatrice illustrates the position of "every woman" in late medieval Florence and the high esteem in which Renaissance women were held.[12] More recent historians continue to interpret the same literary sources and letters across social classes. Richard Goldthwaite has reintroduced the Burckhardtian interpretation of the equality between the sexes in Renaissance Florence.[13] And Lauro Martines, despite his close attention to matters of class and gender, has drawn conclusions about the "feminine intuition" of Renaissance women based largely on the letters of Alessandra Strozzi, a woman from the highest echelons of the Florentine *ottimati*, whose social class might not even be representative of the Florentine ruling class more generally.[14]

Certainly, other historians of Florence have been more cautious about generalizing across social classes from sources that pertain exclusively to the elites. In forming their views about Renaissance women and relations between the sexes, historians have also begun to go beyond literary texts, the letters of elite women, and interpretations taken from manner books and other idealized portraits of women. They have turned to more systematic analyses of sources that record changes in the entry of women into convents, the administration of homes for single women, the recruitment and comportment of prostitutes, ages at marriage, and variations in the values of dowries.[15] Yet, like their nineteenth-century predecessors, these studies also focus either predominantly on merchant and aristocratic women or on high-class courtesans.

In this chapter I will shift the points of reference. Instead of the usual reflections on the habits of the patriciate, their letters and diaries and what might be interpreted from them about the status of women, I turn to sources that center largely on men and women from artisan, worker, and peasant families—criminal court records of Florence from the mid-fourteenth through the fifteenth centuries. As we will soon see, laborers were not the only victims or prosecutors in these tribunals. Nonetheless, the statistics that emerge from these cases, especially for the fourteenth century, shed more light on life in the streets of Florence than on the pomp and circumstance of its patrician loggias and palaces.

Certainly, research on criminal records does not give a complete view of changes in women's status and power during the Renaissance. Such a study does not even begin to penetrate certain vital areas of social interaction, such as the place of work.[16] But, this study represents only a beginning, one that I hope will encourage historians interested in the history of women to go beyond diaries, letters, and other sources that reflect almost exclusively the affairs of celebrated Renaissance patricians and educated prostitutes.

Women's appearances in the criminal tribunals and their actions reported in these records chronicle the deterioration in women's status and power (and especially that of laboring women) over the course of the Renaissance in two arenas: the criminal courts and the streets of Florence. With the consolidation of Medici power by the mid-fifteenth century, women had less access to the criminal courts to resolve their conflicts with men or with other women than they had possessed earlier, in the more open and democratic second half of the fourteenth century. And by the mid-Quattrocento, many fewer women dared to defend themselves or to go on the offensive as Filippa di Matteo did on the eve of the Ciompi revolt of 1378. As with the laboring classes more generally, women (and especially laboring women) suffered the consequences of a change in the balance of power that followed the defeat of the Ciompi in 1382 and the consequent development of the Renaissance state during the fifteenth century.[17]

To propose this hypothesis, I have compiled two initial samples of court cases: the first one covers the period 1343–78, a period of insurrection culminating in the revolt of the Ciompi. The other sample covers a period of relative social calm, comprising the last years of Cosimo de' Medici's rule, 1455–66. A comparison of these two periods of Florentine history, however, is made difficult by changes in documentation. These differences made it necessary to collect different types of samples. By the middle of the Quattrocento, the number of cases tried by the medieval tribunals—the *podestà*, the *capitano del popolo*, and the *esecutore degli ordinamenti di giustizia*—had shrunk dramatically, from more than fifteen hundred cases annually before the Black Death to little more than a hundred annually in the years 1455 to 1466.[18] Two factors largely determined these variations over time: (1) the decline in population; by the mid-Quattrocento the population of Florence was less than half of what it had been on the eve of the Black Death and perhaps as little as one-third the population of Florence at its height; and (2) changes in the system of Florentine criminal justice.[19] Of these judicial changes, the most important was the creation of a new summary court, the *otto di guardia*, in 1378.

Throughout the Quattrocento, the prestige and power of this tribunal, along with the number of cases that fell into its ambit, increased.[20] Finally, in 1502 the Florentine government abolished the remaining medieval courts, the *capitano del popolo* and the *podestà*, and the *otto* monopolized the adjudication of criminal cases in the city of Florence. Yet, until the last third of the fifteenth century (which goes beyond the period of my analysis) only three slim volumes of deliberations and sentences survive from the *otto*, one for the year 1406–7 and the other two for an eight-month period in 1460. In addition, the summary character of these cases restricts but does not eliminate a comparative analysis between the end of the fourteenth century and the middle of the fifteenth.

Because of the enormous case loads of the first period, I selected two sample years to represent the Trecento revolutionary phase of Florentine history. The first of these, the year 1344–45, is within that period, 1343–48, that Gene Brucker sees as the years of most severe social disorder until the revolt of the Ciompi in 1378.[21] It began with major food riots in 1343 and encapsulated one of the most remarkable of preindustrial insurrections: the general strike of wool workers, who had been organized by one of the workers, Ciuto Brandini, in 1343. In the second sample year, 1374–75, the plague returned to Florence for the third time, and bread prices soared. Yet despite these economic conditions and a major crisis in Florentine foreign affairs with the papacy,[22] it was a year of relative social calm before the storm of artisan action that would lead three years later to the Ciompi revolt. Neither the chroniclers nor the criminal records narrate major incidents of urban unrest for this year of economic crisis and pestilence.[23] As for the mid-Quattrocento sample, the diminished case loads make it feasible to examine all the surviving *filze* from the medieval tribunals. In the twelve-year period, 1455–66, sixteen semesters, or eight years, of criminal sentences survive. From these samples, I selected only criminal acts that involve at least one Florentine inhabitant, either as the victim, the prosecutor or the defendant.

The number of women who appear in the medieval tribunals—whether as the accused, the plaintiff, or the victim—drops sharply over time. In 1344–45, 223 women appeared in criminal cases. In 1374–75, after three waves of the Black Death, their number fell dramatically, to 40. Even if we take into account the demographic toll of the Black Death, this figure still indicates a notable decline in the presence of women. To calculate more precisely the per capita number of women who appeared in the courts in these two periods, the nearest point of demographic reference is the *estimo* of 1379 (which comprises 13,779 households, or around 60,000 individuals). Yet, the population figure of 1379 represents a temporary upsurge in population. Because of plague and emigration from the city to the countryside, the Florentine city population probably touched one of its lowest points in 1374–75. The contemporary chronicler Marchionne di Coppo Stefani reports that large numbers of families fled the plague, leaving their homes in the city to return temporarily to their villages of birth in the *contado* or elsewhere in the countryside.[24] According to Richard Goldthwaite, the price of grain in that year reached its highest point.[25] Indeed, the flight to the countryside may not have been only to flee from pestilence but also to find food. But with the end of pestilence, the rural population of the nearby villages began to flow back to their former neighborhoods within the city walls. Even if the Florentine population in the plague year 1374–75 was only half of what it was on the eve of the Black Death, women in the criminal tribunals declined by almost two-thirds (64%) as a proportion of the population.

The third point of observation, 1455–66, witnesses yet an even sharper diminution of women in the criminal tribunals. For these twelve years (eight years of sentences), only 51 cases, or 6.38 a year, involved a woman—a decline of 84 percent from the 1374–75 records. But how did the frequency of women's appearance in the criminal tribunals vary in relation to the total number of cases in these three periods of analysis? Did this decline in female criminality and prosecution result merely from changes in the organization of justice and the forces of social repression? Was it a general decline in criminal prosecution, which affected all cases without regard for sex?

If the fragmentary remains of the *otto di guardia*'s sentences are considered, the transformation of the Florentine criminal system may well account for the difference in number of cases between the Trecento and the mid-Quattrocento. When all criminal cases regardless of sex are considered, the growth of the *otto di guardia*'s case load in the fifteenth century (calculated from the four-month *filza* of 1460) is enough to compensate for the brusque decline in the number of cases adjudicated in the other tribunals.[26] Given this shift in criminal adjudication, the second point of observation, 1374–75, becomes the anomaly as far as the number of crimes per capita for men and women is concerned, and the difference in the total case loads between 1374–75 and the mid-Quattrocento becomes insignificant.[27]

What, then, can be said of the changes in case loads that involved exclusively women? As has been mentioned, the *otto* was a court of summary justice. Unlike the other medieval tribunals—in which the notaries specified the accused, the prosecution, the sequence of events, and when and where the crime occurred—the *otto* usually specified only the name of the accused, the sentence, and in some instances the names of those injured. Yet the summary character of the *otto* does not present insurmountable problems for estimating the appearance of women, as it does for calculating changes in the types of crime committed. In the *otto*'s deliberations, it is possible to establish the sex of the accused and that of the injured party when they are named. In all these cases (unlike those in the other medieval courts, where peasants and citizens alike could bring a case to trial), the plaintiff for the *otto* was the state.

In the four-month period May–August 1460, only seven city crime cases involved women. What is more, the majority of these women were not defendants but the injured parties. In this same period, the *otto* handed out at least 153 sentences.[28] Despite the fact that a small percentage of those involved were women (4.6%), the *otto* cases significantly change the annual number of cases involving women: instead of less that seven cases per annum, around thirty-five cases a year involved women.

Although this second look at the per capita number of female cases still shows a decline from the end of the Trecento to the middle of the fifteenth century, the difference now appears negligible, especially in comparison to the huge difference between the two periods of the Trecento, before and after the Black Death of 1348. Does the absolute difference between these two periods, 1344–45 and 1374–75, reflect a change in women's access to the criminal courts and their presence in the streets for redressing their grievances by extralegal means?

How can we account for the sharp decline in case loads, both the total number and those involving women, from the years just before the Black Death to the eve of the revolt of the Ciompi (1378)? The fall is dramatic even after adjusting for the steep decline in population caused by three waves of pestilence. In the Trecento, the most important organizations for criminal arrests were not the centralized bodies of the *capitano* and the *podestà*; rather, justice rested on a community system that revolved around the parish and depended on locally elected lay chaplains.[29] Unlike the period 1344–45, the registers of the *podestà* and the *capitano* in 1374–75 are filled with cases in which entire parish communities were fined individually or collectively for neglecting to ring the church bells to raise the hue and cry for arresting a bandit, thief, or murderer.

Such a breakdown in the old communitarian forms of obedience and surveillance may well lie behind the deterioration of Florentine control over its urban population on the eve of the Ciompi and, in reaction, may have led to the swift centralization of police functions in Florence during the late Trecento and Quattrocento. By the mid-fifteenth century, lay chaplains had disappeared from the criminal records of Florence, but their decline began before the revolt of the Ciompi.[30] In addition, the change in the prosecution and denunciation of criminal cases may also explain, at least in part, the general decline in the number of cases brought to trial for both men and women in the year 1374–75. Between these two periods of the Trecento, the number of sentences collapsed from 1,682 to 440, and cases involving at least one resident from the city of Florence diminished from 656 to 206 annually.[31]

This decline in criminal cases and its implications for changes in law enforcement did not affect women much differently from men, at least before the revolt of the Ciompi. When the number of cases involving at least one city woman are compared to the total number of cases involving a Florentine resident, no significant change appears between the two Trecento samples. Before the Black Death of 1348, women appear in 22 percent of the cases; on the eve of the Ciompi revolt, they appear in 17 percent of the cases. In other words, the fall in the number of crimes adjudicated (caused no doubt by demographic factors but perhaps even more so by a general breakdown in Florentine police surveillance) affected men and women almost equally. But despite these social transformations, the difference in the proportions of women in the courts between these two dates is insignificant.[32]

On the other hand, the registers from the medieval criminal tribunals of the mid-Quattrocento tell another story: the percentage of women who appeared in these courts falls significantly, to 11 percent; that is, to less than two-thirds of the 1374–75 figure and to only half of the number of cases in the period before 1348.[33] Moreover, when the figures from the surviving registers of the *otto di guardia* are added to the other tribunals, the differences between the Trecento and the mid-Quattrocento become even more accentuated: women appeared in less than 8 percent of all urban criminal cases in the mid-Quattrocento, whether as plaintiffs or defendants—that is, less than half as often as on the eve of the Ciompi revolt and only a little more than one-third during the pre–Black Death period.[34]

The historian can go beyond these comparisons by dividing the cases into categories of crime and comparing them over time. When all cases regardless of sex are compared, little difference is seen between the two periods of the Trecento.[35] On the other hand, striking differences emerge in the patterns of criminality between the Trecento and the mid-Quattrocento. Above all, the relative numbers of assault and battery cases fell precipitously. For all the periods here examined, the crime that overwhelmingly involved the lower classes—peasants, artisans, and urban laborers—is assault.[36] By the mid-Quattrocento, the class nature of conflict in the courts becames more marked; the crimes in which the well-off prosecuted the poor rise. These comprise primarily cases of indebtedness and of urban landlords prosecuting their peasants for cutting or damaging trees, stealing wood, pasturing animals on planted fields, poaching, setting fires, trespassing, breaking *mezzadria* (sharecropping) contracts, and neglecting to work fields and vineyards.[37]

Similar to these overall trends, a close proximity exists in the pattern of

TABLE 2.1. Female Crime and Prosecution, 1344–1466

Type of Crime	1344–1345	1374–1375	1455–1466
Assault and battery			
Of total crime (%)	38.12	47.50	25.49
Women prosecuted	85	19	13
Total prosecutions	402	91	79
Female crime (%)	21.14	20.88	16.46
Murder			
Of total crime (%)	3.14	5.00	7.84
Women prosecuted	7	2	4
Total prosecutions	23	9	27
Female crime (%)	30.43	22.22	14.81
Theft			
Of total crime (%)	6.28	2.50	3.92
Women prosecuted	14	1	2
Total prosecutions	40	8	24
Female crime (%)	35.00	12.50	8.33
Rural crime			
Of total crime (%)	7.17	12.50	23.53
Women prosecuted	16	5	12
Total prosecutions	101	27	88
Female crime (%)	15.84	18.52	13.64
Burglary			
Of total crime (%)	9.42	5.00	7.84
Women prosecuted	21	2	4
Total prosecutions	62	20	19
Female crime (%)	33.87	10.00	21.05
Crimes of immorality			
Of total crime (%)	13.45	17.50	9.80
Women prosecuted	30	7	5
Total prosecutions	38	9	24
Female crime (%)	78.95	77.78	20.83
Indebtedness			
Of total crime (%)	9.87	10.00	13.73
Women prosecuted	22	4	7
Total prosecutions	145	28	19
Female crime (%)	15.17	14.29	36.84
Other			
Of total crime (%)	12.56	0.00	7.84
Women prosecuted	28	0	4
Total prosecutions	212	41	83
Female crime (%)	13.21	0.00	4.82

Type of Crime	1344–1345	1374–1375	1455–1466
SUMMARY			
Women prosecuted	223	40	51
Total prosecutions	1,023	233	363
Female crime (%)	21.80	17.17	14.05

crime involving women in the two periods of the Trecento, while both contrast sharply with the pattern in the mid-Quattrocento.[38] Only theft and burglary diverge significantly from the general pattern of resemblance and diversity among these three periods, but in both of these categories the number of cases involving women becomes negligible after the Black Death (see table 2.1) The two numerically most important criminal categories give a sharper picture of the changes in criminality involving women: crimes of assault and battery and crimes in which urban landlords prosecuted peasants for rural misdemeanors. In all three periods, women, like men, whether as defendants or plaintiffs, appeared in cases of assault and battery more than in any other crime; but over the long term, important changes occurred in the relative predominance of these crimes. Before the Black Death, more than 38 percent of all cases involving women were crimes of assault and battery. At the end of the Trecento, the proportion of these acts of physical aggression increased to nearly 50 percent. In contrast, by the mid-Quattrocento, their proportion had fallen to only 25 percent.

This drop between the Trecento and the Quattrocento is balanced by an increase in the proportion of women as defendants or plaintiffs in rural crime. Before the Black Death little more than 7 percent of all feminine criminal cases concerned urban property holders prosecuting peasants from the surrounding countryside; in 1374–75 it increased to 12.5 percent, then in the mid-Quattrocento the proportion of these urban prosecutions almost doubled, to 25 percent of all crimes involving women.

By the mid-Quattrocento, the crimes that declined sharply were those, like assault and battery, in which woman laborers, artisans, and in general those below the echelons of the patriciate predominated. Thus, to prosecute their assailants and those who threatened their children (and, on occasion, their husbands), women of the laboring classes appear to have had even less access to the criminal courts than their aggregate numbers would suggest.[39] In the fifteenth century, the vacuum was filled largely by a shift to cases involving privileged urban women landowners, who used the tribunals to protect their rural propertied interests. The proportion of women plaintiffs with family names (the most easily recognized sign of elite status in these fourteenth- and fifteenth-century records) further illustrates the shift in the class nature of these cases.[40] For 1344–45, only 12.5 percent of women prosecuting peasants for rural misdemeanors bore a family name, and in 1374–75 not a single woman had one. But, with the mid-Quattrocento, the majority of these landowning women were no longer the widows of artisans or small shopkeepers; instead, almost 60 percent of them possessed prestigious Florentine names, such as Strozzi, Rucellai, and Medici.

The difference between these two principal categories of criminality, the shift from those crimes that concerned most women, especially those from the laboring classes, to crimes that represented only a thin stratum (for the most part widows of patrician origin)—underscores the sharp decline in laboring women's access to the courts and other legal means to defend themselves and their children. The change paralleled the centralization of the apparatuses of criminal justice and police surveillance (the growth of new summary courts and the changes in jurisprudence within the old medieval tribunals) from the eve of the Ciompi to the end of Cosimo de' Medici's government.[41]

This trend, moreover, was linked to other changes in criminal procedure that limited working women's access to the tribunals. In the fourteenth century, women who appeared in court cases represented themselves. Rarely did it seem necessary that they be represented by a male protector (*mundualdus*), as required by Lombard law, or by a lawyer (*procuratore*).[42] Yet, by the mid-fifteenth century, legal practice and custom had changed; Renaissance Florence had revived Lombard law at the expense of Roman law, further constraining the freedom and economic interests of women, from dowry law to the redactions of notarial contracts.[43] According to the communal statutes of 1415, women were no longer allowed to defend their interests in civil courts unless they were represented by a *mundualdus* or a *procuratore*.[44] And although these statutes did not specify the same for criminal cases, by the mid-Quattrocento, unlike the period before the Ciompi revolt, women rarely appeared in criminal cases without them.

Two other statistics illuminate the mid-fifteenth-century decline in women's accessibility to the courts and their opportunities for judicial action against assailants, principally male. The first is the percentage of murders involving women in relation to the number of assault and battery cases involving women. Historically, homicide is the crime least susceptible to changes in morality, custom, or law.[45] Almost always, it has been prosecuted with the most zeal; moreover, the evidence—the body—is more difficult to hide than the evidence in most other crimes. Murders are not usually committed by professionals but are emotive and often unpremeditated, arising from spontaneous disputes between friends, neighbors, or family members.[46]

In assault and battery, occasionally (and often later) the victim dies, and the case becomes reclassified from assault to murder.[47] Indeed, contemporary communal statutes occasionally recognized this contingent relationship between assault and murder.[48] Therefore, if the levels of surveillance and police activity and the practice of the tribunals remain roughly the same over time, a relatively stable relationship ought to persist between cases of homicide involving women and assault and battery involving women. But to the contrary, the number of homicide cases between the Trecento and the Quattrocento relative to assault and battery increased by more than 300 percent. Thus, as with modern ghettos today, law-enforcing agencies and the tribunals of the mid-Quattrocento, reflecting their more centralized and elitist character in Medicean Florence, simply ceased to bother with many of the normal, run-of-the-mill, assault and battery cases involving women from artisan and laboring families.[49]

A second series of statistics similarly reflects on changes in the accessibility of the criminal courts to women. These are cases of immorality—pederasty, sodomy, homosexual and heterosexual rape, adultery, prostitution, blasphemy, and gambling. These crimes, when they involved women, show the most pronounced differences of any category of crime between the Trecento and Quattrocento. For both points of observation in the fourteenth century, slightly more than three-quarters of these crimes against morality involved a woman (79% and 78%, respectively). By the middle of the Quattrocento, crimes against morality had become principally masculine deeds (at least as far as the court blotters are concerned); only 31 percent of the contenders were women. On first impression, these changes may not imply any change in women's accessibility to the courts but instead a change in behavior—perhaps even the spread of Renaissance civilization or manners.[50]

Before speculating about changes in women's behavior, let us consider the most important crime in this category, at least as far as women are concerned: rape. Despite the small number of cases for all three points of observation, the differences over time again suggest that, by the mid-fifteenth century, women possessed fewer possibilities of receiving justice. In both periods of the Trecento, the tribunals failed to prosecute a single case of homosexual rape, while they adjudicated seven cases of heterosexual rape in 1344–45 (22% of the crimes of immorality) and two cases (18%) in 1374–75. These percentages change notably by the mid-Quattrocento. In this twelve-year period, nine cases of pederasty and homosexual rape appear (37.5% of the morality charges), and in only three cases (12.5%) was the victim of sexual aggression a woman and not a boy or a man. Per annum rape charges against assailants of women fell from 2 to 0.37, or about one-sixth of what they were on the eve of the Ciompi revolt.[51]

This shift in the court's preoccupation from heterosexual rape to homosexuality becomes further pronounced when we consider that in 1432 a new juridical body appeared in the Florentine judicial system, the *ufficiali di notte,* whose jurisdiction was almost exclusively acts of male homosexuality.[52] For the year 1461–62, the only year in the period 1455–66 for which its sentences survive, this court tried fifty-one cases of sodomy (all of which involved exclusively males); of these, perhaps only one case could be considered rape.[53] Evidently, other (medieval) tribunals continued to try rape cases, both hetero- and homosexual. Nonetheless, the presence of this new tribunal suggests that comparing only the medieval tribunals between the fourteenth and fifteenth centuries would severely underestimate the Florentine commune's fifteenth-century obsession with homosexuality; the courts' prosecutions of homosexual sex changes in absolute terms as well as relative to the rape of women.

How do we explain this change (at least according to court blotters) from hetero- to homosexual rape? Could it reflect more general changes in sexual preferences throughout Renaissance society? After all, in the fifteenth and sixteenth centuries, some of Florence's most celebrated sons— Marsilio Ficino, Leonardo da Vinci, and Michelangelo—were charged with being, or rumored to be, homosexuals, and the *ufficiali di notte* frequently arrested male lovers in or near taverns, such as one just beyond the gate of Santa Croce and the Buco di Morello, that in these court cases and in carnival songs appear as homosexual hangouts.[54]

Richard Trexler has argued that fifteenth-century Florence witnessed a sharp increase in homosexuality and has given several structural explanations for it: a rise in men's age at marriage, an increase in the values of dowries, and a consequent increase in the number of women entering nunneries (see chap. 5; this volume).[55] Trexler argues that these structural factors resulted in fewer women in the marriage market and an extension of the period in which men had to wait before entering married life. According to Trexler, the result was increasing male frustration and a turn to homosexuality. But would not these same demographic and social structures and the resulting pressures and frustrations for young men have created a corresponding increase in sexual violence against women, as well—and not the decline in heterosexual rape shown by court statistics?

From Leonardo Bruni's *Poliscene*, written at the beginning of the fifteenth century, to Machiavelli's *Clizia* and *Mandragola*, written at the beginning of the following century, Florentine drama revolved around the sexual frustration of young Florentine men. Even if these comedies might contain homosexual allusions, the objects of these men's frustrations were not other men or young boys but young, beautiful, and usually inaccessible women, protected by indulgent mothers and guardians, jealous fathers, and elderly husbands.

As sociologists of crime and feminist historians find for contemporary societies, reported cases of rape bear little relation to their actual number. To the contrary, an increase in the number of reported cases of rape, according to these scholars, often reflects an improvement in the position of women, in that it reflects increases in their accessibility to the criminal courts and in their power to bring such cases to trial. The increase in cases reflects, as well, changes in community consciousness and in police protection and surveillance on behalf of women.[56]

My analyses thus far point in the direction of a sharp decline in women's accessibility to the courts by the mid-fifteenth century—their declining appearance in the court records, both in absolute terms and relative to men, changes in the patterns of women's criminality, and the courts' shift in attention from heterosexual rape to homosexual surveillance. Should we, therefore, conclude that these statistics reveal nothing about possible changes in women's behavior in the Renaissance? In addition to implying that women had less protection from the legal apparatuses of the Florentine commune, might these statistics also chart the diffusion of Renaissance manners throughout society? Had Renaissance women, even laboring women, become more tamed and, therefore, more "feminine," in the victim Piero di Cianchino's as well as Alberti's sense of the word?

Every criminal statistic has two sides: one reflects criminal behavior, the other the intensity with which the state wishes to prosecute—or is capable of prosecuting—certain crimes or social and political behavior. After all, perhaps there simply were fewer women in the streets in the mid-Quattrocento relative to their numbers than there had been in the periods preceding the Ciompi revolt. In addition to structural constraints—most notably, a decline of women in the work force outside the home—consciousness and behavior might have also changed.[57] Perhaps the patriarch Giannozzo's advice given to his wife in Alberti's *I libri della Famiglia*—to learn that her place was the home and that her role in any dispute was to flee and not to fight—was more than simply patrician ideology of the mid-Quattrocento.[58] Instead, it may have been a lesson that had filtered throughout Florentine urban society to the extent that it had even changed the female character.

One way to enter this shadowy relationship between changes in criminal behavior and the accessibility of the courts to women might be to look for changes in the relationship between women as plaintiffs and women as defendants. When we divide these statistics into three categories—cases in which a woman was the plaintiff or the victim, those in which a woman was the defendant, and those in which both were women, that is, conflicts between women—we find once again a notable similarity between the two sample periods of the Trecento and a significant gap between the Trecento and the mid-Quattrocento (table 2.2). In 1344–45, 47 percent of the cases involved women exclusively as plaintiffs, 40 percent involved women as defendants, and 13 percent involved women as both. These proportions changed imperceptibly from the Black Death to the eve of the Ciompi revolt (53, 38, and 10 percent, respectively). But by the mid-fifteenth century, they had changed radically. While in more than 70 percent of cases involving women a woman brought the case to trial, their proportion as defendants dropped to 24 percent, and disputes between women fell to 6 percent. Thus by the mid-Quattrocento, fewer women appeared in the courts as plaintiffs or defendants, both in absolute terms and relative to men, but by far the most important component of this decline was among women defendants.

Moreover, the number of women involved in the two most important categories of crime in these records—rural crimes and assault and battery cases—provides further clues about change in criminal behavior from the late Middle Ages to the early Renaissance. For both periods of the Tre-

TABLE 2.2. Female Crime: Plaintiffs and Defendants, 1344–1466

Type of Crime	1344–1345				1374–1375				1455–1466			
	Plaintiff	Accused	Both	Total	Plaintiff	Accused	Both	Total	Plaintiff	Accused	Both	Total
Assault and Battery	56	13	16	85	8	7	4	19	11	0	2	13
Murder	4	2	1	7	1	1	0	2	1	3	0	4
Theft	2	6	6	14	0	1	0	1	1	1	0	2
Rural crime	6	10	0	16	2	3	0	5	11	1	0	12
Burglary	7	11	3	21	2	0	0	2	2	1	1	4
Crimes of immorality	7	23	0	30	4	3	0	7	2	3	0	5
Indebtedness	13	8	1	22	4	0	0	4	5	2	0	7
Other	9	16	3	28	0	0	0	0	3	1	0	4
TOTAL	104	89	30	223	21	15	4	40	36	12	3	51
Percentages	46.64	39.91	13.45	100.00	52.50	37.50	10.00	100.00	70.59	23.53	5.88	100.00

cento, the majority of women involved in rural crimes were defendants; that is, they were peasant women brought to trial for having stolen or cut wood, poached pigeons or broken work contracts. In cases of arson, they may even have been "primitive rebels," although political motivations are generally left unstated in the laconic texts of the Trecento crime reports. In alluding to motivation of any sort, the records rarely go beyond formulaic phrases such as "spiritu diabolico." But for these acts, peasant women were regularly sentenced with heavy fines and even the death penalty, and the barns and farm houses usually belonged to absentee landlords of the Florentine patriciate.[59]

By the mid-fifteenth century the number of women involved in rural crimes as defendants all but disappeared; only one case charged a woman. For the others (well over 90%) a *procurator* or a *mundualdus* (acting on behalf of a wealthy woman landowner from the city, usually a widow) charged a male peasant for such rural crimes.

Cases of assault and battery confirm even more clearly this change in the behavior of women. By the mid-Quattrocento, the women found in these cases were for the most part the victims of aggression, not the perpetrators or even the contenders. Again, it is as though the feminine manners preached by Florentine moralists—such as Leon Battista Alberti's idealized Quattrocento patriarch, Giannozzo degli Alberti—had penetrated the ranks of urban Florentine society. In 85 percent of these cases, women were either the victims of physical violence or the plaintiffs in these cases. During the Trecento, on the other hand, greater numbers (and percentages) of women came out into the streets of Florence, protecting themselves and their families by cursing, scratching, and stabbing their enemies; women like Filippa di Matteo and, at times, even groups of women protected themselves and their children with extralegal action, directly redressing their grievances against men and other women in the streets.[60] In these cases, women were on the offensive (and thus the defendants in assault and battery cases) in 34 percent of these cases in 1344–45 and even more so on the eve of the Ciompi revolt (1374–75), when more than half of the women (58 percent) involved in cases of physical aggression were the attackers and not the attacked.[61]

Finally, let us return to crimes of immorality, this time to consider not rape (a crime for which the woman was never the defendant and always the victim) but adultery, a crime for which women were always the accused. Before the Black Death, adultery comprised 29 percent of all crimes against morality; in 1374–75 the percentage fell slightly, to 22 percent; but by the mid-Quattrocento, it had fallen by almost half, to 13 percent.

How should we interpret this apparent fall in adultery? Did it result from husbands (who in these cases were usually workers, artisans, and small shopkeepers) no longer possessing the wherewithal to bring such cases to trial? Had they been forced by the centralization of justice from locally elected parish chaplains and syndics to the paid officials of the *podestà* and the *otto* to deal with the infidelity of their wives and daughters in private and by extralegal means, such as by wife beating, which contemporary storytellers and moralists alike encouraged?[62] Perhaps. For this period of Florentine history, however, no records survive similar to the ecclesiastical court records after the Council of Trent, which allow the historian to peer behind the closed doors of artisans' and workers' homes or even into the palaces of the patriciate.[63]

But might the criminal statistics at our disposal nonetheless point to changes that go beyond the courtroom and enter the social realities of relations between men and women? In other words, these statistics, along with others, suggest that women in the mid-Quattrocento were less inclined and less able to circulate as freely through the streets of Florence, meeting other women and even other men outside the home, as they had in the late Trecento. Perhaps a larger social reality lurks in the prologue to Machiavelli's comedy *Clizia,* a reality that, by the mid-Quattrocento, extended through much of urban Florentine society. Adapted from an ancient Greek comedy, the action in Machiavelli's version turns around the sexual lure of the young adopted Clizia—who, however, never appears onstage. As Machiavelli informs his audience, she is never let out of the shelter of her jealous guardian.[64] By the same token, perhaps it is no accident that the well-known Tuscan collections of stories that turn largely on the active and adulterous affairs of married women and widows—those by Boccaccio, Sercambi, and Sacchetti—are Trecento and not Quattrocento creations.

But could it be said that, instead of a decline in women's conditions, these criminal statistics reflect just the opposite—that with the growth of the Renaissance state and the spread of Renaissance manners, both men and women became less violent and that women had less need to be combative or to redress their grievances by physical force? By this view, women would have gained security and honor through the Renaissance "civilizing process." But such an optimistic interpretation of the Renaissance is confounded by the statistics presented in this chapter as well as by other trends that go beyond crime in the streets and the criminal courtroom. First, certain statistics, such as the relationship between cases of murder and assault and battery, do not bear out the conclusion. Instead, the decline in sentences points to a deterioration of artisans' and workers' power to initiate criminal actions in the courts, a point corroborated by historians who have looked at how criminal cases were brought to trial.[65] From a predominance of personal denunciations in the fourteenth century, the pendulum swung toward actions initiated through the inquisitions of the *podestà,* the *capitano,* and the newly created vicariate courts in the territory, along with other summary courts discussed above.

Second, other sources only now beginning to be investigated by historians reflect on noncriminal behavior and association among nonelite women. These studies point in the same direction of change charted by this analysis of women's assault cases: in addition to the sharp decline in women's participation in the work force, women, and in particular working women, became less active in other aspects of public life in Renaissance Florence. Ronald Weissman has studied the membership lists of one of the few religious confraternities composed largely of artisans and laborers, the parish company of San Frediano, from the 1370s through the first half of the sixteenth century.[66] In the last three decades of the Trecento, women comprised 38 percent of the membership of this confraternity (136 women); by the middle of the fifteenth century their number had dropped to only four, and later in the century, they disappeared altogether. Similarly, Richard Trexler has shown that women became a "liminal" group in the fifteenth century, shoved to the margins in public rituals, from festive brigades and jousts to the solemn processions of San Giovanni day.[67]

Other statistics that extend our vision of laboring women's social worlds in late medieval and early Renaissance Florence are needed to test and flesh out the changes charted by the criminal records.[68] But as far as the statistics examined here go, it is clear: the frequency with which women appeared in the criminal tribunals, whether as plaintiffs or defendants, declined markedly from the second half of the fourteenth century to the middle of the fifteenth century, and the major component of this decline was women as defendants, that is, women charged with redressing their grievances directly in the streets of late medieval Florence. Nor, as one might assume on first inspection, was this seeming decline in violence favorable to women's status and power in their everyday lives.

In conclusion, if we consider women in Renaissance Florence not from the perspective of aristocratic letters, such as those famous ones drafted by

Alessandra Strozzi, but through the criminal tribunals, the power and status of the mass of women deteriorated markedly between the more tumultuous period of the mid-Trecento to the period of social calm that dominated Medicean Florence. Despite the statistical problems and distortions in the use of these criminal archives (especially over the long term, with changing demographics and changes in the systems of justice and social control), my analyses show a sharp narrowing in two arenas of action for women—the criminal courts and the streets of Florence. In both, the early Renaissance severely curtailed the possibility of women settling their grievances and protecting their honor.

The general decline in the presence of women in the tribunals, in absolute terms and relative to men, the decline in the percentage of women involved in cases of assault and battery, the increase in female homicide relative to female assault cases, and the steep fall in the relative numbers of rape cases all point in the same direction—a decline in the accessibility of the courts to women from the mid-Trecento to the mid-Quattrocento. From the judges to the law-enforcing agencies, where power devolved from locally elected lay parish chaplains to centralized officers under the aegis of the *podestà,* the *capitano,* the *otto di guardia,* and the new vicariate courts in the countryside, the diminished case loads of the Renaissance state suggest that it increasingly discriminated against the interests of women and, in particular, laboring women.

At the same time, that other face of the criminal statistic suggests changes in the actual behavior of women, pointing to a decline in women's power and status in the streets and *piazze* of Renaissance Florence. As their access to the tribunals declined, even fewer women (as a percentage of the population and in relation to men) appear in court records taking direct action in their neighborhoods and rural parishes by committing crimes such as rural theft, housebreaking, assault, and adultery, despite the myriad causes of such crimes. In cases of assault and battery, in which the frequency of women, as both plaintiffs and defendants, declined precipitously from the Trecento to the Quattrocento, the most important component of this decline was the deterioration in women's extralegal defense of their interests and honor.

These two faces of the criminal statistic were certainly connected. The deterioration in the power and status of women followed that of the laboring classes more generally. With the defeat of the Ciompi and then the government of the Minor Guilds (1382), the consequential tightening of political power and control under the aegis of the Albizzi oligarchy, and ultimately the rise of the Medicean state during the fifteenth century, workers and artisans of both sexes were forced to withdraw into narrower communities for protection.[69] These same mechanisms of the centralization of power forced women to withdraw into even tighter confines. Instead of the parish, their territory of defense became increasingly the home.

Yet is it sufficient to look solely at the development of the state to understand the decline in women's position in the Renaissance? Could concomitant changes also have been taking place within the family itself, which no doubt related to changes in the distribution of power and may have had an ideological life of its own? From the early years of the fifteenth century (as far as the patriciate were concerned), San Bernardino, Giovanni Dominici, and Leon Battista Alberti, were systematizing a new consciousness of the nuclear family—the Renaissance family—investing it with new social and even spiritual significance.[70]

Furthermore, Thomas Kuehn's search through the folds of this ideology for the higher echelons of Florentine society shows that the number of contracts emancipating daughters from the authority of their fathers declined during the fifteenth century, and that the *patria potestà* often extended over daughters even after they married.[71] Did these changes in family practices and attitudes reach the worlds of artisans and laborers? Did the decline in the power and status of the laboring classes after the revolt of the Ciompi and the rise of the Medicean state cause male workers and artisans to impose their power more rigorously in one of the few spaces that remained for their authority and power, the home? To answer this question, new research is needed on the family—beyond three or four patrician houses—to look at the worlds of artisan, workers, and peasants.[72]

From the present study, however, one thing is clear: in the surviving registers of the criminal courts of the mid-Quattrocento, we do not encounter many women like Filippa di Matteo, who redressed their problems by putting themselves on a plane equal to men, even proclaiming the superiority of women over men. On the other hand, the criminal statistics regarding the middle years of the Trecento demonstrate that she was not acting alone.

3. Last Wills

FAMILY, WOMEN, AND THE BLACK DEATH
IN CENTRAL ITALY

Two traditions dominate the study of last wills and testaments in the early modern period. The first, stemming from a long tradition in legal history, considers questions directly related to the family—inheritance patterns—but rarely goes beyond this structural consideration to venture into the realm of sentiment.[1] The other tradition focuses on the history of mentalities—religious piety—but fails to touch the concrete world of property, inheritance, and the family. Historians such as Michel Vovelle, Phillipe Ariès, Pierre Chaunu, and Jacques Chiffoleau do not even mention those "items" that usually comprise half the will: gifts to heirs, friends, and kin.[2] This chapter concentrates on these nonpious final gifts, not so much to chart inheritance patterns in various city-states as to understand differences in mentality between city-states.[3]

My book, *The Cult of Remembrance and the Black Death*, analyzes more than 40,000 legacies in 3,400 wills and codicils from six city-states: Arezzo, Florence, Pisa, and Siena in Tuscany; Perugia and Assisi in Umbria.[4] It chronicles a change that ran though each of these communities, from Franciscan Assisi to the much larger supposed capital of a new Renaissance culture, Florence. In preparing their passage to what Petrarch called "that other side of life," ordinary townsmen and villagers rejected mendicant ideals of charity and began to devise mechanisms for earthly immortality, from perpetual masses and feasts to plaques plastered in sacred places. It was not the first onslaught of pestilence in 1348 that set in motion this transformation in piety. Instead, the break occurred with the relived trauma of the plague's second strike in the summer of 1363. Only at that point did the long, itemized lists of pious bequests with few strings attached disappear from these records.

The six cities, however, do not simply mirror one another but cluster into two camps, and it is this geographical problem that I wish to address here. For three of the cities—Assisi, Pisa, and Siena—the spread of mendicant ideals and preaching transformed late medieval testamentary practice. From the 1270s, whether peasants or patricians, testators strove to avoid earthly hubris by liquidating their estates into small monetary sums, scattering them among numerous pious entities. In Florence, Arezzo, and Perugia, this mendicant pattern of giving was not nearly as pronounced, and testators' desire to leave their marks on the world never disappeared—from the endowment of hospitals to ten-lire altarpieces.[5]

The differences in pious giving between these two triads of cities find resonance in the legacies left to kin and friends. The same zeal for earthly memory is mapped by testators' efforts to extend their earthly influence beyond the grave by placing constraints on their property and dictating the future relations of heirs, attempts that ranged from conditional clauses regarding a son's obedience to his mother to demands that heirs marry specific persons within specified periods of time. The most common of these clauses were restrictions against the alienation of property, from urban palaces to peasant plots. More of these restrictions on property came from testators in Florence, Arezzo, and Perugia than in the other three cities. In Florence and Arezzo, 25 percent of testators placed such restrictions on their bequests; in Perugia nearly 20 percent did. In contrast, testators from the other three towns tried far less often to control their real estate once they had passed to the grave: only 9 percent in Pisa, 8 percent in Assisi, and 6 percent in Siena. If these conditional clauses are calculated as a portion of legacies, the differences among these two triads of cities becomes even more pronounced.[6] Yet, a quantitative analysis alone fails to show the variety and complexity of conditions that swelled in testators' minds as they approached the afterlife.

In Pisa, Assisi, and Siena, these restrictive conditions on property rarely went beyond the notarial formula forbidding the recipient "to sell, alienate, mortgage, trade, or exchange" and often were no more than an entitlement to enjoy the usufruct during the lifetime of the beneficiary. As for the lion's share of an estate, that bequeathed to the universal heirs, testators from these cities rarely specified at what age an heir might alienate an estate, which properties could or could not be alienated, and if alienated, with whose consent or to whom they might be sold. The exceptional cases, when testators went beyond simple transfers of property and entered into the future affairs of relatives and heirs, came predominantly in the latter part of the Trecento and early Quattrocento.

Florence

From the earliest testaments, Florentines were obsessed with the flow of their patrimonies and prized possessions through successive generations down the male line. Such clauses and conditions do not appear in the Pisan records until the 1420s or in the Sienese testaments until the beginning of the sixteenth century.[7] In 1291 a Florentine merchant from the Cerchi family (dominus Consillius filius quondam Ser Olivieri) left his patrimony equally to his six sons and stated emphatically that no daughter born from him or to be born from him or from his sons should inherit any of his houses; they should pass only through masculine hands.[8] If all six sons should die without male heirs, half his patrimony should be spent on building a hospital. The merchant then looked to the future through the ideological prism of the male line. He left the *ius patronatus*, or the right to elect the hospital's rector along with the privileges of overseeing its business affairs, to those at least eighteen years old, of his house, and "descendants through the male line" (*de descendentibus per lineam masculinam*). As for the other half of his patrimony, the merchant again looked to the future of his properties through his lineage and their flow through the male bloodlines. In case all his sons died without heirs, he left it to the male children of his two brothers "and to their male descendants and then afterward through their male line by family stock (*stirpe*) and not by head (*in capite*)."[9]

These strategies and impositions were not the exclusive preserve and ideology of the Florentine *ottimati*. Several years later, Andrea f.q. Manni, a Florentine commoner without a family name, after naming his son as universal heir, added the command "that no woman should inherit or be the heir to the household of this testator at any time," so long as there was any legitimate male members of his family (*in ipsa domo*). Rather, women should have sufficient funds from their fathers for their dowries or for entering a convent, according to the capacities (*secundum facilitates*) of those male heirs down through his lineage (*ex linea masculina*) in perpetuity.[10]

With the recurrence of pestilence, the entailing of property, the granting of special rights, and the devolution of patrimonies through the male line intensified, infiltrating testaments beneath the ranks even of Florentine merchants. In 1364, Alamannus, the son of an ironmonger named Tolosini, appointed his only son as universal heir along with "all others born through the male line and all their sons and all their legitimate and natural male descendants of this Alamannus through his male line" (*seu omnes filios et descendentes masculos legptimos et naturales*). If his son died without heirs, the estate would devolve to his nephew and then, he directed, should pass once again through the male line. In a separate itemized act the ironmonger's son further explained this devolution, boosting further his recently minted family name, de Tolosinis: the estate would pass to his *consortes,* which he defined as the legitimate male descendants of the house and stock of the Tolosinis and "through its great masculine line" (*per lineam masculinam magnam*) and to those kin closest to the testator.[11]

In 1416, the *probus vir* (good man) Johannes, a cobbler from Vinci, who had lived for some time in the Florentine working-class parishes of Santa Lucia Ognissanti and San Frediano before returning to his native village, entailed his house in Vinci along with its small plot of vineyards and olive trees, measuring only eight *starii.* Childless at the time, Johannes gave the house to a friend for the friend's lifetime and, thereafter, to the friend's sons and then to their sons in turn, *in stirpe et non in capite.* This friend and his future sons and grandsons were required to have a mass celebrated for the cobbler's soul once a year at an altar that he had commissioned for his parish church in Vinci. Otherwise, half the property would endow the chapel and half would assist in the dowries of poor girls marrying for the first time. Another itemized act restricted the friend, his sons, and grandsons from selling or alienating the "property in its entirety or in any particular" so long as the sons of this friend and any of their descendants should live "until the infinite degree."[12]

By 1368 the language of family stock and the distinctions in the passage of family properties through individuals or family groups penetrated even lower social levels of the Florentine urban population. Iacobus f.q. Pieri Martelli, a carder in the wool industry (*cardator seu conciator pannorum;* a disenfranchised worker without any guild status), mapped the succession of his properties through various male contingencies. Even though he bore no family name, he demanded that his heirs have his family coat of arms painted on candle holders, which would remain always in the Church of

Santa Maria Novella—thus lending reality to Franco Sacchetti's story of a "uomo di piccolo affare" demanding his coat of arms be painted by the "gran dipintore" Giotto.[13]

The first woman in the Florentine documents to entail property down the male line was a widow of the powerful Strozzi family. In 1377 she named her only son, Alexio, a friar at Santa Maria Novella, as universal heir but left him only the usufructus of a farm. After this son's death, she projected the farm's devolution to her four brothers and then "to their male children and descendants in perpetuity through the legitimate and naturally born members of the male line, by stock and not by head." She further prohibited any of these descendants to sell or alienate this farm or rent it beyond a five-year lease. She also dictated measures to prevent her brothers, after her decease, "from compelling or coercing her son the friar to loan them anything from the revenues of this property." These provisions were certainly not formulaic but instead must have been the fruits of this patrician lady's thoughts after years of court battles initiated by these brothers, who had earlier vigorously contested the young Alexio's paternal inheritance.[14] She further demanded that her four brothers—and after them, their male descendants—once in possession of her farm, pay each year six florins to the nun Nastasia, the daughter of one of her brothers.[15]

In 1313, a doctor, Pierus f.q. Dati from the Florentine parish of Santa Felicità, also tried to continue ruling his roost after death. The doctor named his four sons as his heirs but prohibited them from selling or alienating any of his "houses and lands" without the "permission and spoken consent" (*absque licentia et parabula*) of their mother, "since he wanted this property to remain in the family." The doctor then commanded his sons "to obey, honor, and revere" their mother and "in no way impede or trouble her use of his properties." Each time one violated this condition, he would lose a hundred florins of his patrimony, to be collected by those sons who remained obedient (*applicandum aliis suis fratribus obbedientibus*).[16]

As early as 1301, a certain Florentine, Andrea, left his blood relative Lottus a clothing allowance of five lire a year for ten years on condition that he "behave well and live honestly."[17] In 1319 an emancipated son named Petrus left his nephew an income of a florin a year for four years provided he "stay and practice a trade" that the testator's father, Guido, approved.[18] An international merchant of Florence stated in his testament of 1351 that he possessed two thousand florins or more in money and merchandise in Avignon and required one of his partners to make "suitable yearly accounts of his affairs in that city and to administer these monies, merchandise, and affairs" to the benefit of his heir. If his heir's guardians should judge that this agent was not performing these tasks well, they were empowered to seize the fortune and invest it in the city or *contado* of Florence.[19] Another Florentine merchant, then working in Paris, confessed in his testament to have fathered an illegitimate daughter, whom he claimed to have "nourished" over the past ten or eleven years. He willed her a dowry of four hundred gold francs but only if she married by age sixteen; otherwise, the funds would be spent on the poor of Christ and other pious charities.[20] In a brief will, a widow from a small village in the Mugello left a daughter as universal heir but only if, within five years of the testator's death, she returned to live in the mother's village.[21]

Florentine testators did not simply try to control their heirs; they also wished to ameliorate future conditions to be faced by their kin. Such was the spirit behind the additional comments attached to the end of a testament in 1390: "Mindful of the abundance of his patrimony and the needs of his brother . . . who has eleven children, and being attentive to problems that such a large number of children poses, and having affection for this offspring and his blood relations, and having deliberated and consulted with others, and moved by a fraternal spirit, the testator gives to these children . . . his nephews, four thousand florins."[22] Similarly, the nobleman Niccolò Guicciardini sought to alleviate the possibilities of loved ones slipping into "dishonor" when confronted with unexpected tribulation: "In case any of his daughters should marry and afterward, on account of the impoverishment of a husband, or because of some other misfortune or unforeseen reason, should wish to become separated from her husband and family to preserve her honor or for necessity . . . she should be free to return, to stay and to inhabit [the testator's] palace and home, to live with his sons and to be fed well from the sumptuous inheritance of this testator."[23]

The most common imposition that testators made on the future actions of their beneficiaries, in Florence or any other city, were the demands husbands placed on their widows-to-be. These are discussed later. But one arrangement deserves mention at this point for it reflects the lengths testators could go to in mandating the very movements of their future heirs. In 1371, a Johannes f.q. Dietisalvi Nigri of Florence named his male children still to be born as his universal heirs. If he bore no sons, he left the usufructus of all his property to his sister, although not without qualifications and obligations. She was to spend a hundred florins to construct, within three years, a cottage (*domucula*) in the place of the testator's residence in the parish of San Lorenzo "for the utility and convenience" of living there. He then left his wife, for as long as she remained a widow, the rights to live there as well but mapped out the details: "She might enter by the main passageway (*volta*) and have access to the entire building above the entrance to this passageway, using the steps that lead to a newly constructed passageway, except for that part reserved [for his sister] existing above the stairs and under the study (*scriptorium*) and the cloakroom (*guardarobas*)."[24]

Arezzo

The number of testators channeling property down the male line was almost identical in Arezzo and Florence. Although they appear later in the Aretine samples, the first does not come from a testator of one of the old feudal lineages but from a simple rural notary, suggesting that such practices may already have been well entrenched by the early Trecento, when these documents become prevalent. In addition to sending properties and rights generationally down the male line, Aretines projected communal restrictions over their blood relatives to be held by kinsmen (the "consortium"). For instance, in 1362, a friar, Martinus, left a third part of a house, courtyard, and oven in the countryside to his two illegitimate sons, provided they did not alienate the property until one of them, Iacobus, reached the age of fifteen, and then only with the consent and permission of the testator's brother or his closest blood relative. He, moreover, gave his nephews a third part of the houses in this village, which they held in common on condition that they alienate the properties only with the consent of his *consortes*.[25]

The preponderance of such cases in Arezzo come later, however, after the return of the plague in 1363. The most remarkable of these appears with the third strike of pestilence in 1374. After ordering his arms, plaques, and crests plastered on his ancestral chapel "for his memory" (*ad memoriam*) and that of his ancestors, a notary, Landucius, entailed his residence in the *contrada* of Borgo in the city of Arezzo. Here the testator's reasons for prohibiting alienation were made more explicit than for any such entail found even in the lineage-conscious records from Florence: "The said testator wishes, demands, and insists that his house . . . in no way be sold, alienated, or in any way mortgaged by his heirs or any other person; rather, it is to stay and must stand in perpetual memory (*ad perpetuam memoriam*) of the testator and his ancestors." To concretize the survival of his memory, Landucius went a step further, commissioning one of the very few works of art found in these testaments not destined for display on the walls of an ecclesiastical institution. He demanded that his heirs have his coat of arms carved in stone (*intagliata in quodam lapide*), painted, and displayed "so that it could be seen easily and clearly (*ita quod bene et clare videantur*) on the back portion of his house facing the street of Burgo." He then reiterated his demand for entail, that this urban dwelling should neither be sold nor alienated "but always pass through the direct line" to his sons' sons and, if none survived, to their closest male relatives.[26]

The year afterward, an Aretine Franciscan tertiary divided her estate, giving half to her nephew and subdividing the other half between a fellow tertiary, "the honorable sister" Pia, and the testator's biological sister Cinella. She prevented both from "diminishing" the property by any form of alienation or by any donation "inter vivos." Instead, after their deaths, this portion of the estate was "to be restituted" to "those male descendants" of her brother and then down the male line. If "these male descendants should die before reaching twenty-five and without giving birth to male children, the portion of the estate should devolve to her nephew, Augustinus, and then to his sons and their male descendants."

The testatrix then pried further into the biological futures and sexual behavior of her lineage, ordering that if any of these male descendants should sire "one or more" legitimate daughters, these daughters should receive dowries of three hundred florins apiece. If, instead, an illegitimate daughter (*feminam naturalem vel expuream*) was sired, she would receive two hundred florins, whether she married or entered a convent. Furthermore, if Augustinus happened to sire a bastard son, this offspring would receive four hundred florins, and if he died without legitimate sons, his portion of the estate would pass to another blood relative, a certain Ser Johannes, to whom she attached the same prohibitions against the alienation of properties, the same devolution of property down the male line, and the same price list for legitimate and illegitimate daughters and sons. If any of these stipulations were broken, the properties would pass to the Misericordia.

This tertiary did not, however, let matters rest even here but instead heaped obligations on this contingent heir several times removed. The Misericordia would be obliged to pay the Augustinians, the Franciscans, the Dominicans, the Servites, and the monastery of San Marco six florins a year each for annual offices of the dead for her soul and those of her ancestors. Moreover, this last contingent heir was prohibited from alienating this portion of the patrimony or else this half would pass to yet another degree of contingency, the hospital of Arezzo.[27]

Even more complex was the 1416 division and entail of the estate of an Aretine spice and clothing merchant, who carefully specified the shares, credits, dowry portions, lands, farm animals, shops, and tools to be divided among three sons and then passed on to their children and future heirs. In one of these itemized bequests, two mules were coupled with "all the books pertaining to medicine and its science" and the wine casks found in the merchant's home in Florence. To equalize the patrimony among his sons, the merchant-father even made an accounting of expenses previously incurred by one son: a thousand florins spent on his education, books, and doctorate; three hundred florins that the father loaned him while that son was resident in Florence, seventy-nine florins that the son owed to the father's cloth shop, and so on. More remarkable, the father's plans for his sons extended to the division of the testator's house, shop, and warehouse, demarcating the sons' future rights of way: in the home, one son and his family were to have the ground floor; another son "the second floor with the right to enter and leave the upper bedroom only by the upper veranda."[28]

As the testament above suggests, Aretine testators, like those in Florence, tried to govern from the grave their heirs' futures, down to the intricacies of daily life and business operations. Again, cases of similar complexity and character are almost entirely absent from the thousands of testaments found for the other three towns, at least before the recurrence of pestilence in 1363. In Assisi, Pisa, and Siena, with monotonous regularity, testators simply left their possessions without conditions, restrictions, or other strings attached. On the other hand, Aretine testaments detailing property rights and rights of way in communally owned or occupied homes and palaces outnumber those for Florence and occur further down the social ladder, spreading into the villages and including "houses" no more grandiose than the cottage of a rich peasant.

The first of these future impositions is found in the 1334 testament of a rural notary, which specifies his wife's rights of habitation. If she lived "honestly" and did not remarry, she could enjoy during her lifetime (together with one of her servants) "free habitation" of the first sun terrace off the master bedroom and a kitchen terrace, along with the rights of passage to "come and go freely" by the first stairs leading to the master bedroom.[29]

In 1374, a villager from Fronzola determined through his will the future movements within his house of a cousin and of the testator's brother, Bettino. To his cousin he gave (as a right to be passed down to the cousin's sons) half of a courtyard located behind the house. To Bettino and his family he gave the right to enter this courtyard to fetch water at a well so long as the cousin happened not to be entering the courtyard at the same moment. He further ordered his brother to build a wall to divide it.[30] In 1416 another villager precisely divided the property rights to a small urban dwelling. One of his daughters would receive the rear of the house as far as the pantry (*cellarius*) and might debar the father's son from "its use and habitation." He gave the front part of the house, including the pantry, a bedroom, and a well located in the back part of the house, to his other daughter, with the right to use these portions "communally" with her sister.[31]

Other Aretines imposed posthumous secular construction plans on their heirs. Nor did such concerns over property and its future obsess only the rich and powerful. In 1374, the son of a notary was so concerned to ensure that his house would never be sold or alienated in any form that he forbade it should happen even if his heirs should secure the permission of the commune of Arezzo, the college of cardinals, the pope, or the holy Roman emperor. Moreover, he made sure in his will that if a certain Bernardus did not wish to "repair and ornament" a wall in this house, then a certain Johannes, his debtor, was to spend half the debt for these improvements.[32] A woman from the village of Quarata made only one itemized act in her testament of 1411. It "confirmed" that she had given her husband ten florins, which she obliged him to spend on the house's "improvements, works, and beautification" (*in meliorationem, opere et aconcimine*).[33] On his deathbed, the merchant Baccius was obsessed with details for the future remodeling of a house attached to a stable. He ordered two of his sons to have the stable removed and to construct in its place a balcony "extending from the back to the front" of this house, which he had bequeathed to one of his sons and to that son's lineage.[34]

Besides channeling property through successive generations, Aretines tried to control its future by blocking its flow. In 1340, an Aretine citizen left a maze of contingencies if his son should die without heirs. He then attached a final item to his testament, as though a postscript: "in no way or in any form" might his brother or his brother's children ever assume any rights to his landed property.[35] In the year of the plague's recurrence, 1363, an Aretine notary was even more emphatic in singling out someone never to possess his property. He left his two married sisters as universal heirs, then insisted that "these sisters, neither one nor the other, at no time, through any acquisition or division of the inheritance" should allow the husband of one of these sisters "the [right] of intervention to the succession of his estate." Nor was this man "for any reason" ever to "live, stay, occupy, enter, or come to the testator's residence."[36]

On occasion these blockages came closer to home. For instance, in the year of the plague's second strike, a father "disinherited" his son, leaving him an honorific five soldi and ordering him not to plead for any more, "since he was always disobedient to his father, treated him with malice, and loitered about from place to place" (*cum malis maleficis moratrahit et conversatur discurrendo per mundum*).[37]

Perugia

In Perugia, testamentary entails were significantly higher than in Assisi, Pisa, and Siena and increased in frequency after the recurrence of plague in 1363, but the documents retain a laconic and formulaic character. No examples appear as elaborate as the nouveau riche Alamannus de Tolosinis's attempt to preserve his house through the eternal flow of properties down the male line, or as explicit as the Aretine notary Landucius's attempt to preserve his prized residence for his perpetual memory. Nor does a technical vocabulary rich in new terms for entail, male line, degrees of relation amplify Perugian demands to guide properties down through the generations.

In one of the few instances where the terms *affines* and *consanguineos* do appear, it was not to channel properties down the male line but, instead, to dismiss claims to a testator's patrimony. In 1383, a Perugian knight, dominus Francescus f.q. domini Ugolini, "instituted as his heirs all his blood relatives and those related through marriage, both males and females (*eius consanguineos et affines tam mares quam feminas*) up to the fifth degree of relation," giving them five soldi provided that they keep quiet.[38]

Nor was such wholesale disinheritance the preserve of the nobility. In 1421, a slipper maker with a will consisting of only two items "instituted as heirs" Pellolus Luce and all of his other blood relatives to the fourth degree, giving them five soldi each and demanding that they be content.[39] Notaries and their clients, in fact, employed these tactics for avoiding future claims on estates more often in Perugia than in any of the other city-states. Here, more than three-fourths of the testaments circumvented the possible future claims of friends and kin by such formulaic devices—double that of the Sienese and more than twelve times that of the Pisans.

Testators from Perugia, moreover, tried to influence the future affairs of their heirs, relatives, and friends in other ways. Not only did they prohibit sons and their descendants from selling their ancestral houses; like the Aretines, they asked their heirs for structural changes and specific improvements to their houses. In 1389, a Perugian woman, domina Angela Peruti, gave a married daughter her house with a garden, provided that she spend twenty florins on improvements (*cum accomine et ad edificationem fiendam*) on, not this house, but a cottage given to another, unmarried daughter.[40] The demands of the nobleman Nerus in 1393 reached further into the future business of his heirs. He left his cousin as universal heir but required him to build a bridge leading to their ancestral house. The bridge was to be divided equally between a friend and his wife and then to remain "perpetually" the communal property of "all those from his house" (*debeat comunis dictarum domorum*).[41]

In these laconic documents, emotional attachment to the future relations of testators' progeny on occasion slips into the language. In 1390 a villager left his daughter the customary possibility of returning to his home should she become a widow. He then added that he hoped she would be fed and cared for in this home by his son and heir "with fraternal love."[42] In 1417, a certain Francescus tried to influence the affairs of his kin down the generations. He left his two nephews a farm house with a courtyard and a well, prohibiting any alienation of this property and insisting that his nephews and their descendants maintain it "and live in it always as a family" (*debeant habitare familiariter*).[43]

Concern for the moral and economic well-being of testators' heirs are manifest in other legacies. In 1362, another Perugian left his three daughters a dowry of four hundred florins each but then added that, if one of them had difficulty marrying (*non posset commode maritari*), his executors might augment it to five hundred.[44] Like the Aretines and Florentines, the Perugians demanded the obedience of their children to specially chosen surrogate parents—wives, brothers, or other guardians. The most extraordinary provision made for the future security of offspring and descendants came from a Perugian nobleman in 1383, who made his sons his universal heirs. If they died without sons, the dowry of his daughter was to be doubled to two thousand florins. If all his sons and their male children died without heirs, then his granddaughter's dowry was to be also supplemented by a thousand florins. His residuary estate would then build a monastery on the hill in the village of Cordigliano. After minutely detailing the conditions for the construction and rule of this monastery, the knight required that, if any future progeny of his house, male or female, legitimate or illegitimate (*spureus*), should prove "deficient in some faculty, unable to survive on his own," then the monastery would be obliged to take him in and to provide him with food and clothing as long as he remained inscribed and obedient to the monastery's superiors.[45]

Women and Lineage

The cases above, backed by statistical analysis, show that testators in Arezzo, Florence and Perugia failed to accept their total departure from the present world of mundane affairs. Instead, they attempted to orchestrate from the grave their successors' actions and behavior, with the intent of preserving the testators' earthly memory. The extent to which testators pursued these posthumous worldly designs cuts a precise geography. Where mendicant piety was less influential in structuring the pious portions of wills, testators also strove to hold on to their nonpious property beyond the grave by influencing its future devolution and the behavior of their heirs. In these cities, the male-oriented ideal of lineage was the principle by which testators restricted the free flow of their gifts.

Especially in Florence and Arezzo, testators and their notaries deployed a highly developed vocabulary for directing properties down the male line—*ceppo, agnatio, domus, fidecommissum, consanguineos, affines, stirpes, in ordine successivo, ad gradum, per lineam masculinam*—words and phrases that do not become common in Sienese testaments until well into the sixteenth century.[46] Moreover, testators often prescribed the rules of property division for future generations of heirs. Almost invariably, they favored the property rights of the family stock and lineage (*in stirpe*) over those of the individual (*in capite*). While testators from Perugia, similar to those in Assisi, Pisa, and Siena, rarely relied on this technical vocabulary, they were nonetheless as intent on restricting property rights and influencing the ways of their heirs as their contemporaries in Florence and Arezzo.

In line with the conclusions drawn in comparative anthropological studies of societies as diverse as American Indian tribes in the nineteenth century and Moslems in medieval Spain, women exercised a weaker control over property in those societies of late medieval central Italy that stressed descent through the male line.[47] However, unlike these anthropological studies, my comparison of complex urban societies in late medieval Italy does not provide the sharp and systemic contrasts between societies structured by patrilineal as opposed to matrilineal systems of descent. In all six cities, the general model of inheritance was roughly the same (as can be seen in the intestate laws of their communal statutes). Fathers as well as mothers named their sons as universal heirs with equal rights to the estate, while daughters were granted dowries during their parents' lifetimes and, at their parents' deaths, usually received no more than an "augumentum" to the dowry.

Jack Goody and David Herlihy maintain that this arrangement in fact was generally the model throughout the Christian Mediterranean.[48] For the six city-states, testators named sons and daughters to inherit estates equally in only 13 percent of the cases in which children of both sexes survived a parent (53 of 409 testaments). Goody further generalizes that, "in stark contrast to most of traditional Africa," women in European societies were "seen as the residual heirs in preference to more distant males."[49] But the inheritance patterns of the city-states of late medieval central Italy do not bear out this claim (unsubstantiated by any statistics). Instead, parents chose daughters as their universal heirs before more distant male kin in only 42 percent of the relevant cases (264 testaments of 631).

Despite the general statutory structure of these patrilineal city-states, they nonetheless show significant differences in male descent over time and space. Before the plague of 1362–63, parents chose their daughters over more distant kinsmen as the first choice to inherit their estates in over half the cases (135 of 162 testaments); afterward, the figure plummeted significantly, to 35 percent (129 of 370).[50] Over space, these patterns of descent roughly reflect the patterns of piety and male lineage ideology found earlier for the six city-states. In Florence, where testators were most conscious of entailing their properties through the male line, parents least favored their daughters as heirs over more distant kinsmen (36%, or 44 of 123 testaments). Pisa lies at the other extreme of this spectrum; parents in this maritime city entitled their daughters as universal heirs over more distant kinsmen in 55 percent of the cases (59 of 107 testaments).[51] Nor do these differences result simply from the greater number of women testators in Pisa. Similar patterns are found for Siena, where women constitute slightly less than a third of the testators. Contrary to Eleanor Riemer's claim that only mothers named daughters as their heirs, the majority of those naming daughters as universal heirs in the Sienese samples were in fact fathers (191 fathers, 137 mothers).[52]

The underside of these systems of male lineage was the weakness of women in their exercise of power over property. First, the very act of women redacting wills is testimony to a degree of discretionary power over property. In Pisa, where the entail of property through the male line even among the nobility was extremely rare before the recurrence of plague, women redacted wills almost as often as men (48% and 49%, respectively, before the Black Death). Florence, where the ideology of lineage and entail down the male line appeared earliest and filtered through society most widely, represents the other extreme: less than 30 percent of Florentine testators were women, and before 1363 the proportion was even lower.

These extremes become more patent when the marital status of women testators is considered. Three-fourths of these women in Florence were widows, and less than 10 percent allocated their last properties while married. In Perugia, the highest percentage of married women drew up their own testaments (42%), followed closely by Pisa (38% or four times the percentage for Florence). Before the Black Death, however, Pisa was the leader; and while the percentage was roughly constant for Pisans over time, in Perugia its earlier rate was less than one-third (28%).

Once the testaments of married women are examined more closely, the distinctions among these towns become even stronger, and the wrinkle in these patterns initially presented by the percentages of women testators in Perugia becomes less glaring. While married women constituted a larger percentage of the women redacting wills in Perugia than in Pisa, the act of writing a will for such women appears not to have been the same in these cities. More than half of Perugian women testators simply used their wills to turn over their dotal as well as nondotal properties to their husbands by naming them universal heirs. In Florence nearly 40 percent of married women did the same.[53]

For Pisa the story is entirely different; of 134 wills of married women, not a single one used a testament to transmit the bulk of her property to her husband. The closest any testament came to such a property settlement was in a codicil redacted by the wife of a nobleman in 1311.[54] Its one itemized gift left Chisluccia's husband, Dominus Chellus, not full rights to all her property but the usufructus of all her goods. The testatrix, however, was not a resident of Pisa but came from the village of Podio de Lucca. In Pisa, the customary practice for a married women was instead to leave her husband a mere fifteen lire, which after the Black Death certainly did not constitute a sizable gift even for artisans and peasants.[55] These women, moreover, would "nominate" as their universal heirs nieces, nephews, or even men and women who bore no apparent relation to them—a practice (from testamentary evidence) that was rare for Perugians and Florentines. In Pisa some married women wrote wills without even acknowledging their husbands with the customary fifteen-lire legacy—a far cry from Florence, where a woman had to have the approval of a contracted "protector," her *mundualdus,* who in the case of married women was in these documents almost invariably the husband. It is again telling that of these six towns only Florence retained this Lombard custom in its statutory regulations.[56]

The most common dictate from the grave regarding the future behavior of a beneficiary was the property settlements husbands left their wives. A glance at these again reveals the inferior position of women in Florence, Arezzo, and Perugia vis-à-vis those cities where the mendicant pattern of piety was strong and lineage weak.[57] In all these societies, the individual property settlements that men left their wives show a wide range of possibilities: from one extreme, leaving their wives as universal heirs without restrictions over all the husband's property, without barring the widow's freedom to remarry, and without putting conditions on her future sexual behavior, to the other extreme, in which their wives' dowries were not even returned or were left unmentioned.

In all these societies, however—with the exception of Florence—the husband usually left his wife her dowry without restrictions, along with the usufructus of all of his property so long as she remained chaste (lived the "honest life") and did not remarry.[58] In Florence, this usufructus would often include the husband's gifts, such as her linen and jewelry. By contrast, in Pisa, these properties would be protected as a part of the wife's dowry. Moreover, of the six cities, only in Pisa (and occasionally in Assisi) did fathers and their notaries divide their daughters' inheritances into two legal categories, distinguishing their dowry from their *paraphernalia,* those properties that under Roman law, the daughter would bring into marriage but could control herself without relinquishing them to her husband's administration. Indeed, Julius Kirshner shows that this Roman law distinction between the *patrimonio dotale* and the *paraphernalia* vanished from the Florentine statutes with the redaction of 1322, and Francesco Ercole argues that it disappeared in many regions of Italy during the fourteenth century.[59]

Husbands' settlements were the least favorable to their future widows in Florence. Most often, the husband granted his wife the usufructus of his property (and often, especially among the merchant class, only a portion of his property—her *camera,* linen, and her jewelry), provided that she remain chaste, not remarry, and not ask for her dowry.[60] This arrangement was unheard of in the numerous wills in Pisa and Siena and appears in only a few documents from Assisi (4 of 115 wills redacted by husbands while their wives were still alive). In these three cities, a woman's rights to her dowry after the death of her husband appear nearly unassailable.

Moreover, in Arezzo and Perugia, where the mendicant patterns of piety competed less forcefully with testamentary designs for earthly memory, women also fared less successfully. Although the most common arrangement was one in which the widow's rights over her dowry remained unimpaired, husbands in these towns commonly left their future widows the less advantageous option of taking the usufruct of the husband's estate only as long as she relinquished all rights to her dowry. It constitutes, in fact, the second most frequent formula found in husbands' settlements.[61]

Conclusion

This comparative analysis shows Florence, often taken in the recent literature as typical of the condition of women in late medieval and early Renaissance Italy, as the exception.[62] Of the six societies considered here, Florence was the worst place to have been born a woman, at least in terms of one's discretionary power over property. The situation in Arezzo and Perugia was roughly congruent with practices in Florence, especially in comparison to Siena, Assisi, and Pisa. On this score, the towns divide into the same two triads discovered in the patterns of piety and attitudes toward worldly endeavors and property. With the possible exception of Perugia, whose laconic testaments reveal less about testators' motivations than records in Tuscany, traditions of lineage—the strength of the male line—loom behind the differences in the patterns of piety among these cities: the strength of mendicant ideals of self and worldly denial, as opposed to the quest for earthly memory. Those societies where lineage and the zeal to preserve one's name and the memory of one's ancestors were strongest were also the cities where women's power over property was weaker and where their rights over their most basic economic and social resource—their dowry—was in jeopardy.

A general underlying connection unfolds between the power of women over property and the strength of patrilineal lineage, on the one hand, and patterns of piety and notions of the afterlife, on the other. More than economy, aristocratic alliance (Guelf or Ghibelline), type of regime, strength of one order of mendicancy versus another, ancient settlement patterns and corresponding traditions of law (Lombard vs. Roman), the one structural characteristic that correlates with geographical differences in pious giving is the importance of the male line in property descent—and its corollary, the disadvantageous property status of women.[63] Where concern with remembrance and the devolution of property through the patrilines were strong, mendicant values proved less hegemonic.

At the heart of Jacob Burckhardt's classic formulation of Renaissance individualism lies a crucial contradiction.[64] Those societies where testators were most obsessed with earthly glory and the preservation of memory, whether achieved through clauses blocking the alienation of property or through the construction of burial complexes advertising the profane symbols of family pride, were also the ones where testators were governed most by the constraints of their ancestors. These testators' attempts to govern from the grave the behavior of heirs might well be interpreted as evidence of individualism—the attempt "to fashion other selves."[65] However, at the societal level, these egoistic demands only created barriers to the free and individual disposition of property. As with the choice of burials and chapel foundations, which increasingly became ancestral grounds with ancestral rules, so with the channel of property descent: increasingly, the hand of the ancestor restricted individual testamentary choice. Furthermore, in those societies where the ideals of earthly memory were more in evidence, women exercised less individual choice in their discretionary power over property than where mendicant values dampened the zeal for earthly self-preservation.

Most important, individualism and the cult of fame and glory, which intensified during the late Trecento, were far from being opposed to those ideals Burckhardt identifies as feudal and antithetical to the Renaissance. A new sense of family that Burckhardt and others associate with the supposed earlier ideals of the feudal clan—lineage and the corporate ideology of the *domus*—swept through society, reaching even the ranks of artisans and propertied peasants by the late Trecento. These ties to the ancestors and the values of the male line became the very channels through which testators expressed their desires for earthly fame and glory.

4. Women and the
Counter Reformation in Siena

AUTHORITY AND PROPERTY

IN THE FAMILY

Western Europe of the sixteenth and early seventeenth centuries witnessed the birth of absolutist states and, according to recent literature, the authoritarian family.[1] The dominant religious ideologies, Calvinism and the Catholicism of the Counter Reformation, propagated the ideals of submission and imposed structures of conformism that penetrated society more thoroughly than had been possible in the past. In such a climate, the authority of fathers and husbands narrowed the decision-making power that wives and children had previously enjoyed during the late Middle Ages. In Catholic Europe the condition of women may have deteriorated even further than in Protestant countries, since the antisexual attitudes of Puritan sects sought to eradicate the double standard tolerated by the elites in Mediterranean Catholic societies and raised the image of the good wife to that of spiritual helpmate and companion in the trials and tribulations of everyday life. According to this historiography, there thus emerged what Lawrence Stone calls "the companionate marriage" in seventeenth-century Protestant countries such as England.[2]

This chapter examines a more limited geography: Siena and its surrounding countryside (contado) during the sixteenth and early seventeenth centuries. It concentrates on a type of documentation—last wills and testaments—that is certainly not new to historians of early modern Europe, but that has rarely been used to consider problems other than changes in religious attitudes or the patterns of inheritance. These bundles of notarial formula, itemized legacies, and at times, personal (not formulaic) declarations of sentiment illuminate relations between husband and wives, widows and children, which are left obscure in most other sources that concern social classes below the highest echelons of the elites. These declarations, placed in the context of other social facts gathered from wills and other sources, give a new vantage point for investigating changes in women's decision-making powers within the family, from the aristocracy to artisans.[3]

To assess the impact of the Counter Reformation on Sienese women, I first examine changes in the ways women disposed of their property, ranging from clauses pertaining to the salvation of their souls, to pious and charitable bequests, to last gifts made to friends, kin, and neighbors. Second, I demonstrate that testaments show changes in women's decisions regarding their bodies, at least in regard to their final resting grounds—the choice of their graves. Finally, I read qualitatively evidence not usually expected within the monotonous lists of legacies and the arid and prosaic formulas that structure most last wills and testaments. Beyond the dispositions of patrimonies and the obligations and restrictions of heirs, Sienese testaments of the early modern period began to leave individualistic expressions of respect and gratitude between spouses with increasing frequency.

Before proceeding to a statistical analysis of the testaments, we need to define the chronology of the Counter Reformation: when did this religious movement begin to change the everyday patterns of thought and action of common men and women in Siena? This longest council in the history of Catholicism ended in 1563. The year afterward, the annual synod of the archdiocese of Siena approved the council's canons and decrees.[4] Yet little changed, either in local church hierarchy or in the wills of ordinary citizens and villagers in the territory of Siena. As for many Italian city-states, the Counter Reformation instead arrived in Siena with the first wave of apostolic visitations conducted with a rigor and completeness that cannot be seen in previous bishop visitations of their dioceses.[5] In 1575, Gregory XIII nominated Francesco Bossi, bishop of Perugia, as apostolic visitor to Siena. Bossi quickly established a tribunal and police apparatus in the city's Franciscan friary and began to scrutinize systematically the behavior of both ecclesiastics and the faithful—from members of the aristocracy, even the former papal Piccolomini family, to humble peasants.

The bishop and his officials traveled through city and territory examining the state of church buildings, the upkeep of graveyards, the presentation of the host, the character of religious paintings, and the Latin of parish priests; they interrogated parishioners and priests to ferret out salacious details of moral scandals, principally ones involving sex.[6] Behind this papal visitation, moreover, unlike the earlier ones (which in Siena were little more than inventories of liturgical possessions) lurked mechanisms for persuasion and enforcement.[7] Bossi's court stripped clerics of their vestments and sent lay sinners into exile.

The historian can even gauge the effectiveness of Bossi's work. On 25 January 1598, the reformer and later the archbishop of Siena, Cardinal Francesco Maria Tarugi, conducted another detailed and lengthy visitation. Against the stark inquisitional tones of a generation earlier, Tarugi's investigation was a festive and joyous affair. In nearly every parish, whether urban or rural, the parishioners, both men and women, came to the borders of their parish carrying the host. Their processions "with all those of the *populo*" (parish community) escorted the cardinal from the borders of their parish to the parish church. There, the grand visitor "absolved the dead and after the celebration of mass delivered an Evangelical sermon to those present." Finally, before embarking on the chores of inspection, the cardinal gave holy communion, blessing "as many women as men" (*tam viros quam mulieres*).[8]

Beyond these impressions, a systematic comparison might be drawn between these two points in time. Such a study would be too extensive to undertake here, but a cursory reading of these lengthy visitations reveals a radical change in behavior, architecture, and spiritual life during the intervening twenty-three years. Confession booths, which in 1575 were altogether missing or inappropriately constructed (even in the cathedral of Siena), were in place in the smallest rural churches; graveyards, formerly the feeding grounds for stray dogs, were now enclosed according to the prescriptions of Carlo Borromeo; paintings that Bossi considered either lascivious or ugly (often the comment was simply "too dark") were replaced with new altarpieces; church roofs in need of repair were repaired (except for those rural churches most battered by the war with Florence); the host, often left on windowsills, unprotected and unadorned, were appropriately enclosed in tabernacles with appropriate baldachins.[9] The interrogations of parishioners and priests in 1598 are less scintillating than earlier ones. In Tarugi's ledgers, sexual scandals were few; clerics resided in their rural parishes, and most could pass the rudimentary requirements of their Latin examinations.[10]

Rich as the evidence is from these visitations, space allows for only two observations. Bossi's instructions and condemnations proved to be effective not simply from force or authority.[11] In the visitations of 1575, artisans and peasants expressed resentment of absentee priests who siphoned off their tithes but were unavailable to perform the last rites when neighbors and relatives lay dying. Bossi and his troop listened sympathetically to the complaints of parishioners. Absenteeism led the list. Accordingly, the act most often read to the annually congregated clergy of Siena was the Tridentine decree regarding the residence of parish priests, and perhaps the most effective reform achieved in these years was the residency of parish clerics, who would regularly sing masses, hear confessions, and visit the ill. The enforcers of Trent tapped popular appeal.[12]

Second, Bossi recommended but did not demand the formation of parish lay confraternities and said nothing at all about women's confraternities. The synods of the archdiocese of Siena from 1575 through the early seventeenth century neither required nor urged women parishioners to form or join such companies to praise the holy host. During the intervening quarter century a major transformation had nonetheless taken place beyond the dictates of Counter-Reform enforcement. Parish confraternities, which had been rare in 1575, were almost nonexistent for women. By the beginning of the Seicento, nearly every parish had at lest one lay society; many had two, and women were participating in these new forms of spiritual life in numbers equal to men. In the 1575 records, women were almost totally absent from the spiritual life of the parish. In the visitations of Tarugi, on the other hand, enthusiastic women swelled the ranks of parish processions greeting the cardinal with praises and prayers.

Beyond social status and geography, the division of the population by gender most delineates the early adherents of the new Counter Reformation.[13] The rise in religious enthusiasm of women was both more startling and more enduring than that of urban artisans and petty merchants or of any other group that the notarial conventions distinguish. When we think of the rigorous ascetic regulations and the special discipline that Counter Reformation fathers such as Carlo Borromeo imposed on women, this claim appears even more surprising.[14] At this critical juncture, women deserve especially close attention.

What did the Counter Reformation offer women?[15] First, the numbers and percentages of women who redacted wills suggest that conditions may have begun to change for them immediately after Bossi's reforms. From the mid-fifteenth through the sixteenth centuries, fewer than one-third of the testators were women. By the first quarter of the Seicento, as the repercussions of Tridentine reforms were felt, women nearly reached parity with men. This increase was not simply the result of a long linear progression.[16] By the beginning of the eighteenth century, when indexes of reform vigor peaked, the sex ratio of testators declined once again to the levels of the late Renaissance.

While the numbers of women redacting wills increased, the number and range of their charitable bequests expanded dramatically. From the mid-Quattrocento until the reforms of Bossi, women on average had rarely given more than a single gift to pious causes. The same held for their itemized gifts to friends and relatives; never had these bequests exceeded an average of two gifts per testator, whereas men's gifts to friends and kin in 1551–75 were more than three times that of women (3.55 gifts per testator, see table 4.1).

With the first signs of the penetration of the Council of Trent on the local scene (after the visitations of 1575–76), matters began to change for women. The widening of choices presented in their testaments reflects these changes. In the critical years, the number of nonpious gifts bequeathed by women increased by nearly 40 percent and pious ones by 70 percent. Their trend, moreover, unlike that of artisans and shopkeepers, did not diminish soon after the initial enthusiasm; in the Seicento, the pious bequests of women trebled their pre-Tridentine number. In terms of value, the increase was staggering. By midcentury, the average value of those gifts had soared thirty-five-fold since its low mark in the mid-Cinquecento. Even in terms of constant prices, the change remains impressive; these donations increased in value by a factor of more than sixteen.[17]

With Trent in motion, the pious bequests of women, despite their financial inferiority, exceeded those of men for the first time. These statistics show women clearly in the vanguard of the Counter Reformation. In the critical years following Bossi's reforms, women were fully engaged in the new devotional practices, while men (who controlled by far the greater resources) stuck fervently to their old ways. Their pious bequests (regardless of class or residency) continued to slide in both number and value.[18] The "conversion" of men came at least a generation later.

Why were women the first ones drawn to the Counter Reformation? Not only did the Counter Reformation provide new outlets for women to dispose of their wordly goods; a considerable proportion of the new insti-

TABLE 4.1. Piety by Gender, 1451–1800

Gender and Period	Testators	Percentage of Testators	Number of Pious Bequests	Percentage Monetized	Average Value of Bequest (florins)	Ratio of Values, Male/ Female
Men						
1451–75	40	100.00	96	50.00	26.20	3.25
1476–1500	65	65.35	114	50.88	60.07	2.53
1501–25	65	71.58	92	53.26	50.04	1.74
1526–50	40	66.18	69	43.48	103.10	1.06
1551–75	78	63.36	111	43.24	151.51	13.00
1576–1600	80	67.18	110	41.82	93.33	1.34
1601–25	48	59.52	143	48.95	322.65	1.08
1626–50	62	54.87	168	30.36	260.24	0.64
1651–75	53	58.24	99	28.28	321.55	1.06
1676–1700	59	58.65	153	25.49	312.78	0.55
1701–25	70	67.62	225	31.56	561.69	1.33
1726–50	46	62.16	143	27.97	636.54	1.88
1751–75	59	64.52	99	21.21	155.65	1.32
1776–1800	42	67.19	116	43.97	133.68	2.08
Women						
1451–75	19	34.43	26	57.69	8.06	0.31
1476–1500	34	34.65	49	59.18	23.71	0.39
1501–25	27	28.42	31	45.16	28.72	0.57
1526–50	23	33.82	34	44.12	97.57	0.95
1551–75	48	36.64	53	50.94	11.66	0.08
1576–1600	42	32.82	80	46.25	69.80	0.75
1601–25	34	40.48	110	54.55	297.46	0.92
1626–50	51	45.13	105	28.57	409.77	1.57
1651–75	38	41.76	102	23.53	304.71	0.95
1676–1700	43	41.35	84	9.52	573.47	1.83
1701–25	33	32.38	88	34.09	422.56	0.75
1726–50	27	37.84	65	29.23	339.32	0.53
1751–75	29	35.48	55	21.82	117.71	0.76
1776–1800	21	32.81	30	26.67	64.38	0.48

tutions of reformed devotion directly concerned both the spiritual well-being and the social welfare of women. Women's religious confraternities and women's participation in parish societies devoted to the Holy Sacrament grew by leaps and bounds.[19] The new congregations for the poor mainly ministered to the problems of needy women: the *congregazione delle derelitte,* the *abbandonate,* the *convertite,* the *fanciulle sperse,* the *mulieres de deo*.[20] Perhaps the presence of these new institutions reflects new levels of social need on the part of women during the late sixteenth century. With the emergence of the European marriage pattern, greater numbers of women remained celibate at the very moment when nunneries were either becoming aristocratic in membership or "dilapidated repositories for females."[21] Thus, growing numbers of women were left without the financial support and protection of those individuals more favored monetarily by the inheritance patterns of the sixteenth century—men. From the evidence at our disposal, it cannot be determined whether the social and economic conditions of poorer women suddenly worsened precisely when these new institutions for the care and support of impoverished and usually unwed women began to flourish. But it is clear that the founders of these Counter-Reformation institutions were more sensitive to the problems of distressed women.[22] Most likely, these problems were not new but had been on the social horizons since the reemergence of demographic pressures toward the end of the fifteenth century.[23] One may question whether these new institutions that confined the poor ultimately benefited them.[24] But at the very least they provided new charitable choices to propertied women. These choices, moreover, possessed feminine interest and feminine identification.

The Counter Reformation affected the choices women made with their bodies, at least in the last resort: the choice of their graves. In the late Middle Ages and early Renaissance, women freely chose their place of burial, as the parish and the local monastery competed for the proceeds.[25] Where it is possible to reconstruct the burial choices of both husbands and wives, women often selected places other than the vaults or ditches of their spouses. During the first fifty years of the Quattrocento, five of every six women (based on thirty-six women's wills) who specified their place of burial freely chose places separate from husbands, fathers, or any of the male lineage ("in solito tumulo suorum antecessorum sive precessorum"). In only six cases did women explicitly "elect" the resting grounds of husbands or male ancestors. During the second half of the century the proportion of new graves that women selected independently of husbands and lineage fell by over half (based on forty women's wills), declining still further during the first half of the Cinquecento (based on thirty-eight women's testaments). For the first time since the earliest notarized wills, the dictates of husbands or the male line predominated over the individual choices of those women powerful or independent enough to redact their own wills—a group that, as we have seen, had been shrinking over the course of the late Renaissance. Then with the beginnings of the Counter Reformation the trend reversed: the proportion of women's burial choices apart from husbands and lineage increased to half in the second part of the Cinquecento, then to nearly two-thirds during the first half of the Seicento, and finally to almost three-quarters for the last fifty years of that century of faith.[26]

Nor was this return to independent choice simply a return to the late medieval period, where the choice had been between the parish and the local monastery. To break the hold of the family vaults, the Counter Reformation created entirely new categories of choice, which proved to be of particular significance for women.[27] By the late Cinquecento women could choose among a growing number of places reserved exclusively for them—the burial vaults of women's confraternities and, more important, the new congregations for women such as the *congregazione delle centurate* in the parish church of San Martino, the congregation of the Rosary in the monastery of Santo Spirito, and the congregation of the Conception in San Francesco. In return for dues of only a few lire to the congregation of Saint Peter, women from all social classes might leave their bodily remains under the *pavimento* of the Duomo, once the exclusive burial place of the lay elites and clerics. This congregation, similar to other Counter-Reform institutions, segregated its vaults by sex. Formerly the privilege of monastic orders alone, these sex-segregated tombs provided an alternative to the decisions of male executors, universal heirs, husbands, and fathers as well as the past decisions of the male line. In the first fifty years of the Quattrocento, only two women, both nuns, were buried in communal vaults with other women; by the first half of the seventeenth century nearly two-thirds of women chose such places against their husbands' choices and the traditions of lineage.[28]

The testaments permit us once again to go beyond quantification. The language of these generally laconic contracts was not always formulaic. In addition to property, obligations, and conditions, men and women often left brief personal expressions of gratitude and trust to servants, children, friends, masters, and most often, spouses.[29] These phrases, in aggregate, suggest possible changes in marital relationships. Phrases, such as the one that prefaced the grant of usufructus *ex patrona* to the wife of the butcher

Quiricus olim Pasquini, in 1551, were not untypical of the mid-Cinque-cento: "In consideration of the goodness, obedience, and deserving wor-thiness of this domina Batista, should it be acceptable to her, he leaves her the usufructus *ex patrona* of all of his goods."[30] In other words, for all his attention to her "bonitate et obbedientie et benemeritis," she received only a widow's expected inheritance—the use of her husband's property.

In January 1576, Andrea di Giovanni from Ancaiano expressed gratitude to his wife, which suggests a new spirit behind the living matrimonial re-lationship: "cognizant of the love and benevolence which his most es-teemed consort, donna Margherita, had brought him and her toil through her continuous assistance . . . in managing his properties, causing them to increase in value and to expand in size, desiring to acknowledge and to re-munerate her for so many labors and to ensure that after his death she should not be dispossessed by the heirs . . . and so as never to suffer from need or through any contingencies . . . he left her as *patrona* and *usufruc-taria* of all of his possessions in the hope . . . that she would maintain the honest and widowly life."[31] Although the actual legal conditions do not vary between these two documents, the shift from an appreciation of obe-dience to gratitude for her labors in matrimony and wifely efforts to in-crease the wealth of the household betrays sentiments not so far removed form what Lawrence Stone calls the transition from the "patriarchal" to-ward the "companionate" marriage.[32]

During the Seicento, beneath statutory law, the testaments in aggregate reflect concrete changes in the prerogatives and property rights that hus-bands transmitted to their wives.[33] Husbands' wills over the long haul de-fined with varying degrees of specificity the rights and the divisions of property between widows and surviving children. In some cases, husbands redacted detailed inventories of the property rights of each of these parties. On occasion they specified with architectural rigor precisely the rights of occupancy in the home; the rights of passage to various chambers and the use of wells and stairways were carefully separated for the use of their wid-ows and their progeny. More generally, from the earliest notarized wills through the late sixteenth century, the most common settlement was one in which the husband left his wife her dowry and the usufructus *toto tem-pore vite* to the residual properties of the estate, usually the bulk of real property marked ultimately for their universal heirs, who in most cases were the surviving sons. The usufructus to these properties, however, was rarely given unconditionally. If the widow decided to remarry or was found to be unchaste, she would lose all claims to those properties beyond her dowry, including her right to continue living in the household with her children.[34] Sons, as the universal heirs, were generally also the executors. In addition to receiving most of the property, usually all the landed properties, they assumed the responsibilities for enforcing the wills' instructions. Thus they were entrusted with policing their mothers' behavior, in particular her chastity. Moreover, these sons stood to benefit most directly and immediately from a mother's sexual infraction. Hence, they could curtail the widow's enjoyment of the ancestral properties or prevent her from squandering its future resources, thereby assuming their inheritance earlier.

In post-Tridentine Siena, the power and property relations of widows, at least within the ambit of the family, improved. Although husbands certainly did not suddenly depart from the formulaic grants to wives, curious wrinkles begin to appear for the first time in usufructus clauses. In 1590 a man from the region of Pisa, then living in Siena, nominated his wife as universal heir on the condition that "she remain chaste and serve the widowed life"—not, however, indefinitely, but for one year following her husband's death.[35] Three days later, the testator redacted a codicil to elaborate further his wife's freedom. He repeated that she was to be his universal heir and made explicit that she might remarry, "liberating her totally" from any obligations made in his present testament, "except the prohibition that she should serve the honest and widowed life for one year following the death of the testator."[36]

Husbands, at least by the second half of the Seicento, more often left their wives as their universal heirs with the ultimate rights of controlling the descent of property. Along with these rights often came other prerogatives and responsibilities, such as determining the amounts of the dowries for their daughters and selecting the recipients of certain pious bequests, from the selection of those entrusted with singing masses for the husbands' souls to the election of those poor girls of *buon costume* to receive dowries. During the Cinquecento husbands left their wives as universal heirs between 37 and 31 percent of the cases in which their wives survived them. The figures did not change significantly until the second half of the Seicento, when wives as husbands' universal heirs soared to nearly 60 percent.[37]

When the actual conditions and clauses regarding wives as universal heirs are scrutinized, the changes become more striking. Earlier, when husbands "nominated" their wives they often persisted in attaching the usual conditions found in the other formulaic marital settlements: if the widow

remarried or was unchaste she lost the patrimony. Thus, as the universal
heir in the Cinquecento, the widow found herself in the same position she
would occupy had her husband left her with only the widow's customary
rights; she could not exercise any discretionary powers over the direction
of her husband's estate. During the late century sixteenth century a quali-
tative change occurred; the formulaic conditions placed on widows disappeared altogether when they succeeded as their husbands' universal heirs.

The wills reveal other changes that undercut the prescriptions of statutory law. The number of mutual and reciprocal wills made by husbands
and wives together, usually while both enjoyed good health, was negligible
before 1575.[38] Only one of these partnerships appears during the Cinquecento, but for the second half of the seventeenth century, my sample contains nine. Of those identified by profession, all were from humble back-
grounds: a cobbler, a barrel maker, a mason, a silk weaver, three *maestri*,
and a sharecropper. In these wills each spouse entreated the surviving
spouse to say prayers or have masses sung for the other. Each became the
executor of the other's will, and each proclaimed the full faith and confidence in the other's devotion, which "so many years of marriage and com-
panionship would have led each to expect." Further, the widow was more
than the *usufructaria* of her husband's estate; no conditions were attached
to her enjoyment of the patrimonies in these mutual testaments. Instead,
their property rights were exactly identical. For instance, the "Provido
huomo" Cristofano, from the village near Monteriggioni of Abbadia Isola,
currently residing in Siena, and his wife Madonna Maria drew up a will together in 1642. Cristofano named Maria, Maria named Cristofano as universal heirs to their mutual estates and then appended the following:
"They wish not to impose any weight or aggravation on one another, because each of them confides in the good conscience of the other, that the
one who survives will have performed as many suffrages as possible for the
health of their souls."[39] But even before the diffusion of these practices in
the second half of the Seicento, testators expressed similar sentiments in
other wills. In 1611, for example, a baker for hostels in the rural villages of
Pontremoli explained why he chose his wife as universal heir: "for her infinite loving deeds" and the services she rendered him while he was ill. He
began his praise by claiming that "there has always been between them a
reciprocal love and benevolence."[40]

Finally, the appearance of new hortatory phrases reveal other changes in
property rights between widows and sons. By the mid-Seicento, husbands

reflecting explicitly on the doctrines of Trent, on the importance of hierarchy and obedience, placed their wives at the apex of the family and urged them to assume responsibility, as surrogate fathers, the education of their children in "the holy fear of God." In 1663 the sharecropper (*mezzaiolo*) Austino del gia Francesco Marianini, who worked the *podere* of San Maffei owned by the Dominican order, named his wife along with his daughter and son as universal heirs to the estate.[41] Quite out of line with Cinquecento property arrangements for widows—the grant of the usufructus—Austino gave his wife the explicit rights of selling property and using the house according to her judgment. Instead of *patrona usufructaria,* the sharecropper left his wife as the *padrona assoluta,* which meant that "she might do whatever she pleased" with his property, since "he was certain that she would be accountable for her children as indeed she had been in the past." He did, however, burden her with the "weight" of "educating" the children "in the holy fear of God." But the nature of the obligation was again quite unlike those conditions men placed on their wives during the Cinquecento. Instead of instituting watchdogs, either *fidecommissarii,* other relatives, or as was often previously the case, the sons themselves to oversee the behavior of the mother, the Seicento notary for the peasant merely added, "and all of this because he places faith in her goodness and integrity." In closing, the peasant besought his spouse "for the love of God" to dower "according to her capabilities" their daughter when she attained marital age.[42]

Other cases of husbands' mutual respect and affection rather than discipline and control over the future behavior of their widows come from the second half of the Seicento. In August 1678, Iacomo di Antonio Benvenuti from Florence, who "had lived for many years" in Siena as a commissioner in the office of the tobacco tax collection, left expectations and instructions in addition to property to his nearest kin—his wife and a fraternal niece who had lived in the household "for many, many years" and now "merited to be considered as his own daughter." He named his wife universal heir and "appealed to her charity and love . . . that she educate and rear his niece in the service of God and for the health of her soul and that she feed her as best she could." Iacomo was quick to add that he was not, "however, placing any obligations on his heir, but only appealing to what could be expected from her will and desire." He made it clear to his niece that she might not pretend to any gifts other than the ones previously enumerated in the will; she was expected to live with his wife "with the obedience and love toward his heir that should be expected from a daughter, serving and assisting her in all her needs."[43]

In another seventeenth-century will, the nobleman Tullio del gia Nobile Fausto Ugurgieri began the sections pertaining to his wife: "Having known through practical experience the cordial love that his most loving consort, domina Giulia, had always brought him, and confident that she would continue that same love and affection that she bore him toward their dearest children." He left her the rights and responsibilities as *curatrice et amministratrice* over the children and the household and then added: "because he trusts in an especial way that his wife will carry out the responsibilities for their dearest children, and since he hopes that she will always retain with maternal affection the responsibilities of educating their children, he beseeches her in the love of God to stay with the children, to educate, feed, and clothe them . . . and to govern the household through divine and human laws." The noble testator next appealed "with paternal love" to his eldest son, Signor Francesco, "to assist lovingly" the needs of his other brothers and wished his son to show his mother "the eminent deference" (*la grande obbedienza*), which hitherto he had accorded his father. The father, moreover—in striking contrast to Cinquecento formulas that granted the sons ultimate rights in the house of residence—obliged his son to leave to his mother the house *in promiscuo uso*. The son was not to make any demands on his mother's dowry or its fruits. If the testator's wife did not wish to remain with her children, then the children were to provide her with an annual income of thirty scudi.[44] In the sixteenth century, by way of contrast, when an annual income was to be provided for the widow, it always had been the sons' prerogative whether to live with their mother or to expel her from the household with some compensation.

After the spread of Tridentine culture through the local parishes, husbands entrusted their widows more often than surviving sons with the ultimate rights of overseeing the moral order of the household. Here, concerns for religious education "in the holy fear of God" outweighed the old preoccupations with the widow's remarriage or chastity. Earlier matters of remarriage and chastity, after all, had not been simply concerns of morality; they threatened the flow of properties to the husband's progeny and the splintering of patrimonies.[45]

To understand further what Trent offered to women, the historian must understand the world of property relations and the role of women in property descent on the eve of the Counter Reformation. In late Renaissance

Siena, notaries and testators turned their attention from the lists of legacies to concentrate on the final section of the will—the property obligations attached to the universal heirs and the succession of future heirs, given the wide array of demographic contingencies that these testators often listed. Not only did this change in attitude result in a sharp diminution in the number and values of legacies left to the church and pious causes over the course of the sixteenth century, but last gifts to relatives who were not designated as universal heirs as well as legacies to friends and neighbors also declined in number and value. The role of Cinquecento testaments were first and foremost to channel landed property through generations of male heirs and to dictate in detail the future behavior of these heirs to ensure against the alienation or dispersal of the ancestral landed properties beyond the lineage.

By the sixteenth century, these concerns over the preservation of properties within the male lineage were not only the preoccupations of the old Sienese magnates, both male and female, but had penetrated Sienese society, characterizing even the last wills of peasants from the surrounding countryside. After compressed lists of individual legacies came long and complex clauses to ensure the preservation of the male line and to govern the flow of property and family names to the next generation. Testators specified in smallest detail the flow of their properties: who should inherit, given a complex web of demographic contingencies or if a future heir should violate a condition of the inheritance. At times, testators pondered the extinction of their biological male lines and devised conditions for the selection of a new heir who would consent to the conditions of the original testament as well as to adopting the family coat of arms, the chapel, and above all, the family name of the original and, perhaps by then, ancient testator. In this sixteenth-century world of property transmission, women were little more than cogs in a mechanism bent on directing property through the male line. Even powerful aristocrats, such as the "Honesta ac nobilissima" domina Camilla, the daughter of the deceased magnate Raynaldi de Tolomeis and the widow of Niccolai de Petruccijs (1560), had made few individual decisions in their testaments.[46] Beyond long and complex clauses regarding the channeling of her patrimony through male heirs and the preservation of the lineage, this extraordinarily wealthy woman, related to two of the most powerful of sixteenth-century Sienese families, left only four separate bequests, and one was the repayment of a debt. As we have seen, these patterns of property descent and the ideology of lineage went beyond the social ambit of the aristocracy.[47] They permeated Sienese society, reaching even peasants proud of their recently minted family names and possessing the wherewithal to leave notarized testaments.

By the early Seicento, noble women were the first to break ranks with their class in regard to property strategies benefiting the male line. Thus "la nobile et honestissima" Signora Erminia Bellanti, the wife of Bernardo Francesconi, named all eight of her children as the universal heirs, "the daughters as much as the sons." Again, against the grain of Cinquecento family and property strategies, the noble Erminia maintained that her inheritance was given "as much for their [her children's] possession as for their alienation of the properties." She further prohibited her husband from "acquiring any of the usufructus" to this inheritance. Rather, she wished her children to enjoy "its income, returns, and fruits . . . freely, fully, and immediately . . . especially her daughters, since they have the greater needs and the less security." Signora Erminia's final comment appended to her final disposition gave a new twist to the meaning of family—one that went to the immediate concerns and well-being of the then-living children as opposed to the Cinquecento ideology of lineage, the generational flow of property through the male blood. She asserted "that her husband should be the first to approve" these special provisions because they were made "for the benefit of the family."[48]

Other noble ladies, such as "the most chaste" Elisabetta q. Domini Michaelis Angeli de Ferrandinis, gave preferential treatment to nieces over nephews. She left her married niece, "the most chaste" Lisabetta, as universal heir, while her nephews were left holding the household linen (la biancheria).[49] The humble tertiary of the Dominican order, monna Cassandra del gia Francesco Bianchi, went the furthest in her Counter-Reform policy of affirmative action. In reaction to the Cinquecento ideology of blood and descent through the male line, her testament of 1691 left as universal heirs "all the legitimate and natural female children born or to be born of the said Chiara Papari," the testator's niece. She further clarified her decision over the future devolution of her property "excluding always and in whatever case or time, with the greatest of precautions, all males so long as there are female children."[50]

Changing notions about the family were not all that was at stake. My statistics show that the growth of the Cinquecento strategy of the afterlife of lineage robbed the church of sacred space and cut deeply into its revenues. Again, harking back to the years of Catherine and the reformers of the late Trecento, ideologues of the Counter-Reformed church sharply contrasted attachment to family and worldly goods with the grander sanctity of the spiritual life achieved through ascetic ideals and, at least in part, through the loosening of transient familial affections.[51] The militant church's attack on the interests of lineage had an unintended ally. Women had also suffered from the practices of late Renaissance property transmission.[52] Unlike the mechanisms of inheritance through the male line, Trent (again, without intent) opened new possibilities for women: participation in the spiritual life of the parish, new women's confraternities, new organizations that assisted impoverished women, new burial societies where women could make decisions independently of their husbands and fathers, and a new authority in the household once their husbands had died. As the life of Siena's Passitea Crogi illustrates, these new opportunities were not simply matters offered by the Church Fathers at Trent; rather they were opportunities taken through women's initiatives during the crisis of ideologies at the end of the Cinquecento.[53] Indeed, the testaments reveal ordinary women, a full generation before their brothers and husbands, as the vanguard of the Counter Reformation.

One question, however, remains unanswered. Why did husbands change their minds? Why did they reduce the previous restrictions on the properties they granted to their wives? Certainly the Counter Reformation had not transformed men into paragons of feminism, ever attentive to their wives' rights and needs.[54] Perhaps because women enjoyed a relatively stronger position in Sienese society and were better protected by church courts, which were more sensitive to the routine violence against women, testaments after the papal visitations of Bossi in fact give more evidence of women's complaints with married life and with their husbands' behavior.[55] In a testament of 1580 a man bequeathed the usufructus to his small shop (*botiguccia*) in the "Third" of Camollia near the Fonte d'Ovile to assist his daughter Laura, who was married to a tanner. He granted her this "subvention for her needs" because, "he attested," she "is poor and has been abandoned by her husband and does not possess the means to live except from her own toil."[56] In a will of 1602, monna Silvia gia di Pierantonio Ciappettini, the wife of Savino Locci, thanked her brother for all she had received from him "in her adversities. . . . Among many other courtesies and loving gestures" she had been able "to stay in his house and at his table for a long time. He had fed her and had seen to her every need, not only in health but also in her troubles, especially in her long litigations with her husband, Savino." Because of this and "moved by other reasons of conscience," she bequeathed to her brother and his heirs one-fourth of her dowry and property, "praying that he would with charity make the necessary arrangements for her body and soul, once she had passed to the other life."[57]

Nor had the Counter Reformation altered fundamentally the parameters of welfare and financial security for the majority of women—namely, the dowry. This long-entrenched custom could prove precarious even for those women most favorably situated in early modern society. The "nobile and honestissima" Signora Camilla alias Caterina, daughter of the nobleman Cesare Bianchi and widow of a nobleman from Florence, named her son universal heir. If he should die before the testator, she "substituted" her brother, the nobleman Signor Alcide. She was greatly obliged to him "for his trouble and for the expenses he incurred during her prevous adversities," particularly in the litigation for recovering her dowry in Florence. For five years he had assumed her financial burdens and those of her children when they were young and most in need of assistance.[58]

The Counter Reformation had not produced a new feminist man. Nor had it overturned the most fundamental material bridge between the sexes, the dowry. Nonetheless, attitudes as well as property, social, and legal relations did not remain hardened in some ideal-typical premodern mold. As we have seen, husbands' attitudes toward their wives moved from suspicion requiring legal force and outside agencies of surveillance to appeals to conscience, mutual respect, and a new confidence, which they claimed was rooted in lives of affection.

How do we explain these changes? Again, the testaments provide clues. The culture of the Counter Reformation changed the ways in which both men and women imagined the afterlife and lived in the present. During the late fifteenth and sixteenth centuries, while the number and value of pious bequests declined, testators were preoccupied less with their souls and more with the survival of their family names. In less than a quarter of a century, the reforms instituted at Trent transformed, first for women but finally for both sexes, that investment in lineage and the materialist hope for the afterlife. After the reforms, testators once again filled the treasuries of religious corporations and even alienated ancestral properties for the sake of the soul. In the charged atmosphere of seventeenth-century spiritual fears, obsessions, and expectations, men such as the "Illustrious" Annibale Piccolomini relied much more heavily than during the sixteenth century on the terrestrial intercession of their wives to say prayers and masses, to organize their funeral processions, to select the most deserving persons and charities. In the new spiritual ambience of the Counter Reformation, the wife had become, a generation ahead of the men, the spiritual smiths of the household. Husbands preparing for death, now pondering their soul's passage more than the devolution of their properties, found their wives' assistance of more use than trust mapped through the notaries' legalistic contingencies on property.

The supposed analogous developments of absolutism, the authoritarian Reformation, the authoritarian Counter Reformation, and the authoritarian family must be reexamined. First, the Counter Reformation was not a single phenomenon that pointed solely in one direction, as Protestant propaganda has held since the sixteenth century. Especially during the last quarter of the sixteenth century, it did not always develop from top to bottom; nor did change arise from the imposition of conformity and orthodoxy through force and repression.

In Siena, the apostolic visitations of 1575 gave rise to a more complex conflict, which (at least in its early stages) saw the alliance of peasants, artisans, and religious reformers against a corrupt and complaisant clergy and a church structure based from top to bottom on the nepotism of the old noble elites. Second, the "authoritarian" Counter Reformation had unintended and surprising consequences within the ambit of family life. After the death of husbands, widows and mothers acquired responsibility and authority within the household, often against the wishes of surviving sons, male relatives of the deceased husbands, and the executors of the estates. Instead of the authoritarian demands and controls that husbands of the Cinquecento before the Counter Reformation imposed on their widows, Sienese husbands of the Counter Reformation turned instead to appeals of love and affection. They placed trust in mutual loyalty acquired (as they declared) through the travails of married life and from what "practical experience" had led them to expect from one another. Thus, they explicitly renounced the controls that their fathers and grandfathers had imposed on their wives during the earlier part of the sixteenth century.

The Counter Reformation signaled a clear break with earlier strategies for the preservation of the male line and the transmission of landed property only to "male hands." At the end of the sixteenth century, unexpectedly, women and the church found themselves with a common enemy—a structure and an ideology of inheritance that saw salvation in the eternal continuity of male bloodlines. By the end of that century, in the era of a new Catholic devotion, women had ceased to be simple cogs in the transmission of property down male family lineages and, instead, could dispose of their patrimonies more fully and freely, choose the final resting places for their bodies, and plan for the salvation of their souls.

5. Nuns and Dowry Funds

WOMEN'S CHOICES IN THE RENAISSANCE

Last wills and testaments in Siena portray women as the shock troops of the Counter Reformation. They were the first to adopt the new patterns of piety—numerous masses, baroque funeral preparations, elaborate supplications to patron saints to intercede in the afterlife, and above all else, bequests to a plethora of new charitable groups that attended to the care of poor women, such as the "dispersed girls" and the "destitute women" who hung out in the piazza of the hospital of Sant'Onofrio.[1] With the rise of new charitable institutions that addressed women's problems and with the largess of propertied women who directed their charity toward such causes and institutions, late-sixteenth-century Sienese wills embodied new forms of women's consciousness.[2]

To further understand women's pious reactions after the Council of Trent, this chapter focuses on an earlier transformation in piety, against which these Counter-Reformation women would later rebel. This earlier shift in religious mentality came in the wake of the Black Death. Its arrival, however, coincided not with the cataclysmic events of 1348 but with the return of pestilence in 1362–63 and its relived trauma. The systematic study of hundreds of last wills and testaments chart this transformation in religious mentality. Instead of a change in pious choices, say from bequests to nuns to bequests to hospitals, it was the structure of giving itself that changed. From the late thirteenth century until the second attack of pestilence in the 1360s, testators fragmented and spread their wealth across a wide array of pious institutions.[3]

After 1363, such testaments disappear almost entirely as testators began to reconsider the mendicants' preaching about the fleeting significance of earthly endeavors and the sinful hubris of earthly pride. They began to stockpile their pious funds to support a small number of carefully selected charities in order to be remembered in both this world and the next.[4] For this change in psychology and piety after the Black Death, class, gender, and city-rural distinctions appear at first glance not to have been as important as they were to become during the Counter Reformation. In psychological terms, little distinguished Francesco Petrarch from the Tuscan peasant drawing up a testament at the same time. For both, the return of plague (for Petrarch, in 1361; for Tuscany and Umbria, in 1362 and 1363) brought back the trauma of 1348. It was this that broke patterns of belief and giving that had structured the majority of wills since the late thirteenth century. In both cases, mendicant disgust with worldliness was transformed into its opposite—a new obsession with earthly remembrance and the legal mechanisms to ensure its possibility. By the end of the fourteenth century, patricians and peasants alike were directing their pious funds toward ends that would prolong their earthly and spiritual memories.[5]

This first rupture in the deep structure of piety, at the second coming of the plague, was undifferentiated, I originally thought, because the plague struck the Italian population (at least in its earliest assaults) with no great regard for class or gender.[6] By comparison, the later break in piety of the Counter Reformation was more complex in terms of social class, gender, and politics, because toward the end of the sixteenth century peasants, women, and the new Counter-Reform church found themselves with a common enemy: the old aristocracy, whose ideology was deeply rooted in the symbols as well as the economic structures of property transmission down the male line.

But even if the Black Death struck the entire population of a village, city, or territory more or less the same without much regard for class, did men and women react to it in the same way? Did they adopt the new Renaissance forms of charity and spirituality that blossomed in the last decades of the Trecento with the same intensity? And if so, who were the leaders? While the structural changes in Renaissance giving were more striking than any transformation in testamentary choices, two changes in the destinies of pious recipients nonetheless stand out. Both concern the activities and welfare of women—on the one hand, bequests to nuns and nunneries; on the other, the testamentary foundations of dowry funds to initiate family life for poor nubile girls of *buon costume*. What was the fate of these institutions aimed at women over the late middle ages and early Renaissance, and did men and women support them equally?

In the last years of the thirteenth century, women in orders as well as a plethora of small semiofficial clusters of pious women vaguely described by a variety of labels—*donne, mulieres, recluse, incarcerate, romite*—had garnered over a fifth of all pious bequests in Florence, Siena, Pisa, Arezzo, Perugia, and Assisi, more than any other charitable category for that period or any other that I have uncovered from more than twenty thousand pious legacies (table 5.1).[7] With the beginning of the fourteenth century, bequests to nuns declined steadily, until by 1400 they constituted less than 6 percent of all pious legacies. In monetary terms, these gifts had become even more negligible, amounting to less than 3 percent of pious funds, or one-third of what they had been in the earliest testaments until 1275 (9.28%).[8] Yet the decline in value was less smooth than in the numbers of bequests, resulting in part from the occasional large bequest (figures 5.1, 5.2 and 5.3).

In Perugia, the value of bequests to nuns soared to nearly 22 percent in the years 1301–25, the highest levels found for any of these city-states. After falling steeply in the next period, 1326–47, it rose sharply again in the year of the Black Death, 1348, to more than 35 percent of all pious expenditures (figure 5.3). This deviation from the general trend of the other cities, however, needs to be treated with caution. The first jump is based on a small sample of twelve testaments, including one relatively large bequest of 31 florins to a convent in the *contado*.[9] Similarly, in the year of the Black Death, 1348, the average was inflated by a single bequest, in this case a contingent one that straddled the often thin line between the pious and the nonpious. Niccolaus f.q. Bernardoli Andreuti from the parish of San Pietro promised the usufruct of his "paternal inheritance," which he valued at 400 lire, to the nunnery of San Niccolò if his widow did not remarry and instead took vows. If his son should die without surviving children and his widow should join the nunnery, his bequest would double to 800 lire (372 florins), the largest bequest granted in these samples from any Perugian for any pious cause at the time of the Black Death—and the eighth largest for any cause.[10] If the medians instead of the averages of pious legacies are calculated for 1348, Perugia's proportion of pious expenditures, while remaining high and out of line with trends in the other cities, falls from 35 percent of all pious sums to 22 percent.[11]

After 1348, testamentary support for nunneries in Perugia followed the trends sketched for the other city-states. In the years immediately following the plague, the values of its bequests to nuns fell dramatically, to less than 1 percent of the value of all pious bequests, and remained at roughly

TABLE 5.1. Pious Bequests, by Sex, 1200–1425

Type of Bequest	Number of Bequests	Average Value of Bequest (florins)	Total Value of Bequests (lira)
Miscellaneous bequests			
Men	1,626	18.79	30,552.54
Women			
Raw figures	958	6.92	6,629.36
Wgt by testators	1,657		11,468.79
Wgt by wealth	3,631		25,125.27
Wgt by wealth × testators	6,495		44,947.06
Ratio M/F (raw figures)	1.70	2.72	4.61
Ratio M/F (wgt by testators)	0.98		2.66
Ratio M/F (wgt by wealth)	0.45		1.22
Ratio M/W (wgt by wealth × testators)	0.25		0.68
Priests and parishes			
Men	2,094	6.24	13,066.56
Women			
Raw figures	1,107	3.41	3,774.87
Wgt by testators	1,915		6,530.53
Wgt by wealth	4,196		14,306.76
Wgt by wealth × testators	7,505		25,593.62
Ratio M/F (raw figures)	1.89	1.83	3.46
Ratio M/F (wgt by testators)	1.09		2.00
Ratio M/F (wgt by wealth)	0.50		0.91
Ratio M/W (wgt by wealth × testators)	0.28		0.51
Friars			
Men	2,412	18.52	44,670.24
Women			
Raw figures	1,945	6.92	13,459.40
Wgt by testators	3,365		23,284.76
Wgt by wealth	7,372		51,011.13
Wgt by wealth × testators	13,187		91,254.73
Ratio M/F (raw figures)	1.24	2.68	3.32
Ratio M/F (wgt by testators)	0.72		1.92
Ratio M/F (wgt by wealth)	0.33		0.88
Ratio M/W (wgt by wealth × testators)	0.18		0.49
Monks and monasteries			
Men	797	7.72	6,152.84
Women			
Raw figures	608	2.15	1,307.20
Wgt by testators	1,052		2,261.46
Wgt by wealth	2,304		4,954.29
Wgt by wealth × testators	4,122		8,862.82
Ratio M/F (raw figures)	1.31	3.59	4.71

(continued)

TABLE 5.I. (continued)

Type of Bequest	Number of Bequests	Average Value of Bequest (florins)	Total Value of Bequests (lira)
Ratio M/F (wgt by testators)	0.76		2.72
Ratio M/F (wgt by wealth)	0.35		1.24
Ratio M/W (wgt by wealth × testators)	0.19		0.69
Nuns and nunneries			
Men	1,322	2.84	3,754.48
Women			
Raw figures	1,175	3.19	3,748.25
Wgt by testators	2,033		6,484.47
Wgt by wealth	4,453		14,205.87
Wgt by wealth × testators	7,967		25,413.14
Ratio M/F (raw figures)	1.13	0.89	1.00
Ratio M/F (wgt by testators)	0.65		0.58
Ratio M/F (wgt by wealth)	0.30		0.26
Ratio M/W (wgt by wealth × testators)	0.17		0.15
Hospitals			
Men	1,525	19.56	29,829.00
Women			
Raw figures	1,117	5.08	5,674.36
Wgt by testators	1,932		9,816.64
Wgt by wealth	4,233		21,505.82
Wgt by wealth × testators	7,573		38,472.16
Ratio M/F (raw figures)	1.37	3.85	5.26
Ratio M/F (wgt by testators)	0.79		3.04
Ratio M/F (wgt by wealth)	0.36		1.39
Ratio M/W (wgt by wealth × testators)	0.20		0.78
Confraternities			
Men	821	11.21	9,203.41
Women			
Raw figures	389	4.47	1,738.83
Wgt by testators	673		3,008.18
Wgt by wealth	1,474		6,590.17
Wgt by wealth × testators	2,637		11,789.27
Ratio M/F (raw figures)	2.11	2.51	5.29
Ratio M/F (wgt by testators)	1.22		3.06
Ratio M/F (wgt by wealth)	0.56		1.40
Ratio M/W (wgt by wealth × testators)	0.31		0.78
The "Poor of Christ"			
Men	799	40.38	32,263.62
Women			
Raw figures	479	11.90	5,700.10

Type of Bequest	Number of Bequests	Average Value of Bequest (florins)	Total Value of Bequests (lira)
Wgt by testators	829		9,861.17
Wgt by wealth	1,815		21,603.38
Wgt by wealth × testators	3,248		38,646.68
Ratio M/F (raw figures)	1.67	3.39	5.66
Ratio M/F (wgt by testators)	0.96		3.27
Ratio M/F (wgt by wealth)	0.44		1.49
Ratio M/W (wgt by wealth × testators)	0.25		0.83
Dowry funds			
Men	170	115.59	19,650.30
Women			
Raw figures	88	46.01	4,048.88
Wgt by testators	152		7,004.56
Wgt by wealth	334		15,345.26
Wgt by wealth × testators	597		27,451.41
Ratio M/F (raw figures)	1.93	2.51	4.85
Ratio M/F (wgt by testators)	1.12		2.81
Ratio M/F (wgt by wealth)	0.51		1.28
Ratio M/W (wgt by wealth × testators)	0.28		0.72
Servants			
Men	234	10.43	2,440.62
Women			
Raw figures	155	8.29	1,284.95
Wgt by testators	268		2,222.96
Wgt by wealth	587		4,869.96
Wgt by wealth × testators	1,051		8,711.96
Ratio M/F (raw figures)	1.51	1.26	1.90
Ratio M/F (wgt by testators)	0.87		1.10
Ratio M/F (wgt by wealth)	0.40		0.50
Ratio M/W (wgt by wealth × testators)	0.22		0.28
TOTAL			
Men	12,071	15.93	192,291.03
Women			
Raw figures	8,129	5.74	46,660.46
Wgt by testators	14,063		80,722.60
Wgt by wealth	30,809		176,843.14
Wgt by wealth × testators	55,115		316,357.92
Ratio M/F (raw figures)	1.48	2.78	4.12
Ratio M/F (wgt by testators)	0.86		2.38
Ratio M/F (wgt by wealth)	0.39		1.09
Ratio M/W (wgt by wealth × testators)	0.22		0.61

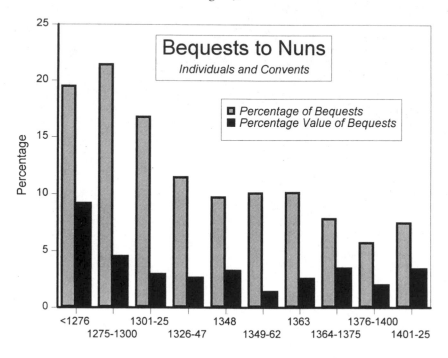

Figure 5.1

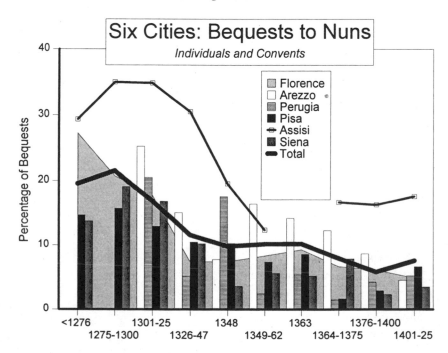

Figure 5.2

Figure 5.3

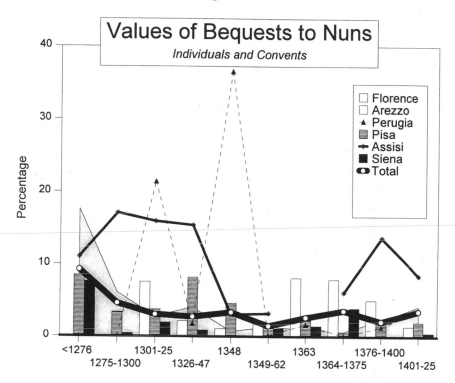

this low level through 1425. In the period following the second onslaught of pestilence, the number and values of these bequests sank to the lowest levels registered for any of these cities and for any period (1.52 and 0.10%, respectively).

In contrast with the Perugian experience, 1348 sparked a different reaction in testators' charitable decisions in the rest of these six cities; the proportions of funds to nunneries continued to tumble, in some cases more radically than at any other moment in the two centuries covered by these samples. With the Black Death of 1348, the values of legacies to nuns reached their lowest proportions in Assisi, Arezzo, and Florence, 3.52, 1.07, and 0.85 percent of all pious values, respectively. This general pattern of decline in testamentary support does not appear to have arisen from the institutional behavior of a dominant nunnery, the decisions of a local bishop, the politics of local clerics, or the secular policies or family strategies in any given city-state. Rather, the pattern was unmistakable in all six city-states (figure 5.1). Bequests to nuns and nunneries fell most precipitously in Pisa and Perugia, to less than 2 percent of all bequests in the years immediately following the plague of 1363.

In numbers of bequests to nuns and convents, only Assisi is at variance with the other Tuscan and Umbrian cities. In the city of Saint Francis, where mendicant ideals persisted longer than elsewhere, cloistered and individual penitent women fared better as the recipients of pious largess, drawing more than one-third of all pious bequests from the earliest testaments through the plague of 1348.[12] Yet Assisian nuns and recluses registered a decline to just under one-fifth of all pious legacies in the last quarter of the Trecento and the early Quattrocento. Similarly, the values of these Assisian legacies hovered above those in the other cities, but they too fell with the onslaught of plague in 1348 (figure 5.3).

Although tallies and percentages of testamentary gifts can by no means serve as a census of the numbers of nuns or nunneries, the trends uncovered by these samples are broadly commensurate with the conclusions of those who have studied nuns, recluses, and convents from the institutional perspective. In places where historians have attempted to estimate changes in the numbers of convents and nuns—Milan, Bologna, and Borgo San Sepolcro—they have observed a pattern of steady decline in the numbers of cloistered communities of women from the late Duecento and the opening years of the Trecento through the fifteenth century.[13] Gabriella Zarri's study of Bologna, the most meticulous survey to date of the demographics of nuns and nunneries from the central Middle Ages through the Counter-Reformation, shows that nuns and nunneries reached their numerical apex around 1315 and then declined rapidly through the fourteenth century. By the mid-fifteenth century, the numbers of nuns sank to their lowest level, and rapid recovery did not come until after the Counter Reformation; only in the late sixteenth or even the early seventeenth centuries did their numbers begin to rise.[14]

The one exception to this pattern comes from the seminal study by Richard Trexler, "Le célibat à la fin du Moyen Age: Les religieuses de Florence."[15] Although Trexler emphasizes the dramatic increases in nuns and nunneries from the third quarter of the fifteenth century through the period of the Council of Trent (on which my study does not bear), he also argues that the proportion of nuns in the city of Florence had doubled from Giovanni Villani's number found in his famous synopsis, "The Greatness,

Status, and Magnificence of the Commune of Florence" in 1336, to the *cat-asto* tax enumeration of religious institutions in 1428–29.[16] In a comparison with late medieval England, where, according to Eileen Power, nuns and nunneries fell on hard times from the reign of Edward III to the Reformation, Trexler claims that the sharp and exceptional increase in the enrollment of nuns in Florence resulted from changing family strategies among the middling merchants, or the Florentine bourgeoisie.[17] In the face of increases in dowry prices, Florentine fathers forced increasing numbers of their daughters into nunneries to avoid financial ruin.

But did dowries increase in Florence significantly more than in the neighboring city-states of Tuscany and Umbria, where (supposedly unlike Florence) the number of nuns and nunneries fell in number?[18] Or more than in Venice, where Stanley Chojnacki argues that patrician dowries increased by 4.6 times (in nominal values) from the mid-Trecento to the beginning of the sixteenth century?[19] Or in Siena, where at least by the end of the fifteenth century dowries of the elite were as high as in Florence?[20] If last wills can be taken as a guide, then nunneries in Siena, as in the larger and more prosperous territories of Milan and Bologna, appear to have declined in number and resources, despite rises in dowry prices. Nor had matters improved over the fifteenth and sixteenth centuries. In both spiritual and economic well-being, most Sienese convents endured intolerable conditions, described in vivid detail in the apostolic visitations of 1575.[21]

To return to the samples of last wills and testaments: in both proportions and values of bequests to sponsor nuns, Florence was not the exception but fell in with the general trend discernible in the other five Tuscan and Umbrian centers. In fact, its decline was even more pronounced than elsewhere. From their earliest testaments until 1275, Florentines bequeathed almost 30 percent of their pious legacies and almost one-fifth of the values of these bequests to nuns and nunneries (figures 5.2 and 5.3). By the early Quattrocento, such gifts to nuns and nunneries had dwindled in number to less than 5 percent of all pious bequests and in value to just above that figure.

Why should such discrepancies arise between the growing numbers of nunneries stated in chronicles and enumerated in tax records, on the one hand, and the dwindling pious legacies compiled in my samples, on the other? Could there have been a shift in funding for nuns from testamentary gifts to other sources of incomes (that is, running in just the opposite direction of the funding trends for confraternities and, possibly, hospitals)?[22] Might convents have increased but have become more impoverished or more reliant on dowries from their recipients' own families? To answer these questions, one must await studies on the finances of Tuscan and Umbrian nunneries comparable to the studies by James Banker and John Henderson for religious confraternities. But I suggest that the discrepancies arise largely from a radical shift in the communities that comprised religious and penitent women in later medieval Italy. Neither Giovanni Villani's mention of twenty-four nunneries in 1336 nor the *catasto* listings of 1428–29 would have charted the large array of small, short-lived, and fluid communities of amorites and recluses—tiny groups of women who appear with great regularity in thirteenth- and early fourteenth-century testaments throughout central Italy.[23]

Nor would Villani's number have included many of the tiny houses of unofficial nuns in the surrounding suburbs, which, Mario Sensi argues, increasingly sought security within the town walls through the late Duecento and the Trecento.[24] Earlier, in wills like that of Contessa Beatrice da Capraia, redacted in the city of Florence in 1279, itemized bequests sprinkled small sums among numerous peripheral groups, which disappeared, at least from last wills and testaments, over the course of the fourteenth century: the "donne rinchiuse dala Crocie a Montesoni," "le donne del monasterio rinkiuse da Gingnoro," "le donne rinkiuse da Maiano," "le donne rinkiuse da Santo Stefano da Boldrone," the more obscure "ale donne da Fonte Domini e a quelle ke stanno nela casa ke sue di frate Iacopo Sigoli a Pinti, ke ssi chiamano le fratelle," and many others.

The contessa, moreover, reserved her smallest legacies (three lire apiece) for individual penitent women, such as "madonna Contelda, vestita dele donne di penitençi di Santa Maria Novella," as well as to those with no institutional association, "madonna Giemma, donna di penitençia, ke sue matringna di Guido Paçço, se viva in quel tempo."[25] As the research of Gabriella Zarri, Anna Benvenuti Papi, Giovanna Casagrande, Mario Sensi, and others shows, these small groups as well as other unofficial nunneries of *carcerate,* without formally accepted rules, increasingly came under attack from papal as well as local church authorities, from the Second Council of Lyon, 1274, to the promulgations of Pope John XXII's *Altissimo in divinis* and *Sancta Romana,* and then to the political zeal of the early Quattrocento Franciscan Observants.[26] In places as disparate in size and religious history as Milan, Bologna, Padua, Borgo San Sepolcro, Città di Castello, Rome, Perugia, Pisa, and smaller towns in Tuscany, Umbria, and Lazio, these groups peaked in the late Duecento or early Trecento and declined rapidly in number after the Black Death through the fifteenth century.[27] Giovanna Casagrande argues that these demographics of pious women were universal in northern and central Italy.

As the testaments make clear, these are the groups that, from the early years of the Trecento and increasingly after the Black Death, fell from the lists of pious legacies throughout the Tuscan and Umbrian city-states. The tiny sums of money, ranging from pennies to several lire for *recluse* and *carcerate,* hardly occur in these documents by the Quattrocento. Either their beneficiaries were rapidly reined into established convents with officially recognized rules, as happened with the late Trecento Florentine Murate, or they ceased to attract pious legacies.[28]

These changes in the institutional character of women's houses and in what papal and local religious authorities regarded as legitimate forms of penitent living account in part for the differences between numbers and values of pious bequests to nunneries. While in 1348 their numbers had fallen by two-thirds since the beginning of the century, their values had fallen by only about half (table 5.1, figures 5.1, 5.3). This change reflects the near disappearance of small bequests to individual nuns and especially to the more fluid *carcerate, romite,* and pious women "who walked the streets" in certain pious places, such as around the seaside suburban church of San Piero a Grado outside Pisa and, presumably, their concentration into larger established orders.[29] But had there been simply an organizational reshuffling of nuns away from unsanctioned forms of spirituality, often found on the suburban fringes of cities, to large urban nunneries?

At about the same time, the testaments give witness of the disappearance of the hospices and two-bed hospitals mentioned in the pious legacies of late Dugento and early Trecento and their absorption into the expanding postplague monopolistic hospitals: Santa Maria Nuova in Florence, Santa Maria della Scala in Siena, and Santa Chiara in Pisa.[30] The same, however, did not occur with nunneries. No new increases in the values of testators' patrimonies rolled into the coffers of women's houses forming new meganunneries, either after the Black Death or in the early years of the fifteenth century, as had happened with hospitals. Instead, bequests to nuns and nunneries, whether calculated by numbers or by values, registered the most decisive decline of any set of charitable or pious institutions in all these city-states, from the late thirteenth through the early fifteenth centuries.

While bequests to dower young girls of "good behavior" never equaled those for nuns and nunneries, they ran the same course in near reverse (table 5.1 figure 5.4). Before the Black Death, dowry funds were hardly known as a form of charity, especially entire dowries contributed for a small, specified number of girls, instead of dowry fractions parceled out to numerous girls.[31] But by the early fifteenth century these new dowry bequests accounted for over 7 percent of all pious legacies in Florence and over 9 percent in Siena.

Moreover, bequests for dowries differed from those to nuns in another regard: while gifts to nuns comprised the lowest values found in these testaments (on average, only 3 florins, about the monthly wage of an artisan at the end of the Trecento), legacies to fund dowries for poor girls were the largest of any charitable bequest. These legacies (91 florins on average) were nine times the value of the average pious bequest and thirty times that of bequests to nuns. Furthermore, they grew in value, reaching 162 florins by the early Quattrocento, without the appearance of any one fund dwarfing the others.[32] In Florence, funds to dower a select number of nubile girls soared even higher, averaging 227 florins by the early Quattrocento, two-and-a-half times the average dowry fund and more than the average price of even a chapel foundation (table 5.1).

Thus, if we consider the value of pious legacies rather than their number, dowry funds assume a different scale of magnitude. With the Black Death of 1348 the values of these funds for the first time outstripped the values of bequests for nuns and nunneries, and by the early Quattrocento, they had increased in value far beyond their number. In the portfolios of the pious, such bequests attracted 35 percent of all pious expenditures, as opposed to only 2 percent for nuns. In addition, dowry funds supplanted the earlier forms of poor relief—handouts to "the poor of Christ"—in all six cities after the second pestilence. In Florence the shift was the most spectacular: legacies to dower poor virgins rose from 0.05 percent of the sums bequeathed to "the poor of Christ" in 1348 to more than twenty-five times that value in the early fifteenth century.[33]

The shift in testation from "the poor of Christ" to the dowry fund marked more than a simple change in pious choices; it paralleled other

Figure 5.4

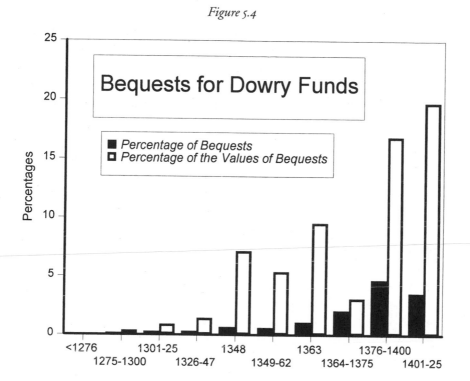

changes taking place after the second wave of pestilence—a decline of the mendicant worldview and the rise of a cult of remembrance.[34] While testamentary gifts to the poor were one-shot, indiscriminate, doles of pennies, crusts of bread, or scraps of clothing, the dowry fund initiated an ongoing, self-perpetuating institution—marriage and the family. But demographics alone fail to explain the shifts in pious attitudes toward these two late medieval forms for supporting women (dowries for initiating married life or gifts for avoiding it in cloistered communities of women). True, a shift from sheltering women from the trials of childbirth to funds that encouraged the formation of families made ostensible economic and demographic sense at a time when, following the Black Death, Tuscan and Umbrian city-states suffered most acutely from labor shortages and began to grant tax relief to attract foreign workers.[35]

Popular preachers such as San Bernardino of Siena harangued their audiences, largely composed of women, to pursue such a change in consciousness.[36] Moreover, as Anthony Molho shows, "publicists and political theorists advocated ideas exalting the family and favoring married life over the monastic condition."[37] Such natalist preoccupations can be seen in the decrees establishing a special fund in Florence (the *monte delle doti*) to help finance dowries and, thereby, to facilitate marriage. In the early rulings of this dowry fund, fathers lost their investments if their daughters took vows in a nunnery, thus treating girls who so joined "the celestial spouse in marriage" as if they were "truly dead" (*tamquam vere mortua*).[38]

The trend of pious legacies to nuns and nunneries, however, made little demographic or economic sense before the two plagues: the decline in testamentary support of nuns had already begun in the last decades of the thirteenth century, when population levels and the economic hardships of overpopulation were continuing to mount in Tuscany and Umbria. As evidenced by waves of famine and rising grain prices, these were the most depressed decades since the eleventh century, not only for Tuscany and Umbria but for large areas of Europe.[39] Thus they were times when, had economic or demographic motives alone been at work, bequests to nunneries, instead of falling, should have registered vigorous growth as a form of conscious family limitation at least through the plague of 1348.

As with other changes in mentality that followed the plague's second strike in 1363, so with piety: it did not abide solely by any simple economic or demographic rules. Nor do economic or demographic changes help to explain the gender differences in the sponsoring of the two charities earmarked for women. Relative to men, women supported nunneries and nuns more than any other pious cause. In number and value of bequests it was the only category of piety where women's legacies approached those of men (table 5.1).

That men left more than women to charitable causes does not, however, signify that men were more pious than women. Only a third as many women's testaments as men's survive in the samples from the six city-states, probably because women had less latitude to dispose of their property, both real and moveable. Further, men controlled more than twice the resources that women did.[40] Relative to their wealth and number, women spent nearly twice as much as men on charity and other pious causes and outspent men in every charitable endeavor (tables 5.1, 5.2).[41] Perhaps Lauro Martines's hypothesis based on the letters of elite Renaissance women in Tuscany should be expanded to Renaissance women, writ large: "In a word, owing to their more confined state, they were more likely than men to be loyal repositories of traditionalism."[42]

TABLE 5.2. Pious and Nonpious Bequests by Sex, 1200–1425

	Testators	Wealth (in florins)	Nonpious Bequests (florins)	Pious Bequests (florins)
Men	2,138	685.29	545.39	127.74
Women	1,235	180.88	122.48	60.42
Ratio M/W	1.73	3.79	4.45	2.11
Women, adjusted by number	2,138	313.13	212.03	104.60
Ratio M/W, adjusted by number	1.00	2.19	2.57	1.22
Women, adjusted by wealth	4,679	685.29	464.03	228.91
Ratio M/W, adjusted by wealth	0.46	1.00	1.18	0.56

But is this truism valid through the medieval and early modern periods? By the end of the Renaissance large numbers of last wills and testaments in Siena show women as the radicals, breaking out of the Renaissance confines and expectations of patrilineal property succession. On the other hand, perhaps eighteenth-century Protestant women and later moral writers had it right: religion and charity are more "natural" to women's sensibilities than to men's.[43] Even if true, the pious choices men and women made with their estates varied widely and must be explained. Most significantly, women's average legacies to nunneries exceeded men's almost two to one and, in terms of their relative wealth, six to one.

More surprising is the place dowry funds occupied in women's pious choices. Here, the expectation that women, more than men, supported women's pious causes is called into question.[44] This other charity marked exclusively for women—in this case to start, as opposed to avoid, family life—was not central to women's testamentary consciousness in the later Middle Ages or early Renaissance. Instead, it was one of the most "masculine" of all charities. Dowry funds were one of only three categories in which, relative to their resources, men outspent women. Men made more bequests only to religious lay confraternities (table 5.1), whose memberships were mostly male in these six cities until after the Council of Trent.[45]

Although they later took the lead in supporting new charities of the

Counter Reformation, women were not at the forefront in sponsoring this new Renaissance form of charity—dowry funds that offered entire dowries for a small and selected number of "well-behaved" girls—which rapidly took the lead as the principal form of poor relief by the last quarter of the fourteenth century. Before the "boom" in dowry funds that followed the second strike of pestilence in 1362–63, three of every four legacies to support this basic fund for a woman's welfare in the secular world came from men's estates. By the first decades of the Quattrocento, women were slowly conforming to the new forms of early Renaissance piety, contributing one out of every three legacies that offered dowries to younger and perhaps less fortunate nubile girls.

Furthermore, women not only gave more to nuns; they persisted longer than men in channeling substantial portions of their estates to nuns and nunneries. Before the plague of 1362–63, men's legacies to cloistered women were almost 20 percent higher than women's, and their value exceeded women's by half. But during and after the second plague, women's legacies to nuns outnumbered men's by 25 percent, with an average value over two times that of men's, despite their much smaller estates. Once adjusted for differences in disposable property between men and women, women's post-1363 bequests to nuns surpassed men's by almost four times in number and fifteen times in value. Thus, women resisted the rupture with the older mendicant habits of piety and adopted the new forms of Renaissance charity slowly, after they had become firmly implanted in men's wills.[46]

This divergence in men's and women's pious comportment is most clearly seen in the year of the second plague. In that year, men suddenly and decisively embraced the new desire for earthly memory by concentrating their pious legacies on a few selected charities, a pattern that would persist through the early modern period. While earlier they had scattered their bequests to an average of 15 pious causes, in the year of the plague's return men reduced their pious bequests (but not the value of their charity) to fewer than 5 bequests. On the other hand, women resisted the sudden change with a vengeance, marching in the opposite direction from men by increasing the fragmentation of their estates from an average of 9.6 to 15.9 pious gifts, three-and-half-times the number found in men's testaments in that year of crisis, despite the considerably smaller worth of women's estates. Moreover, women in 1363 and afterward persisted in scattering their bequests over the landscape of pious institutions. They were the only ones to continue to splinter their estates by endowing 35 or more pious causes.[47] Most spectacular was a widow from the Albizzi family who left 78 pious bequests, a number of which were small sums between one lira and one florin to support individual nuns in small and now obscure nunneries in and around Florence's periphery—places such as the donne of Sant'Anna in Verzaia, Santa Maria Urbane, and San Silvestro in the via San Gallo.[48]

How are these differences in men's and women's sponsoring of women, and women's pious causes, to be explained? Men predominantly gave dowries to assist poor adolescent girls to become wives and mothers in the secular world, while women assisted other women to do the opposite—to refrain from marriage and family life by choosing holy orders. Here, differences in gender were more important than class (at least as far as these documents allow the historian to make class distinctions).[49] Throughout this period, the wealthier half of testators (both men and women) donated a larger share of their legacies to women's charities in general, consistently supporting both nunneries and dowry funds with a greater proportion of their bequests than did the less wealthy. Nor did the second round of plagues change this class bias in the support of women's causes, despite the fact that throughout these testaments women belonged to the lower economic half of testators.[50]

The sexual divergence in charity becomes all the more perplexing considering that the vast majority of women testators were in fact women who were either married or widows and who had raised families at the time of making their testaments. Nuns and young girls form only slightly more than 1 percent of women testators. Of course, a cynical view might have it that widows' bequests to nunneries were a ploy to gain a nun's social security (*corody*) in their own old age. Indeed, a handful of testaments cut such deals: that is, a testator would donate the usufruct of an estate to a religious house in return for rights to join the order and be fed, lodged, and protected thereafter. But such clear exchanges, while they may have become more important later in the fifteenth century with the recruitment strategies of Le Murate, were extremely rare in these testaments, and they all concerned men or married couples.[51]

If not because of immediate self-interest, how then can this divergence in men's and women's charitable choices toward women be explained? Despite carnival songs and other literary scraps showing daughters cursing fathers who placed them against their wills in nunneries, women's persistent support of nunneries casts doubts on the nineteenth-century gothic view of the horrors of the medieval nunnery—or at least women's perception of such horrors in late medieval Tuscany and Umbria.[52] We might even question the applicability for central Italy of certain contemporary statements, such as that registered in the Venetian Senate's preamble to its dowry legislation of 22 August 1420, which claimed that the inflation of dowries had "forced" fathers to imprison their daughters in convents, "amid justified tears and wailing."[53] Equally, it may be wrong to read back into the fourteenth and fifteenth centuries the sad state of nunneries described in 1575 by the apostolic visitor to Siena, Francesco Bossi, who found conditions of the "clausure" unacceptable "for various causes and especially their poverty and discomfit."[54]

We might even wish to smooth the sharp distinctions that Katherine Gill draws between "the vitality and creativity" of "open monasteries" of third-order women as opposed to "the traditional virginal dependency and obedience" of the cloistered medieval world during the late Middle Ages and the Renaissance.[55] The multifarious and unofficial groupings of women disappear almost totally from the testaments of these six city-states after the second strike of pestilence, and these documents register few bequests to those specifically called *pinzochere* or labeled as belonging to "third orders" (whether Franciscan or Dominican) or to their houses, despite their presence as benefactors in these samples.

Siena leads the list with a mere fifteen bequests to those belonging to third-order *pinzochere*. For Arezzo, Perugia, and Assisi, the samples record only a scant appearance of legacies for third-order women. Moreover, places run by third orders, such as the hospital of San Paolo in Florence, received only a negligible number of legacies compared to what women bequeathed to cloistered nuns, both before and after the plagues of the 1360s. Do these absences arise from evidentiary problems of notaries failing to identify further those *donne* or *incarcerate* that belonged to third orders? Or did these institutions amass their wealth by means other than testamentary bequests, at least before 1425?[56] In any case, it was the traditional orders that continued to elicit the sympathies and financial support of women across social classes through the early Renaissance, even as men withdrew their support and turned their devotion toward funding women to endure the secular world through marriage. Indeed, Gabriella Zarri and others have shown the positive side of cloistered life for women's intellectual development from the end of the Quattrocento through the Counter Reformation.[57]

Should the historian then conclude that these sexual differences in charity for women meant the opposite: that married women and widows valued the cloistered life above their own lot, locked within the confines of married life and the secular family? Without actuarial knowledge, did married women realize that nuns outlived them (as Judith Brown has shown for Florentine nuns, at least in the early modern period) or that nuns lived better and more merrily, as tales by contemporary storytellers often suggest?[58] As K. J. P. Lowe has posited for early fifteenth-century Florence, "religious life on a large scale and in a large city offered opportunities for the exercise of power by women not available to those of the female sex who stayed within the structure of the family."[59]

Evidence supplied in other chapters in this volume corroborates the view that women were becoming increasingly restricted in occupation, in accessibility to the courts, in religious and civic participation, and in other aspects of public life and could exercise fewer options within the household as Renaissance models of behavior and lineage-oriented property rights developed throughout the fifteenth century.[60] In Florence, models critical of secular marriage and patrilineal strategies of property succession touched the ranks of the patriciate with the spread of Cathar religiosity in the thirteenth century and the popularity of penitential blessed ones, such as Umiliana dei Cerchi.[61] According to Carol Lansing, incidents of forced monasticism were rare in the thirteenth century, and "by contrast women who chose the church over marriage against the wishes of their families are much in evidence."[62]

Moreover, given the dominant view of Trecento mendicants that the monastic life was superior to that of secular marriage, did married women in making their wills suddenly feel they had made a mistake and wish with their final charities to spare other women the toil and humiliation of married life?[63] Had they been persuaded by the pastoral and pedagogical literature, whose ideal figure was that of the nun?[64] Perhaps. But in addition to this possible growing discontent with family life, these sexual differences in the pious designs for women also fit a larger pattern.[65] Indeed, the reasons for women resisting the Renaissance shift in piety in the late fourteenth century—the move away from a mendicant disdain of what Saint Catherine of Siena called "the earthly cell" and toward the Renaissance cult of remembrance—were not so different from the reasons that later guided women during the Counter Reformation, when, after two centuries, they would be the first to break with these same Renaissance patterns of charity and agnatic property succession.

The study of last wills and testaments shows that the Renaissance cult of remembrance was no Burckhardtian celebration of the individual.[66] Through legalistic webs of contingency clauses, which increased in complexity from the late fourteenth century through the apostolic visitations of the late sixteenth century, testators sought to limit the possibilities for individual action of both their pious and nonpious beneficiaries. This was especially true of rights of future generations in the alienation of landed property and the rights of women in making decisions over their inheritance and even over their own dowries. As Julius Kirshner has shown from statutory evidence, and as I have argued from statistics of widows' settlements, the property rights of women declined notably over the fourteenth and fifteenth centuries.[67]

Instead, the cult of remembrance, which took hold after the second strike of pestilence in 1363, was grounded not in the individual but in the celebration of the memories of the ancestors—male ancestors, that is. Moreover, it sponsored a new sense of family, which earlier had been known only within the ranks of the aristocracy.[68] This notion of the family, made clear in hundreds of testaments across social classes, was centered on the flow of property and memory down the male line. After the second strike of pestilence in 1363, this strategy for the afterlife penetrated even into the wills of wool workers.[69]

Thus, women in the early Renaissance would have had the same reasons for persisting with the earlier mendicant forms of piety that women in the sixteenth century had for becoming the Council of Trent's most avid supporters. These later women finally broke with Renaissance forms of giving by breaking the stipulations laid down by their Renaissance fathers and husbands. For nearly two centuries, these stipulations had funneled property down the male bloodlines, forming a strategy for the afterlife that often forbade landed property to females, even if they were next of kin, and that understood salvation in terms of the regeneration of memory through male offspring.[70] This strategy for the afterlife threatened the economic interests of both women and the church and, thus, by the late sixteenth century unwittingly made them common allies in the battle for new forms of religiosity.

On the other hand, dowry funds turned charity away from church hands. Unlike allocations of pennies, tunics, or bread for "the poor of Christ," which often followed funerals and relied on the mendicant orders or parish priests for their distribution, the administration of dowry funds and the responsibility for selecting their beneficiaries fell mostly to surviving kin or the executors of estates (at least before the Council of Trent). To repeat, the dowry fund was not a single-shot palliative but an ongoing institution that initiated family life and its reproduction. Moreover, by the late fourteenth century, at least in the city-states across central Italy, family life—its structures as well as its ideology—was changing across social classes.[71] Increasingly, the male lineage came to define the family over competing notions of the domestic conjugal cell, as men more tightly controlled dowry properties and determined the flow of ancestral goods down the male line.[72] As a result, along with enabling the formation of new nuclear families, the dowry fund was an investment in the perpetuation of male bloodlines.

6. Sex and Violence on the Periphery

THE TERRITORIAL STATE IN EARLY

RENAISSANCE FLORENCE

Over the past several years historians have been finding a rich lode of sex and violence in the vicariate court cases of the Florentine territorial state. The final resting place of these documents is the deposit of the Appellate Court (Giudice degli Appelli e nullità) housed in the Florentine state archives (ASF). Yet these are not appellate court records but the summaries and sentences of criminal cases adjudicated by the Florentine vicars (*vicarii*) and captains (*capitani*) sent off to some of the furthest reaches of the Florentine state, including Anghiari (Angularis), on the other side of the Casentino valley in the Aretino, and the Rocca di San Casciano, in the Apennine mountains of Romagna.[1]

As the memoirs of patricians Jacopo Salviati and Buonaccorso Pitti reveal, however, these commissions had not yet become the dreaded outposts that Ariosto would later complain about in the sixteenth century while serving as vicar of the Garfagnana.[2] Nor were they necessarily the first posts of patricians beginning their political careers in the Florentine civil service, again as these memoirs attest. Rather, patricians alternated throughout their political careers service as ambassadors, as priors in Florence's highest ruling councils (the Signoria), and as vicars in the territory. Storyteller Franco Sacchetti died as vicar of San Miniato. Indeed, the office of *vicarius* was seen as a plum position, for the accumulation of both honor and profit.[3] From the earliest vicariate records, the names of those nominated to these offices comprised families well known to students of Florentine history: the Machiavelli, the Rucellai, the Salviati, the Guicciardini, and the Pitti.[4]

As the fifteenth century progressed, these political appointments became ever more desirable, fetching salaries as high as ten thousand lire, boosted by bribes and other extraofficial payments, which the chronicle of the vicar Salviati makes appear a normal part of the job's perquisites.[5] Moreover, as the Florentine territorial state bought or conquered neighboring city-states, the places patricians might be sent off to could become more "civilized"—the cities of Pisa, Cortona, and Livorno, for example. At the same time, the boundaries of these courts extended inward, appropriating jurisdictions previously under the purviews of the medieval tribunals, the *podestà* and the *capitano.* By the second decade of the fifteenth century, Florentine patrician vicars made arrests and adjudicated cases from parts of the traditional countryside (*contado*) of Florence as close as the *podesterie* of Carmignano to the east, the Valdelsa and Pesa (the Chianti) to the south, and the Mugello to the north.[6]

This chapter examines only a small fraction of the documents that survive in the *extrinseci* criminal records of this *fondo,* a series that begins in 1398 and continues through the fifteenth century.[7] First, I read and selected for study only two categories of crimes, moral crimes, which were almost exclusively sex crimes, and political crimes, usually identified by the court as acts of conspiracy and rebellion.[8] Second, my survey covers the first thirty-six years of these records, from 1398 to the rise of the Medici in 1434.

Instead of the usual search for colorful or bizarre cases, which might then be corroborated by selected citations from contemporary literature, at the outset my approach rejects recent claims that storytelling and statistics are, or should be, mutually exclusive.[9] I instead mix narrative and quantitative methods, placing and testing the extraordinary within the context of the ordinary. One mode of analysis raises questions and tests hypotheses from the other. Literary evidence is used to draw meaning from the statistical evidence, while the statistical analysis is used to question certain literary topoi that have become commonplaces about Renaissance sexuality. Further, this essay breaks through the usual assumptions about the private and the public, placing the state's surveillance of sexual offenses in the larger political context of territorial conquest and control.

I am by no means the first to tap these sources. In the 1960s Gene Brucker foraged through these vast documents, often difficult to read and, given their overstuffed bindings, even difficult to open. He used them to describe outbreaks of political unrest in the Florentine territory and translated several bizarre, picturesque, and gruesome examples of social behavior for his book of late medieval and Renaissance documents.[10] One case of infanticide from Ponte Bocci in the *contado* of Pistoia near San Miniato has been translated into English and is the topic of an entire article.[11] More recently, Maria Serena Mazzi combed through these records to describe in full those cases of sexual offense that she claims were "exemplary" of daily life on the Florentine periphery.[12]

The cases selected for publication, and commented on to date, however, do not constitute the usual but, instead, the extraordinary. The most published case is that of a woman who drowned her "beautiful male baby" in the Arno River at Ponte Bocci. The court's detailed description of this woman's drowning of her only child—the product of a second, clandestine, bigamist marriage—is matched, even exceeded, by the state's reaction: the authorities sent this "crudelissimam mulierem" to Pisa, where with the recovered baby's corpse tied to her neck, she was to be led down the streets of the city until reaching the accustomed place of execution. There she was to be "burnt and cremated" alive in a little wooden hut especially constructed for the occasion, her dead baby still attached to her neck.[13]

In several respects, this remarkable case is typical, if not of criminal comportment, then at least of the infanticide cases found in these records. First, all the "murdered" babies were products of adulterous, often incestuous, relationships. Second, in all but one case, women and not their partners faced the courts alone as the defendants. In the one case where a man was prosecuted for infanticide, it was, nonetheless, a woman (his mother-in-law) ordered by her lover who was accused of carrying out the deed.[14] Third, most of the dead babies (four of seven) were male.[15] Fourth, in all but one case (where neighboring peasants found and revived the abandoned baby) death was the penalty; and in half of these cases, that penalty was the same as that for the bigamist murderess of Ponte Bocci—cremation alive in a straw or wooden hut—otherwise a rare form of execution in Renaissance Florence.[16]

The state's preparations for these death penalty ceremonies were sometimes even more elaborate. After ten years of marriage, a woman from Castel Bonizi in the *podesteria* of San Casciano just south of Florence had an affair with a man whose name the court wished for the present to conceal. Separated from her husband (*divortium fecisset*), she became pregnant but insisted to her neighbors that she was only ill.[17] When her pregnancy came to term, she allegedly suffocated the baby in the house where she lived alone, then placed it on her bed and announced to her assembled neighbors that it (in this case, a girl) had died at birth.[18] Evidently, neither the neighbors nor the vicar believed her story, and she was sentenced in 1433 to be burnt in the accustomed place of the vicariate of Valdelsa, which for this occasion was to be painted inside with "ugly pictures" (*in dicto loco cum intera picta ad picturas turpes*).[19]

Notaries relished presenting infanticide cases in gruesome detail, even details not relevant to the guilt or innocence of the defendant. Such was the proceeding against a married woman from Casaboccaccio in the *popolo* of Santo Stefano a Castiglione in the hills above the val di Sieve who strangled her child (here, again, born from an affair with an unnamed man) and buried it in the sand near the Sieve River. The following Saturday a pig herder from a neighboring village discovered the "creature" when one of his pigs dug it up and began to rip it apart with its teeth.[20]

The thin line separating these early Renaissance men and women from the animal world and their fear of it finds further expression throughout these criminal cases. In another case of infanticide, the notary describes the actions of "a most nefarious female murderess" who, having become impregnated by her father's brother, retreated to her father's "twisted, semidilapidated, and debased" pigsty, where after "lingering" there for many hours gave birth to a "living male boy" (*puerum maschulum vivum*).[21] Wishing "to liberate herself from that bulk stretching her vagina" (*gula*), she cut the umbilical cord.[22] "And not being content with this but adding worse to bad, with her most cruel hands, she took the said boy, her own living son, and with shame and perfidy left and exposed him naked without any cloth to wrap or cover him. And without any food, this most cruel mother left him on the ground between two stones squashed into a corner of the pigsty." From the notary's rhetorical description, it is not altogether clear whether this was a case of simple abandonment, as I assume, or whether squashing the baby between two stones actually did the infant physical harm. At any rate, once dead "from the acts of the most cruel mother," and after several days, the "boy's" cadaver was found by a passing dog, which ripped him apart with its teeth, thus "bringing to light" this "horrendous and polluted" act.

Bestiality was the term generally used by the courts to describe any sexual act deemed *contra naturam,* from sodomy, hetero- as well as homosexual, to incest. Such was the court's verdict on an incest case involving a brother and sister from the village of San Gueninello near San Miniato al Tedesco in the vicariate of the Valdarno inferiore.[23] One day in September

1414, according to the court's inquest, Nera grabbed her brother, Maso, by the hand and said: "Let's go out to the hut." Maso followed her and, once arrived, "she threw herself on the ground and the said Maso pulled off his britches (*sarabolis*) and hopped (*sallavit*) on her, knowing her carnally, her virginity [until that moment] intact, inviolate, and immaculate, corrupting her in incest and deflowering her." Later in September, Nera again called her brother and said, "Let's go to the hut and do the deed" (*ad fare quel facto*). Maso "so moved" went with his sister to the hut, and when they arrived, Nera said to Maso, "[this time] you go under, and I will go on top" (*va di sotto tu et jo andarò di sopra*). Whereupon Maso threw himself on the ground and, lying prostrate, took off his britches and Nera hopped on him and "the said donna Nera carnally knew this Maso." (This is the only instance I have found in these documents, when the verb *to know carnally* is given in the active voice for a woman.) "And this Maso knew carnally Nera his sister many times on various days and hours during the month of September, as did the said domina Nera, this Maso. And from this carnal knowledge, corruption, deflowering, and incest Nera became pregnant," which disgraced and dishonored her blood kin all the more by the fact that, meanwhile, her kin had promised her in marriage to another Maso, this one named di Nanni from the Garfagnana, with whom she had exchanged rings.

Despite the fact that by the court's account his sister had initiated their illicit love affair, Maso appears to have suffered the graver penalties. He was to be led to the accustomed place of justice in San Miniato "clothed in skins" (*indutus pellibus*) "to denote the irrationality and bestiality of his beastly act and crime."[24] Once arrived at the accustomed place of justice "with gallows and other necessary instruments his testicles were to be severed and detached from his body, that is, cut off entirely and thus he is to remain forever neutered" (*denatura*).[25]

Edward Muir describes in gripping detail how such obsessions with the animal world structured conflict and revenge among political factions in early sixteenth-century Friuli, contrasting them with the manners and civility of Renaissance cities.[26] Yet the vicariate court cases of Florence—and in particular the sentences adjudicated by those from the highest reaches of the Florentine patriciate, bearing family names well known to the student of Renaissance history—show that such obsessions were not marginal to Renaissance manners or solely the residue of backward feudatories but could be central to the mentality of Renaissance urban elites, at least as regards their rule over the newly incorporated districts on the periphery.

As Maria Serena Mazzi has shown, in her detailed and careful descriptions of approximately thirty sex cases from the vicariate court records of 1427, such materials illuminate another side of Renaissance life often lacking in humanist texts and chronicles of high-level political history. They show another, darker Renaissance, far removed from our general assumptions about modernity: not that the modern world, or Jacob Burckhardt's perception of it, was free from violence; far from it. Burckhardt defines the state in large part as the dexterous use of violence.[27] Yet he saw this violence in Machiavellian terms as rational, instrumental, and pragmatic. While, qualitatively, the libidinous violence of these mountaineers and *mezzadri* from the territorial outskirts may not shock a reader hardened by present day tabloid horror stories, the counterobsessions and violence of the vicariate courts, officiated over by prominent members of the Florentine patriciate, strike different psychological chords. As for the patrician Jacopo Salviati, who served as vicar of several posts in the Florentine territory in the early fifteenth century, almost the only cases "worthy" (*degne*) of memory were those in which the defendant was tortured, mutilated, or executed.[28]

Before trying to place these and other extraordinary cases in the larger context of early Renaissance criminal prosecution and Florence's strategies to control its outer hinterland, I would like to consider these individual cases in order to explore further early Renaissance uses of violence and its concretization or fetishism of evil. In particular, these courts saw sexual crimes as originating from bodily parts that thus needed to be punished and removed.

In 1413 the vicar of Anghiari charged a certain Muccino from the mountain village of Rassina with raping his eleven-year-old grandniece (*pronepte*), Angela, the daughter of the son of his sister. While Muccino's wife was off in the market town of Bibbiena and he and Angela were sleeping together in the same bed, Muccino, prompted by "impulses of his libido, acting from animal instinct (*bestialiter agendo*), through force and violence, violated and corrupted her, causing her to roar with immense pain, from which she screamed 'Oyme, Oyme.'" The notary continued: "Her great uncle ought to have stopped at this point; but moved by his bestiality and nefarious cause, he consummated this violation and his iniquitous purpose. . . . Not content, but adding evil to evil, consummated with the said iniquitous pollution, and because Angela was still roaring from the pain she had suffered in her coitus, he kicked her and slapped her across the face, breaking one of her teeth, saying 'Shut up and stop crying.'"

As heinous as Muccino's crime may strike us, the Florentine state proved itself again capable of matching violence with violence, striking directly at what they perceived as the concrete cause of his evil.[29] Muccino was to serve as an example; "stripped to his kidneys" and led through the market of Anghiari, he was to be whipped with branches and switches until reaching the place of justice, where his penis was to be sliced in four places and then burnt in each by a red-hot iron.[30]

Another case that might make us bristle is the remarkable sexual career of a boy (*puerum maleditum*) about sixteen years old from Campi, just to the east of Florence, who had moved to the city of Pistoia.[31] Here, the court reported retrospectively his sexual exploits going back six years. In all but the final case, which brought the boy to trial, he had seduced infant girls, from three to five years in age, from noble Pistosese families. With flattery (*blanditoriis verbis*) and presentations of flowers picked in the gardens and courtyards of Pistoiese noble palaces, the boy knew carnally his victims "not in the customary libidinous place" but "inter tibias", whose meaning in sodomy cases becomes clear—"ex latero posteriori."[32] For the most part, these seductions were not one-time encounters but, according to the crime reports, were romances that continued for days and, in one case, a month. Moreover, they occurred in rather open places—the courtyard of the palace of the Fioravanti, under the pergola in the gardens of the de Orsi palace, and even in the fireplace of the palace of the ruling priors of Pistoia. In each case, the court refused to name the victim, protecting the little noble girl's reputation and presumably her value on the patrician marriage market.[33]

Finally, the boy violated a commoner, a five year-old girl, first in the cellar of his own house and later at her house, where he seduced her over the space of eight days. In this last instance, her parents demanded the girl's future dowry; thus she alone of his conquests was recorded by name.[34] But little girls were not the only objects of this boy's sexual appetites; the notary in his last "item" adds that the boy also had "many and diverse adulterous liaisons with married women from both the city and the countryside of Pistoia over the course of these years and months, at various times and places." Perhaps they were the mothers of the seduced little noble girls, who permitted him such open space in their courtyards and a free hand with their daughters.

Despite his tender age and that his mode of conquest was with flattery and flowers, not *per vim et violentiam* (the formulaic phrase used in rape cases), the Florentine vicariate court did not treat the boy's sexual adventures as the peccadillos of an age of innocence. Instead, he was to be led to the public place of justice in Pistoia, whipped all along the way (*semper fustigando*), and once arrived, was to be castrated, "his testicles cut and extracted from their place, to deprive him of them in perpetuity." Nor was his punishment to end here; afterward, he was to serve a life sentence in the prison of Pistoia, the only life sentence I found meted out by these vicariate courts. Finally, under threat of decapitation, he was required to produce a fifty-lire dowry for his last victim, Caterina di Antonio.[35]

While these cases shed light on a Renaissance violence not reflected in the darkest stories of Machiavellian-calculated murders, such a survey—with the eye searching for the most gruesome or salacious stories—can also lead to mistaken conclusions. For instance, from the above sampling, the reader might well conclude that the vicariate courts were specialized tribunals concerned overwhelmingly with matters of morality and, in particular, sexual morality. Indeed, Maria Serena Mazzi says so in introducing her "exemplary" stories from these court records of 1427. But such was not the case, as any casual counting of cases quickly reveals. Sex crimes, no matter how broadly defined, never constituted more than 5 percent of these courts' annual caseloads, and indeed for 1427, the year from which Mazzi draws her examples, they constituted little more than 2 percent.[36]

Moreover, the reader of the criminal stories presented here might well imagine that infanticide cases figured prominently in the vicariate cases. Instead, I spotted only seven cases of infanticide among the massive numbers of cases (about eight thousand) that survive from the thirty-six years of my survey, 1398 to 1434. Unlike seventeenth-century England, where these prosecutions could surpass the number of cases for other homicides or rival witchcraft for the burning of women at the stake, cases of infanticide in the vicariate courts were extremely rare, as indeed they were in the other criminal courts of Florence—the *podestà*, the *capitano del popolo*, the *esecutore degli ordinamenti di giustizia*, and the *otto di guardia*.[37]

If in shunning quantitative treatment of such cases—as Mazzi, Edoardo Grendi, and others insist we must do—and if in their place we are to present "exemplary cases," how are we to know which cases are exemplary?[38] And exemplary of what? Criminal behavior? The obsessions of the state? Or of our own wandering eyes through the documentary thicket of everyday crime, which largely comprised cases of assaults and battery, burglary, and petty theft in agricultural communities?[39] Certainly, the last of these criteria is behind the selection of cases for "thick description." To be sure, the analysis of such cases can uncover mental structures not always visible in the run-of-the-mill cases: the pathological can be a privileged peephole into the normal. But as criminal or inquisitional cases, they remain truly the exception—a fact that the new "microhistorians" often wish to blur.

On the other hand, as Grendi, Lenman, Parker, Sharpe, and others have shown, a counting of pre-nineteenth-century criminal cases and their characteristics is perilous for any reconstruction of criminal behavior. Should we infer, for instance, that infanticide in rural areas was indeed rare, was always the product of adulterous, usually incestuous, relations, and finally that infant boys, not girls, were its most common victims? Instead, a statistical analysis of tax records for the traditional Florentine *contado*—perhaps the earliest records in Western Civilization that list entire households by name and age—reveal skewed sex ratios and suggest strongly that, as in Asiatic societies, girls were the usual victims of infanticide or abandonment and that these practices were normal means of family limitation within wedlock and not the products of adulterous affairs.[40] These conclusions, moreover, are corroborated by quantitative studies of foundling homes in Florence, Prato, and San Gimignano, which received a surfeit of abandoned infant girls from their rural hinterlands.[41]

Should we then, as Grendi advises, distrust completely and discard the counting of criminal records and their trend lines? Instead, I would argue that even seven cases can be significant and can be read in the context of other statistics, giving texture and meaning to other data distilled from archival research. The fact that these infanticide cases are rare, result entirely from illicit affairs, and decry the death of baby boys more often than baby girls lends further credence to the high sex ratios for infants in contemporary tax records.[42]

Such sex ratios favoring male infants, as we shall see in the next chapter, were not wholly the result of error or underreporting. Instead, they suggest that infanticide usually happened in wedlock, not in incestuous or bigamist relations as in all of the court cases brought to trial, and that female babies, not male ones, were its usual victims. The high infant sex ratios in the countryside, along with the complete absence of prosecutions of women who killed or abandoned their infants in legitimate marriages, suggest that these acts were kept quiet, tolerated as a normal means of conscious family limitation in the territory of early fifteenth-century Florence, and that the punishments when meted out were displaced with a vengeance onto illegitimate offenders.[43] But can we read criminal statistics as more than reverse images of the societies from which they were drawn? If not to deduce precise "crime trends," can they be used to corroborate, nuance, or question time-honored impressions gleaned from prescriptive as well as descriptive literary works, which social historians today often accept as being reliable and necessary to lend credence to their archival findings?[44]

To return to the vicariate courts: certain cases, for instance, do reflect contemporary literary depictions of nuns as readily available and valued objects of sexual desire. Remember Boccaccio's day 3, story 1, about the pretended deaf-mute, Masetto da Lamporecchio, and day 9, story 2, about the abbess who in haste runs out of her cell mistaking the priest's underpants for her veil.[45] In the day-to-day cases of the vicariate courts, few were as clever as Masetto or as foolish as the hypocritical abbess of Lombardy, and many were more violent.

For instance, the Valdarno inferiore court's notary describes a Giovanni alias Nanni di Salvino from Agliana in the district of Castel Fiorentino (not the Agliana in the *contado* of Pistoia, near Lamporecchio) as "wanton, obscene, and incestuous." In the summer of 1413, while on his donkey returning from Pisa, this Giovanni came across four women on a pilgrimage to Rome, "the junior" of whom was dressed in a nun's habit, and it was she (whether because of her age or her habit is not made clear) whom he *per vim et violentiam* jumped. He held a sword to her throat, knocked her to the ground, and would have raped her (according to the notary's description) had she and her fellow travelers not frightened him off by screaming "Accorruomo!"[46] Despite this account and "because of his poverty" (*respectu paupertatis*), he was let off with seemingly one of the lightest sentences for attempted rape found in these documents. He was to be led barefoot to the accustomed place of justice in San Miniato and left there in infamy and shame.[47]

This was the only case, however, where a man just so happened to meet a nun along a "public road." In other cases, men crossed monastic walls to satisfy their "libidinous desires." In March 1417, while engaged in on-going business dealings (*circa quasi continuam conversationem praticam habuit. . . in eorum negotiis exercendis*) with the abbess and other nuns of the Pisan convent of Sant' Agostino just beyond the gate of San Marco, Bartolommeo di Michele di Luparello, called Centosanti from Pisa, hid in the convent all day and part of the night. After waiting for the nuns to go to bed, he tried to rape one of them. But he was caught and was led to the palace of the captain and sentenced to a six-month exile in the city of Naples.[48]

But not all these cases portray the nuns as unwilling victims of men's libidinous desires, and some may cast doubt on nuns' "dedication to the service of God," at least as far as sexual abstinence is concerned. Two years later, another Pisan, the Magister Andrea di Francesco (perhaps also transacting business with nuns), was more successful: against the wishes of the presiding Dominican friars, he managed to move in and live with the nuns of San Silvestro in the city of Pisa from January through May of 1419. But he too was caught by the *capitano*'s police and sentenced to a two-year exile ten miles beyond the city walls of Pisa.[49]

The sexual lure of the convent and the threat it posed to the honor of cloistered women and of Florentine communities could go beyond what these mild sentences might imply. The year 1422 saw a series of sentences all involving the convent of the Clares at the low-lying marshland's *borgo* of Fucecchio in the Valdarno inferiore (less than fifteen kilometers across the Arno Valley from Boccaccio's infamous nuns at Lamporecchio). These cases, moreover, make the nocturnal male population of Abbess Usimbalda's Lombard nunnery in Boccaccio's day 9, story 2, pale by comparison. First, some time after the ides of March, a former chaplain of the parish church of Fucecchio, then a chaplain at the hospital of Bonifazio in Florence, returned to Fucecchio, secretly climbed over the town walls, and entered the convent of the Clares, where he stayed "many days, knowing carnally day and night one of the recluses who wore the nun's habit and had dedicated her life to God." Word leaked out to the townsmen of Fucecchio, and a group of men entered the nunnery and assembled the nuns to question them about this affair, but the priest had by then escaped over the walls. In absentia, he was fined the hefty sum of five hundred lire.[50]

Although his was the first case to be heard, the chaplain was not the first man to taste the earthly delights of the Fucecchio Clares. In June of the previous year, a man from nearby Castel Fiorentino, bearing the family name de Activantibus, had also secretly climbed the town walls and had entered the nunnery, where he lived with a certain nun (whose name the court wished to keep silent) for the next ten months—that is, until about the time the chaplain joined him in this otherwise women's community "dedicated to the service of God." And from "the seed of his libidinous pleasure" he impregnated his holy consort, who gave birth to a girl. In March, this man similarly escaped over the town walls, taking his newborn daughter with him. He was also fined five hundred lire.[51]

By March, the fame of this nunnery had spread beyond the confines of the Valdarno inferiore. A man from Ghizzano in the former *contado* of Pisa—described as a vagabond but who was also the son of a lord (*domini*)—entered the *castrum* of Fucecchio at night, climbed over the nunnery walls, entered a nun's room (*camera*), and raped her (*violentie strupavit*). Despite the violence of his act in comparison to the apparent consensual and long-term nature of the others, he was fined the same, reflecting the court's (and possibly the larger secular community's) view that it made no difference whether a nun's sacred vows of chastity were violated by consent or by violence.[52]

Nor were these acts the whole of the outside world's interaction with the Clares of Fucecchio during 1421–22. On the same day, the vicariate court of the Valdarno inferiore brought to trial three other men, all from the town of Fucecchio, for crossing the wall of these nuns' confinement.[53] Their objectives, however, were different from those of the chaplain, the man from Castel Fiorentino, and the vagabond son of a lord. Instead of seeking virgin sex with those dedicated to serving God, in November and again in December 1421, armed with both offensive and defensive weapons, these townsmen entered the monastery, not secretly or over its walls like the others but directly through its doors, and captured and beat up a man whose name (unfortunately for the historian) was kept silent by the court. Could it have been the man from Castel Fiorentino, then living with a nun who gave birth to a baby girl? Since his case was already on trial, there would have been little reason to keep his name silent. Most likely, the three men of Castro Fucecchio were morally outraged with yet another man never apprehended or prosecuted or whose records are lost and who was living at the same time with these poor Clares. At any rate, for their moral outrage and assault, these vigilantes of the local vice squad were fined the much lower sum of twenty-five lire apiece.[54]

Perhaps other monastic walls in the Florentine territory during the early fifteenth century may have been as porous to men's sexual desires as those confining the Clares of Fucecchio. Perhaps there were other men, like the Clares' battered but unnamed illegal resident of November and December 1421, who outraged the moral sensibilities of other men but who escaped the clutches of the vicariate's police as well as the notary's pen. And to be sure, saucy nuns who were the perpetrators of sexual license or moral misconduct without implicating a layman would have been tried in ecclesiastical courts and thus would have escaped the purview of the vicariate courts.[55] Nonetheless, despite the richness of these individual cases and their parallels to a supposed Boccaccian world of the early Renaissance, sexual cases involving nuns were rare, comprising only 7 of 241 sentences for sexual misconduct, or less than 3 percent of these cases.

Nor do these records suggest that the Florentine authorities turned a blind eye, tolerating the occasional transgression behind cloister walls. Instead, the courts judged the violation of a nun's spiritual marriage, whether or not with her consent, as a crime of incest, which tarnished the honor of the secular community and its jurisdiction as well as violating canon law, God, and the Virgin Mary. A final case of a nun's love affair shows the extent to which the civil authorities might go, crossing decades and territorial jurisdictions in pursuit of retribution for such tarnished secular honor.

A sister Vangelista from Caprona in the former *contado* of Pisa had lived as a nun in the convent of Santo Stefano just outside the Pisan gate of Perlati. According to the court's notary, she practiced the nun's "profession," performing "the customary sacred chores" (*sacratas*), as did the other nuns, "dedicating her life to God" in this convent "through enduring [*protrassit*] the honest and virginal life for twenty years and more." Afterward, "necessity" demanded that along with several other nuns of good and honest reputation she leave this nunnery and go to the city of Lucca to enter the convent of San Cerbone, where for months she led an honest and laudable monastic life. At this point in the story, a certain Michael di Coli of Lucca appeared in sister Vangelista's life, with no other explanation from the court's scribe than that the "spirit of the devil" was in him and that he was filled with the "intent and ardor" to kidnap her and have sex with her—which he did, though not *per vim et violentiam* but, seemingly, through mutual consent. At any rate, the two were married for ten years, or "circha."

In 1416, even though the marriage was contracted by a public notary in Lucca, where the two remained residents, and despite the fact that Lucca was not only beyond the jurisdiction of the vicariate of Pisa but outside the Florentine state altogether, the vicariate of Pisa suddenly intervened, deciding (again for undisclosed reasons) that the marriage was *inutelem,* "against human and divine law and against the jurisdiction and order of the city of Pisa . . . injurious to men and the reverence of God Almighty."

For these reasons, the court sent one of its notaries, Ser Niccolò, to Lucca to demand Michael's extradition and to lead him back to Pisa, where he was to serve a four-year sentence in the *stinche* (named after the Florentine prison). The first year, he was to be enclosed in a cage (*in quadam cabia recludatur*) locked in the tower of this prison. Having survived this ordeal, he was to pass the next three years as a normal prisoner.[56]

Thus, the cases surrounding the Clares' seeming open-door policy at Fucecchio in the early 1420s may lure us into believing that the Boccaccian world of lusty nuns evoked by Masetto da Lamporecchio's fate and by the pleasure of the abbess who wore the priest's underpants on her head was larger than fiction in the territory of late medieval and early Renaissance Florence. But here, even within fiction itself the power of a good story can twist our perceptions. After all, Boccaccio's statistics differ little from those taken from the vicariate sex crimes: only two or possibly three of his hundred stories concern sex with nuns.[57]

The walls separating nuns from the outside world, at least as far as sexual encounters are concerned, may have been higher and more difficult to scale than recent historians of the Renaissance might wish to believe.[58] The horrible end to Michael of Lucca's love affair and the anger and violence of the townsmen of Fucecchio who sought to avenge the dishonor brought on their nuns—and by implication on themselves—show that both secular courts and communities in early Renaissance Florence insisted on the sexual purity of their nuns and would take extraordinary measures to preserve it.[59] Once again, the historical realities appear different from, even the opposite of, what a few good stories might suggest.

Another topos from contemporary literature—not only for Boccaccio but even more so for later storytellers at the end of the Trecento and early Quattrocento (Giovanni Sercambi, Franco Sacchetti, and Gentile Sermini)—is the high profile of priests and friars in sexual adventures, and exclusively heterosexual ones. Yet clergymen appear even less often than nuns in these criminal cases involving sexual offenses. Most surprising is the complete absence of monks and friars, prime butts of the storytellers' mockery of heterosexual intrigue. The closest approximation is a case of sodomy against a Spaniard who lived with the friars (sic) of San Benedetto in Lucca (*cum dictis fratribus*) but who was the servant (*famulus*) of the prior. Perhaps he was a conversus. The Spaniard abducted a boy and, according to the notary "made him into a wife" (*sibi in uxorem eligit et cum eo in cubiculo et in aliis locis occultis dicte domus sepissime peccavit*). After three months of this "marriage," one day while mass was being performed the Spaniard ran off with the boy, first to Castelfranco in the Valdarno inferiore, then to Genoa, and finally to Sarzana, where he became employed (*ad stipendium*) by the duke of Milan. In this capacity, he was captured, tried for sodomy, and beheaded.[60]

As defendants, only two priests appear. Accused of a three-month love affair with his cousin, which produced a daughter, one priest was acquitted.[61] The other sustained a long love affair with a married woman and then hired an outlaw (*exbanpnitus*) to kill her husband. The plot was successful; the priest was indicted for homicide as well as adultery and was decapitated.[62] More than in sex crimes, priests were found in village rebellions and "conspiracies." Indeed, they were often the ringleaders, which, in contrast to heterosexual adventures, the contemporary storytellers did not apparently wish to joke about. In cases of rebellion, priests appear more than any other named profession, with the possible exception of notaries.[63]

But here the bias of our source is clear. Crimes against the state, like murder, were a different matter from moral transgressions. Well into the Renaissance, ecclesiastical courts must have exercised considerable authority in trying crimes of the clergy, except for murder or lèse-majesté.[64] Hence, they escaped the net of secular jurisdiction at least in the territory, even for serious offenses, where their secular coconspirators received the death penalty. Such was the case of a woman living in the parish of San Lorenzo a Monteguscone in the *podesteria* of Montespertoli, the vicariate of the Valdelsa, who, during an April evening in 1416, together with the local parish priest, and "against the will of the superiors of the church and its congregation," robbed the church of various altar furnishings and priestly robes valued at eighty-eight florins. For her sins, the court sentenced the woman to be burnt to death: no sentence was mentioned for her clerical collaborator, who no doubt was handed over to ecclesiastical tribunals.[65]

In addition, clerics—as part of local elites, often with connections to the Florentine oligarchy and even with interregional patronage ascending as high as the pope—may well have been shielded from the clutches of the vicar's police and court.[66] Certainly, Buonaccorso Pitti's experience as captain of Pisa conveys this impression. During his six-month term in 1409 as Florence's highest magistrate in the newly conquered city-state, he attempted to remove the Pisan nobleman Messer Mariano Casassi as head of the hospital at Altopascio. Casassi, according to Pitti, was destroying the hospital's patrimony by selling off its properties for his own aggrandizement. To remove Casassi from his benefice, Pitti had to use his family's patronage and his connections within the *signoria* of Florence as well as engage in international diplomacy, writing supplications to Pope Alexander V in Rome and to the college of cardinals' legate then residing in Bologna, Baldassarre Cossa (who became Alexander's successor, Pope John XXIII). These were followed by secret meetings in Florence with some of the most powerful men in the oligarchy.[67] But during his term of office, Pitti was unable to remove Casassi from his benefice. Pitti was able to do so only later, after further secret meetings with patricians in high places in Florence and after two trips to—and three months of residence in—Bologna, negotiating with the future pope and his secretary.[68]

But local elites were not immune from the pressures of either the Florentine state or their own constituencies, as the vicariate cases reveal, even when their adversaries were less powerful and zealous men than Buonaccorso Pitti. In addition to numerous cases of local officials and elites brought to trial for tax fraud, other officials who used their office to abuse their subjects could be tried and convicted in the vicariate courts.[69] Such was an elaborate case of 1406 that has the ring of a contemporary novella. It resulted in the conviction of the *podestà*'s notary in Barbialle (in the vicariate of San Miniato). On numerous occasions, with flattery and offers of money, Ser Lucas tried to seduce domina Gemma, the wife of Corsino. "Seeing that neither flattery nor money were sufficient to fulfill his proposition," one night "without any legitimate charge" he locked her husband in the local jail located in the palace of the *podestà* and then went to Gemma's house pretending to be her husband. Believing the ruse, she opened the door but on recognizing her tormentor threatened to scream and promised "that the whole neighborhood would come running." She managed to slam her door shut, but the persistent Ser Lucas returned later that night and afterward, according to the court's report, persisted "day and night with words and deeds pestering and bothering the said domina Gemma, desiring to soil her honesty through the crime of adultery."

To settle scores and end the harassment, domina Gemma, her husband, her brother, and other relatives hatched a plot: Gemma convinced the insistent officer that she was finally ready to sleep with him, that her husband had been called out of town by Count Robert, and that she would be waiting for him that night "nude in bed." The eager notary fell for the story, entered the house, and indeed found Gemma nude in bed. But after having stripped and gotten ready to indulge his long-frustrated desire, he also found the bats (*mazze*) of Gemma's husband, brother, and kinsmen, who beat the notary to a pulp: after many strikes, and as he was struggling to crawl out the door, one relative stabbed him with a sword, giving him a "large gash" in the chest. While he lay on the ground, the others rallied round and continued beating him with their bats. Yet, despite this aggravated assault, the officer of the court was fined 160 lire, while his adversaries were fined half that amount.[70]

But, back to clerics: even given the blind spot created by the absence of church court records and possible behind-the-scenes protection and patronage, we can see priests in court descriptions as collaborators, whether the case is one of theft or adultery with consenting women brought to trial by disgruntled husbands, relatives, or the vicar's inquisition. Indeed, a sprinkling of such cases do survive in the vicariate records. Over a sixteen-month period during 1418 and 1419 a married woman from Uzzano in the vicariatus of the Valdinievole had a love affair with the local parish priest, who was also godfather to her daughter (*contraxit in fide in sacrosancto batismale*).[71] For her crime, the adulteress wife was forced to wear a crown of shame and to ride seminude on a donkey through the countryside of Pescia to its place of justice and, all along the way, be whipped severely (*acriter fustigetur et scopetur*). Afterward, she was exiled for life from Pescia and from the district of the Valdinievole.[72] The adulterous priest—hardly innocent in the court's eyes—who had "knowingly, premeditatedly, and deceitfully sinned against God and the Glorious Virgin Mary" was not sentenced but most certainly was handed over to a church tribunal.[73] If we can take Sacchetti's stories of similar libidinous priests at face value, the penalty would not have been light; at the very least, he would have been castrated.[74]

The courts tell a similar tale three years later (1422), again in the vicariate centered in the town of Pescia. In this case, an official of the court caught a married villager in bed with her local priest, who again was bonded to her through the spiritual relation of the baptismal font, "calling one another godmother and godfather." In this case, the notary was more specific, accusing the couple of adultery and incest, but once again, only the woman was charged. For unexplained reasons, this woman was sent to Pisa, where she was to be whipped "until blood should appear," but unlike her compatriot of a few years earlier, she was not exiled.[75] Finally, in 1430, a woman from the village of Marti (in the former *contado* of Pisa) was accused by her husband and fined the substantial penalty of three hundred lire for fornication with the local priest, "against the statutes of the commune of Marti and canon law."[76]

These cases of priestly libidinous desire may have provided the raw materials for a Boccaccio, a Sacchetti, or a Sercambi; indeed, Sacchetti was *podestà* of Mangona, Bibbiena, San Miniato, and the vicar of Portico di Romagna and San Miniato.[77] What is surprising, however, is how few priests appear in these sex scandals, given the large number of cases of adultery that these vicariate courts tried and given our expectations shaped from contemporary storytellers and, more recently, by masterpieces of microhistory such as *Montaillou*.[78] More than in Boccaccio's stories, in nearly half of Sacchetti's tales that joke and moralize about sexual infidelity, the protagonist is a libidinous male cleric.[79] These stories, moreover, turn on adulterous relations between consenting adults, not rape. In other words, they were cases where clerics may not have been tried in the secular courts but nonetheless would have been present in the notary's description of the case, since it involved an adulterous lay woman.

Another statistic from the vicariate court that may not contradict but does confound the view of Florentine life taken from the prescriptive literature—even if that literature was produced by merchant writers for an urban merchant class—regards the marital status of those women who aroused men's libidinous desires. From Giordano da Pisa to Paolo da Certaldo to Giovanni Morelli to San Bernardino to Machiavelli's *Clizia*, it was unmarried women who posed the greatest threat to men's reputations.[80] According to Paolo da Certaldo: "Woman is a very vain thing and light to move, and, therefore, when she is without husband she is in great peril."[81] And thus he advised fathers to punish their young girls and to restrain them at home. Similarly, the other side of marriage—widowhood—evoked men's distrust and fear. According to Mazzi, "the negative elements [of Boccaccio's *Corbaccio*] finish by concentrating on the figure of the solitary woman—the widow."[82] And it was this state that, for Boccaccio and his contemporaries, spurred the most distrust, "since these women enjoyed a discreet sexual liberty."[83]

Yet, the objects of men's desires as far as these court proceedings reveal were more often married women, whether the case concerned rape, attempted rape, or a consensual love affair. Over two-thirds of the women in these cases were married (140), and of these the court specified that only two were young newlyweds.[84] One was an eighteen-year-old, who, because of her age (according to the court), was susceptible to "the blandishments and promises" of her seducer; the other, an adolescent girl (*iuvenis et puella*), whom the court also judged unable to defend herself against her lover's "false words and flattery," was "extracted" from home and seduced in a nearby hut.[85] Some of these cases of adultery sketch scenes of the hopelessness of married life, not uncommon for any historical period; others can be seen within the context of wife beating, justified and lauded by contemporary moralists and even advocated in communal statutes. Still others involved women who rose up against their husbands' battering and, often with the assistance of other women, plotted to poison their husbands.[86]

One such case of adulterous love brought to trial Niccolò di Francesco of San Severino, an unmarried employee of the vicar of Anghiari, then living in Borgo San Sepolcro, who every day fed a certain woman prisoner (whose crime is not stated) through her jail window. From these daily encounters he became infatuated with her and one day entreated her to run away with him, abandoning her husband and children. To which she inquired, "Who are you? And do you have a woman or not?" He responded: "I am from San Severino. I live with my mother and don't have a woman, and when we get away from here I'll never abandon you." At this promise, the imprisoned woman resigned herself to his getaway plot and their future romance, saying that her husband was a drunkard and that she would not mind "to be taken somewhere for a thousand years where he would never hear from her again."[87]

The preponderance of married as opposed to single women who appear in these records as consenting partners or victims of male lust or love is, moreover, slightly understated by a simple counting of cases. Serial adulterers were rare in these documents, especially in comparison with *famosi sodomiti*.[88] While nearly half of those convicted of homosexual sodomy were charged with more than a single affair, only 18 percent of those convicted of heterosexual crimes were accused of more than one affair, and only 13 percent with more than two.[89] Nonetheless, the rare heterosexual Don Giovanni who was brought to trial was indicted for relations mostly with married women. Casinus olim Johannis from San Clemente in the league of Terranuova, the Valdarno superiore, described as "captorem et subtractorem mulierum et aliarum uxorum furem venenatorem aggressorem et fractorem stratarum hominem vagabundum" led the list for numbers of adulterous convictions (eight). He was charged first with stealing domina Antonia, the wife of Matteo from neighboring Treggiaia, running off to Siena with her, "keeping" her there for twelve years, and siring six children by her. Next in the court's charges, but chronologically not necessarily distinct from the previous case or the cases that followed, he "stole" domina Katerina from her husband (of his own village), taking her to the castle of the powerful Count Francesco de Battifolle in Poppi, where he kept her "for many years" and sired two children by her. While still in Poppi, he stole domina Santa from her husband and brought her back to his "cell" in the castle at Poppi, where he "knew her carnally many, many times."

Casinus next led domina Lucretia from her husband in Trappola (Valdarno superiore) to Lucca, where he knew her carnally, stopping off along the way at Cerreto Guidi to perform a robbery. Next, while an employee (*famulus*) of the *castellano* of the castle of Mammi in the *contado* of Florence, he was charged for his only exploit with an unmarried girl, a *puella* from Castiglione Aretino, whose name the court "did not remember," keeping her for ten days or so, not only for his own sexual pleasure but sharing her with the other *famuli* of the castle, "much to the detriment of the young girl." Next, he abducted and seduced Katherina, the wife of Angelo from Poggio, taking her out of the territory of Florence to the village of Lizari de Montegutolo. He was also charged with stealing property from her husband. During these decades of travel, of multiple sexual exploitation—long sexual liaisons mixed with brief adventures—Casinus may have been married to another. At any rate, in the court's penultimate charge, he was accused of having tried twice to poison his own wife, Frea. Finally, he was charged with kidnapping men and holding them for ransom in Siena over a twenty-year period. For all these transgressions, Casinus was sentenced to be decapitated.[90]

Even more surprising than the predominance of married women as the objects of men's extramarital appetites is the near absence of widows from these blotters of sex and violence (fourteen cases, or less than 7%), especially given contemporary suspicion of widows' sexual liberty and prowess and the fact that high mortality rates resulting from war and plague left many women widowed in their sexual prime. Stories by contemporaries about this predicament abound. One of Giovanni Sercambi's *Novelle*, story 70, "De vidua libinosa" (The Horny Widow), tells of a young widow of the Strozzi family who, to satisfy her sexual *rabbia* after the death of her husband, consumed sausages in her *bocca senza denti*, which finally provoked her brother into allowing her to remarry.

Did widows really enjoy discreet sexual liberty unharrassed by the local authorities, or did they simply lack the power to bring their grievances to trial? While the vicar himself or his rectors denounced a number of sexual violations as cases against decorum and mores (one often wonders how cases such as incest came to the attention of these courts), cases of rape, attempted rape, and adultery were often brought to trial by close relatives.[91] Yet this was not the case with raped or harassed widows who came before the vicar's court. Unlike the sexual violations of young girls and married women, "blood relatives" did not denounce a single case of a widow's misadventure in these samples and rarely put forward claims as injured parties whose honor was at stake along with that of the victimized widow.

Indeed, in every case involving the sexual mores of a widow, when the person bringing charges was named, it was the rector of the village or another official of the state.[92] And in only two cases of the fourteen involving widows in sex scandals were relatives mentioned as members of the violated party. Significantly, both were cases of incest. In the first, a brother of a recently deceased husband seduced his sister-in-law and, from their affair, sired a child. The court considered this affair not only a violation of the widow but of public decorum and of his brothers and other kinsmen (*suorum fratrum et aliorum consanguinorum et actinorum*).[93] Moreover, to my reading, it is ambiguous whether the "suorum" refers to his or her blood relations.

The second case involved an incestuous affair between a father and his recently widowed daughter-in-law. They mutually agreed to a love affair, which lasted seemingly without any problems for the community or the courts from March through August 1433. In September, however, the father "adding evil to evil," decided to move in with his daughter-in-law and his grandchildren, "knowing her carnally, and living with her as though she were his own wife, against all mores and the honor of these children, his grandchildren, and to their serious detriment."[94]

As Isabelle Chabot and Christiane Klapisch-Zuber argue (largely for urban, elite widows of the Renaissance), less powerful and less wealthy country women also found themselves ripped from the protective structures of kinship with widowhood.[95] As Klapisch-Zuber puts it, "women were passing guests" in the larger family, or *casa,* of kinship and lineage.[96] Based on the percentage of widows who remained in the countryside, Klapisch-Zuber and my statistics in chapter 7 suggest that widowhood may well have been worse for women in the country than in the cities.[97] Thus, like the "cruel mother" caught within the contradictions of male lineage strategies—damned by her kinsmen if she did not remarry and by her children if she did—so too was the widow in the countryside cast out of the net of both her kin groups, cut from the protection and concerns of affines as well as her own blood kin, at least as far as her sexual honor was concerned.[98]

The presence of young unmarried women in the vicariate records as the objects of men's desires also runs against expectations derived from contemporaries' deep concerns about preserving the honor of unmarried daughters. Only slightly over a quarter of the victims and woman participants in sex crimes had not yet married (fifty-seven).[99] What is even more surprising, the majority of these girls were not the pubescent ones of thirteen to eighteen imagined by Paolo da Certaldo and other contemporary moralists but were younger, ranging from the three-year-old seduced by the Pistoiese boy Don Giovanni to the prepubescent early teens. Nor were these country girls especially well guarded by their guardians or parents, as the prescriptive literature might lead us to believe. Unlike the place of rape, attempted rape, or seduction of married women—her house or occasionally the communal well, and usually at nighttime—the unmarried girls in these sex cases were found almost invariably accosted outside the home, in open fields or on public roads, and were assaulted in broad daylight. Many of these young victims were shepherdesses tending their animals in pastures alone, sometimes far from home.

Such was the 1418 case of a girl "about ten years old and no more than eleven," who, while tending her pigs, was seduced and sodomized (*inter cossias*) and then taken to woods in several places through the *contadi* of Agliana and Vignale in the Valdarno inferiore, where she was repeatedly raped.[100] A year later, a nine-year-old girl alone on a public road near the Ponsacco in the former *contado* of Pisa was sodomized by a traveler from Perignano in the *podesteria* of Crespina.[101] In 1422 an eight-year-old from Ricasoli in the Valdarno superiore, tending her herds "in a certain pasture," was taken to a nearby dense patch of broom, her underpants were lifted, and she was sodomized.[102] Even more disturbing was the rape of a six-and-a-half-year-old traveling with her flocks (*cum certis castratis seu bestiis pecundis*) during the transhumance from Verghereto high in the Romagna Apennines (beyond the present borders of Tuscany) to the parish of San Cristofano in Lucignano in the southern Chianti. (Given the circuitous route through the mountains, the journey was certainly no less than one hundred kilometers and no doubt required several days or more.) She was sodomized by a "vagabond" from Ischia in the Maremma senese, most likely also a shepherd on the transhumance. The case makes no mention of parents or a guardian who might have been traveling along.[103]

Nor do these country and small-town girls always seem so simple and naive (*simpliciter et bona fide*), as the court notaries often alleged or as the contemporary moralists' instructions to jealous fathers might lead us to believe. In 1427, a "libidinous man" from Poggibonsi propositioned a nine-year-old girl, who just happened to be by his doorstep: "You want me to make you?" (*Vuoi mi che ti fai?*) She responded: "Sure, if you give me a few coins and don't take them away from me afterward" (*Si bene se voi mandate pauchi quatrini et non megli toglate poi*). He then gave her four coins, led her into his house, and sodomized her on his bed.[104] Was the Tuscan preacher at the turn of the fourteenth century, Giordano da Pisa, not far off the mark when he claimed that Florentine boys and girls never came to marriage as virgins?[105] Perhaps. But again, the historian should be leery of assuming that the "exceptional" was the "normal." To be sure, country girls and their blood kin may well have had different mores from urban artisans, shopkeepers, and the merchant elite to whom da Certaldo or San Bernardino and others were preaching. On the other hand, the relative rarity of young nubile girls in these cases compared to their younger sisters or their mothers suggests that country fathers may have begun to guard their daughters' honor with much sterner resolve once they reached puberty.

And, as always, the "dark figure" of unreported crimes and crimes settled out of court looms over these criminal statistics.[106] Perhaps cases of rape or fornication with pubescent girls were resolved out of court more often than cases involving married women, since marriage could have been the resolution.[107] Indeed, at least two statute books from the territory of late Trecento and early Quattrocento Florence—those from Firenzuola and the Podere Fiorentino—gave the rapist the opportunity of marrying his victim as a way of avoiding the full force of the law.[108] Yet in spite of the Florentine statutes compiled in 1409 and published in 1415, the sentences from the surviving court cases suggest that the territory of Florence may have been different in this regard from villages in the Liguria and from Renaissance Venice and its hinterland, where regularly, according to Guido Ruggiero, rapists were required to marry their victims or face graver penalties. (The consent of the victim was not stated as a prior condition for the marriage.)[109] In the Florentine hinterland, such "agreements" between rapist and victim appear as an option in only one case, and even in that case the victim was not yet nubile, but only ten years old.[110] To conclude, even if we can say nothing more, these court cases defy a neat concordance between literary evidence and social statistics, correspondence now taken for granted in the historian's effort to corroborate social facts with contemporary opinion.

What more, then, can these statistics and their stories tell us? To answer this question, it is best to leave the sex cases, to consider them not in isolation from other cases, as though within a private realm sealed off from questions of state policy.

The years circa 1401–5 marked a watershed in Florentine policies toward the welfare of its *contado* and especially in regard to taxation. Renewed hostilities between Milan and Florence set the stage, as warfare spread across the mountainous borders to the north and east of Florence. But Florentine changes in politics did not hinge on diplomatic history and external warfare alone. The provisions of Florence's highest councils—the Tre Maggiori—and the court records of the *podestà* and the *capitano del popolo* disclose that, unlike previous military encroachments across the Apennines, those of the first years of the fifteenth century sparked widespread peasant revolts across the mountain zones dividing the Florentine state from Modena, Bologna, Forlì, and parts farther east. Except for the Sambuca resistance led by the Pistoiese patrician Ricciardo Cancellieri, these peasant uprisings are unchronicled by historians but are reported in great detail in the criminal records and the day-to-day business of Florence's highest councils, records called the *provvisioni*.[111]

Rural Florentine tax registers—the *estimi* and the *catasti*—also show a turning point circa 1400. The tax rate on the *contado* increased steadily from the earliest records in the 1350s to the *estimi* of 1401 and, afterward, began to fall steadily. Not all rural communities were taxed alike, and the discrepancies widened progressively as the total rate burden increased; by the time of the *estimo* of 1401–2, some communities were taxed as much as thirty-two times that of others.[112] The communities most burdened by Florence's increasing fiscal crisis were those farthest from the city and highest up—those close to or straddling the sensitive political borders separating Florence from its enemies to the north—and which would revolt against Florentine sovereignty in 1402–6. Finally, migration out of the Florentine state increased steadily in the last decades of the fourteenth century, reaching its zenith in 1401. Those who migrated in the greatest numbers and whose village populations dwindled most rapidly again came from the overtaxed mountain hamlets to the north. The *provvisioni* of the Tre Maggiori corroborate this last point, as the demographic circumstances of the Florentine hinterland weighed on the minds of its patrician rulers. Increasingly, Florence passed legislation to attract foreign rural laborers into the Florentine *contado* and, by the 1390s, gave moratoria on previous debts and tax concessions for as long as twenty years in order to entice back its own rural inhabitants, who had left their farms in flight from the tax collectors and the *berrovarii* of the *podestà*.[113]

The earliest vicariate records for the mountain zones north of Florence appeared just at the moment when the *podestà* and the *capitano del popolo* criminal records reveal conflict heating up in these borderlands—the Alpi fiorentine and the Podere Fiorentino, which straddled the border with Romagna. The first extant volume of the vicariate court records is a treasure trove of collective peasant violence, a mix of rebellions, cattle raids, kidnapping, and armed invasions. These were sometimes organized by Florence's ancient feudal enemies, the Ubaldini and the Ubertini, but they were executed by the indigenous peasant populations. Space does not allow a descriptive recounting of these events or a more careful typology of the forms of rural violence directed against the Florentine state and its officials. Suffice it to say for now that the insurrectionary activities ranged from widespread collective military action of peasant communes against Florentine dominion (mainly in the mountains) to efforts by wives and children to liberate their husbands and fathers from their creditors and from the clutches of the *podestà,* which often resulted in rural women pummelling armed officers of the Florentine state with sticks and stones and their own bare hands.

But let me recount briefly two of these uprisings, in the tradition of microhistory—not because they are typical but because they are the exceptions that may reveal underlying tendencies about insurrection and the mentality of this period not unveiled readily from other sources. The first occurred in 1399 in a small market town, the Rocca di San Casciano in the Florentine Romagna.[114] It was the only insurrection in the mountain hinterland organized by what seems to have been a local bourgeoisie, and it is one of the few in which any inkling of ideology and social motivation was allowed past the prejudicial eyes of the vicariates' notaries.

A Ser Matteo di Ciandrino and Maestro Giovanni di fu Niccola, both of Rocca di San Casciano and described by the Florentine notary as plotting to subvert the peace and "wishing that the people of Romagna should live in tyranny," had sold the bread *gabella* to a Cristoforo di Drudoli of this Rocca without authorization from the district's *podestà*. According to the court's scribe, "these men had raised a major disturbance and acted as tyrants by speaking injurious and ugly words to the Florentine authority in the district, charging that the Lord Captain ought not to interfere in their business" (*de negotiis nostris*). Several days later, Ser Matteo appeared before the court of the captain, speaking on his own behalf and that of Maestro Giovanni, who then sat as an elected councilman of this rural commune (*qui nunc est ad consilium comunis*). Ser Matteo submitted a formal petition protesting the exile that had been placed on them and claiming indemnity for all penalties and expenses. The captain, seeing that he did not have the force to arrest them at that moment, demanded that they report back at his court on the following day. Ser Matteo replied, "yes we shall appear, and we shall bring with us men and women from throughout the province of Romagna." Among "many other vituperous and offensive words against the Magnificent Comune of Florence" spoken by Ser Matteo were, "One day, we will leave this tyranny once and for all" (*Noi usciremo pure una volta di questa tirapnia*).

Later in the month, with others whom the court for the time being refused to name, Ser Matteo and Maestro Giovanni held secret meetings, constructed ladders for scaling the *borgo*'s walls, and negotiated with the feudal lords of Romagna to intervene on their behalf. Thereby, they planned a revolt appealing to feudal powers against further encroachments by the Florentine state into the economic liberties that had been granted to them in their original treatises of submission to Florence in 1382. The two ringleaders of the revolt were sentenced to death in contumacy. Two months later they petitioned the *consiglio maggiore* of Florence to drop the charges and were absolved of their crimes.[115] Indeed, increasing warfare and peasant insurrection in the Romagna must have conditioned the *signoria* of Florence's mercy as it had in their cancellations of death penalties charged against peasant insurgents across the northern boundaries, from Sambuca in the Pistoiese to Palazzuolo in the Podere Fiorentino.

In 1425–26, after twenty years of relative calm throughout the territory of Florence, at least as regards internal (but not external) affairs, resentment in the countryside began to stir again, by 1430 leading to major insurrections in Arezzo, Pisa, and Volterra. In this new wave of insurrections, the mountain village of Pontenano, on the southern tail of the Pratomagno, was one of the first to welcome the military assistance of Milan in an attempt to throw off Florentine dominion. The village elected its own revolutionary council, and in a meeting in front of the parish church one old man from the crowd yelled out: "I have a flag that I have kept hidden away in my chest for forty years" (that is, since about the time Arezzo and its *contado* had passed into Florentine hands), "which I'll run and get." The court scribe then interrupted his narrative of events to describe the flag in detail: on it was painted a bridge, a black eagle, and the coat of arms of the Pietramala (the feudal lords of Arezzo throughout the early fourteenth century). The old man presented the flag to Ser Domenico, the parish priest and leader of the village revolt, who hoisted it above the campanile of the church.

The crowd began to chant: "Long live the duke! Duke, duke, duke, and death to the *marzocco* [the symbol of the Parte Guelfa] and to whoever painted it and to whoever wishes it well."[116] Then the revolutionary committee formally turned the village over to Captain Guidone, acting on behalf of the duke of Milan, and "these men and women understood themselves to be the duke's subjects, faithful and obedient to the duke, his officials, and his mandates."[117] Thus, as in the case from the Romagna village of Rocca di San Casciano twenty-six years earlier, feudal lords both past and present (the early fourteenth-century Pietramala and the duke of Milan) were seen as the villagers' liberators from the tyranny of an urban republic and its rapid territorial expansion.

In subsequent months, men from the village led raiding parties through the mountains, stealing cattle and taking hostages.[118] They joined up with other adversaries in Borgo San Sepolcro and invaded the neighboring mountain district of Castel Focognano, cajoling the peasants there to rise up against the Florentine state, claiming that they had the better part of them, and that the Florentine troops would "flee like whores."[119] In other villages of the vicariate of Anghiari, the symbols of the Florentine state were again assaulted. In Castel Ranchi, the villagers with their weapons attacked and devastated the painted coat of arms of the commune of Florence and again of its Parte Guelfa—that is, "the lily, the *marzocco,* and the red eagle holding a green dragon under its feet"—and chanted, "Death, death to the *marzocco,* who has skinned the rope [ripped us off; most likely a reference to Florentine tax policy], and to the Parte Guelfa and the commune of Florence and its protectors (*conservatori*) and those who wish them well."[120]

In Pontenano the attack on the symbols of Florentine power went beyond the stabbing and devastation of coat of arms and entered the realm of street theater, as these mountain peasants dressed up a donkey as the *marzocco,* led it in mock fashion around the village piazza, and then cut its head off. Back in Florence, in its highest councils, the insult was not taken as a joke but struck tender nerves. It was one of the few acts of insurrection to reach the highest level of the Florentine state for debate and consultation, the *Consulte e Pratiche,* since Ricciardo Cancellieri's 1401 revolt against Florence, his capture of the castle at Sambuca, and his two-year control of the Montagna Pistoiese.[121] In describing the village's rebellion and its attacks on the sanctity of Florence's symbols of authority, Ser Tommaso di Ser Luca di Francesco, speaking on behalf of both colleges in the Florentine *signoria,* advised that Pontenano be leveled to the ground "so that no stone should remain on top of another and neither rooster nor hen ever crow there again, that its properties be confiscated, its church deconsecrated, and that no one should [be able] ever to settle there again."[122]

Through these revolts and others, the student of popular unrest can glean the vital importance of the symbols of power and the power of words like *tyranny,* which the Florentine tribunals contorted to justify their own ideology, at the same time that those in the subject territories used it as a rallying cry to throw off Florentine dominion. Despite five hundred years of political thought and propaganda, in large part initiated by Florentine humanist statesmen at this very moment in Florentine state building, villagers on the periphery did not find that "city air made one free"; instead, they saw feudal lords as their liberators, freeing them from the tyranny of the republic's taxation and dominion.[123] These insights into early republican political propaganda, state building, and the use and abuse of words and symbols defy any quantitative analysis. But my more modest objective here is the opposite: to show that a quantitative reckoning of court cases can provide clues to the past that no individual case study, no matter how "thickly" described, and no narrative treatment of the most exceptional cases can possibly reveal. Edoardo Grendi and the historians of *Quaderni Storici* may be right: the quantitative study of criminal records for discerning comportment is fraught with problems, but concluding as he does that the exercise is without any value now deserves the same skepticism that Grendi, Bailey, Pastore, and others have given quantitative studies over the past two decades.[124]

Not only are criminal statistics, past and present, records of comportment; they chronicle state actions—strategies of political and social control and attempts at the acculturation of mores.[125] In proclaiming the uselessness of criminal statistics before the nineteenth century, historians have

Figure 6.1

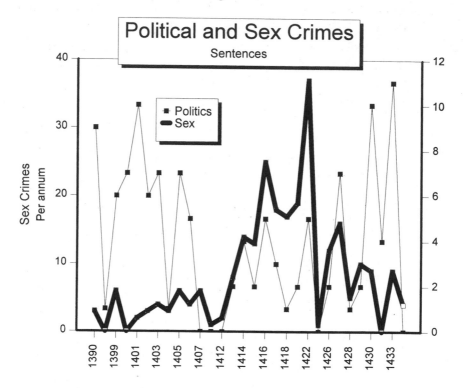

recently shoved this political aspect of premodern criminal statistics aside as though only criminality could be the objective of a quantitative inquiry of judicial data.[126] But I would argue that it is this underlying chronicle of politics, far more than delinquency, that a quantitative treatment of criminal court records can bring to the surface; more than criminal trends, this record provides a new perspective for viewing political conflict and territorial consolidation.

Viewed from the side of state behavior and quantified accordingly, the vicariate court records chart a tripartite periodization from the earliest records to the rise of the Medici in 1434: (1) a period of insurrection on the periphery from 1398 through the end of the war with Milan, Siena, and Pisa in 1406; (2) a period of social calm from about 1406 to 1425; and (3) the rise of new internal hostilities and the outbreak of a new wave of peasant insurrections from 1425 to 1434.[127]

In addition, quantification of these records shows a strong inverse rela-

Figure 6.2

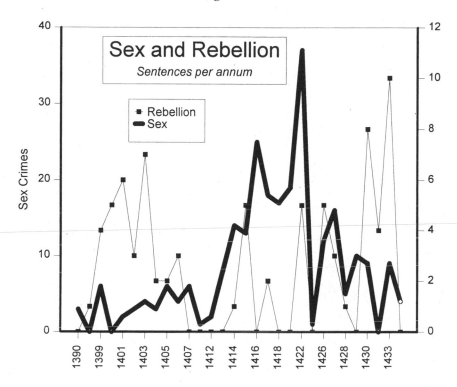

tionship between periods of political crime and insurrection, on the one hand, and the prosecution of sexual offenses, on the other (figures 6.1, 6.2, 6.3). When peasant insurrections were rife, at the turn of the century, prosecutions for sexual crimes, whether rape or the affairs of consenting couples, were rare. When insurrections subsided, after 1406, prosecutions of sex crimes brought before the courts rose absolutely and soared over political charges. When insurrection returned to the periphery in 1425, prosecutions of sex crimes once again dipped. If we narrow the category of political crime to include only those cases in which the law officers and their notaries explicitly judged the actions of peasants, mountaineers, or townspeople as subversive to Florentine dominion, calling them acts of conspiracy or rebellion, this negative correlation between sex and politics strengthens to −0.74, one of the strongest inverse correlation coefficients I know for medieval data.[128] Nor were these changes simply a matter of the courts being blocked from regular criminal prosecution during periods of insur-

Figure 6.3

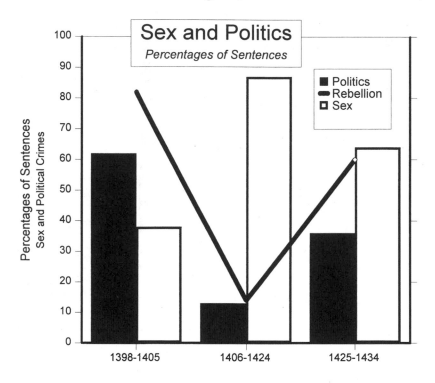

rection. A glance through the records reveals that the vicariate courts continued to function, apprehending criminals and prosecuting the normal caseloads of crimes such as assault, theft, fraud, and trespass. For no year did sex offenses or insurrection ever constitute more than 5 percent of the caseloads found in these documents.

Do these trends underlie patterns of behavior similar to football hooliganism, which journalists and sociologists have claimed declines in times of national crisis or war?[129] Or again, was it like the relationship between drugs and political activism in the black ghettos of inner-city America, the argument being that drug use declined in the 1960s when political activism gripped these communities and, afterward, increased sharply in tandem with political apathy? Perhaps. But more likely, these sexual acts seen as criminal were earlier either tolerated or dealt with by more informal, extralegal means, which the centralizing arm of the vicariate later snatched from the authority of local families and clans.[130] Certainly, this is the impression given in the Mugello, where the records of traditional medieval courts existed before its criminal jurisdiction was reorganized as a vicariate in 1415. In the earlier records of the traditional medieval tribunals, sexual offenses were extraordinarily rare both in absolute numbers and relative to what they would become once the vicariate court was put in place. In addition, those crimes of sexual misconduct that did come before the medieval tribunals were unlike those later to be sentenced in the vicariate courts: earlier, they had been almost exclusively ones of sexual assault rather than crimes of the heart.[131]

Indeed, earlier, at least in the territories under Aretine control and in the Valdinievole when it belonged to Lucca, communal statutes protected families from the direct intervention of the state and from the accusations of others in matters of adultery and incest. Such cases were invalidated if initiated by state inquest (no matter whether served by the village rector, the *podestà*, or any other official). Only members of the immediate family could bring such crimes to trial.[132] In late fourteenth-century commune of Santa Maria a Monte (later incorporated into the vicariate of San Miniato), protection against such charges and state intervention extended even to rape.[133]

More clearly than possible changes in criminal behavior, further quantitative treatment of the vicariate records also highlights the other side of these criminal statistics—prosecution and the state's strategy to control its hinterland more rigorously. Of course, this control might not be seen entirely as outside repression but rather as the "civilizing process," protecting women, in particular, in a world of male dominance and violence.[134] Indeed, historians and sociologists have claimed that, as the centralized state and its police developed, the general level of interpersonal violence declined.[135] Yet as far as the criminal records show, sexual violence increased both absolutely and relative to political crime in these years of Florentine conquest and the consolidation of its territorial state. From one rape reported every two years in the first revolutionary years, the annual number of violent sex crimes increased by more than eight times in the middle years of internal political calm and then fell by more than half when insurrection again spread through the mountain districts of the Florentine state.[136]

The character of these prosecutions also changed in the middle years of relative social peace, 1406–25. The courts' surveillance and protection crept more often into the bedroom, prosecuting more cases of attempted rape, adulterous relations between consenting partners, and seduction between unmarried partners in which flattery and gifts were the keys of conquest (or who knows, even romantic love) and not *per vim et violentiam.*[137] With the second wave of peasant uprisings in 1425, sexual crimes of mutual consent shot up by three times in these middle years of social calm, from 18 percent to 63 percent of all sex crimes, and then fell again to 37 percent. In addition, for the most secretive act of sexual misconduct—incest—the middle years again reveal the closer surveillance and moral intervention of the state. Florentine vicariates sentenced two-thirds of these cases between 1406 and 1425 (the denominator for sexual crimes remains approximately the same for all three periods: sixty-one, sixty-five, and sixty cases, respectively, and the number of complete years of surviving documents for each period is the same, eight).

Moreover, the fines for sexual crimes nearly doubled in these middle years, from a mean of 99 lire to a mean of 182 lire, even though the severity of these crimes had declined, at least in terms of violence. (The higher fine was at the top end of what the richest peasants in the Casentino could give to dower their daughters during the mid-fifteenth century.)[138] Nor was this a matter of inflation in this period of stable population and prices; when insurrection returned to the countryside in the mid-1420s the fines for sexual offenses (a mean of 98 lire) sank to almost exactly what they had been at the beginning of the century. Furthermore, if only attempted and consensual sexual offenses are considered, the differences in the fines charged by the vicariate courts became more accentuated, rising from 48.5 lire in the first years of the century to 81.2 lire in the middle years of relative social quiescence, then falling precipitously to a mere 9.5 lire when insurrection returned in 1425, only one-ninth of what they had been in the period of social peace.

These increases in the middle period are the more remarkable given recent historians' arguments that the harshness of penalties and the amount of fines declined as the incidence of arrest for a particular crime increased, their argument being that community cooperation with law enforcers was made more palatable when the fines were lowered.[139] If we accept this logic, then the reverse phenomenon in the territorial periphery of the Florentine state further suggests the outside, oppressive nature of these arrests for alleged sexual transgressions.

In addition, the court's sentences do not chart a progressive decline in mutilation, whipping, and torture, as general theorists of crime and punishment have speculated and as historians have recently argued for Renaissance cities.[140] Instead, the middle years register an increase in punishments that cut off bodily parts of sexual offenders and paraded both men and women, although usually women, sometimes stripped "to the kidneys," sometimes wholly nude, through the streets of the vicariates' centers, flogging them until, as the notarial formula demanded, she (less often, he) showed signs of blood (*ita et taliter quod sanguis appareat*).[141]

Furthermore, this middle period of relative social peace witnessed the most heinous penalties meted out to political prisoners—live burials in the accustomed place of justice—even though the threat of internal insurrection had declined.[142] One such sentence gives off the scent of ancient Greek history, perhaps a contribution from humanist historiography. The vicar of the Valdinievole condemned four men from Montecatini for insurrection resulting in the death of an official of Florence's Parte Guelfa. The four were to be led to the place of justice in Montecatini, where a round ditch two arms'-length (*braccia*) deep (about five feet) was to be dug. The men were to be put in on their heads, their feet pulled upward, and the ditch then filled until they died. Once dead, their bodies were to be hanged from the gallows and left in perpetuity wherever they happened to fall; that is, they were to be buried alive but left unburied when dead.[143]

Like late nineteenth- and twentieth-century liberal democracies, which preached and mostly followed practices of due process at home but exported torture, concentration camps, and other forms of repressive brutality to their client states and colonies, Renaissance Florence appears also to have had a Janus head in its strategies of political control and social repression.[144] As Rocke and Zorzi claim for urban Florence and Dean for Bologna, the harshness of penalties from the frequencies of the death penalty to various forms of mutilations may have declined in fifteenth-century urban centers.[145] Yet, at the same time and with the judgments of the same Renaissance patricians who held offices in the *signoria* as well as being vicars in the outlying districts, the vicariate records reveal that early fifteenth-century Florence meted out penalties in its newly consolidated territories that reversed the more "civilized" clock followed at home.

Finally, a quantification of these records reveals a geography of crime and prosecution that raises other hypotheses for the political history of the Florentine territorial state. Sexual offenses were not spread evenly across Florence's dominion; instead, three vicariates stand out: first, the two newly incorporated zones of the mountainous Aretine *contado,* the vicariates of Anghiari and the Valdarno superiore, which swept down from the high slopes of the Pratomagno to the Arno River and into the eastern boundaries of Florence's traditional *contado;* and second, the low-lying hills and marshy valleys of the Valdarno inferiore, centered on the town of San Miniato al Tedesco and bordering the former *contado* of Pisa.[146]

Over a third of the sex cases (34%) came from the two contiguous mountainous vicariates of the Valdarno superiore and Anghiari. But next in line was the Valdarno inferiore, with 15 percent of the sex cases. Thus, if we are to take these statistics as reflecting anything about behavior, certainly no mountain versus valley explanation or comparison with isolated, supposedly incest-ridden, Appalachian communities holds water. Indeed, sexual offenses hardly appear in the vicariate records for the mountainous Florentine Romagna and the Alpi fiorentine above Firenzuola, which had led the peasant insurrections in the early fifteenth century.[147]

Moreover, crimes of incest were not particularly pronounced in the mountains of the Florentine territory. One gripping tale from these records does, however, conjure up Appalachian images that, in isolation, might well satisfy the present-minded historian's taste for continuity over the *longue durèe.* In 1416, Cardone, the son of the former Cardone from Camerino, then living in Villa Marsane in the mountains north of Borgo San Lorenzo, "affected by wickedness and beastly will," attempted to know carnally his own daughter Lisa. "In his wife's absence and even in her presence, with deception and flattery, Cardone would hold his daughter in his arms as though she were a whore, both at home and outside of it, to fulfill his bestial desire." One day while in the Grezani Alps in a place called Frassino with his daughter Lisa, he embraced her, threw her on the ground, and began to know her carnally (*ipsam lisam anplettens et sternens eam in terram coatus fuit ipsam carnaliter congnoscere*) but was unable to execute his iniquity because of "her filial rebellion," she protesting many times, "Leave me alone or I'll tell." Yet, with power and fatherly authority, he persisted in urging this beastly union (*bestiali coytu*), which he would have realized had she not been able to escape. One night in December of the same year, while in bed with his wife, his daughter, the said Lisa, and his other children, Cardone tried again "to rape and have incest and beastly union with Lisa." When his wife arose to relieve herself and was wandering through the house tending to her business (*cum dicta domina piera eius uxore surgens tempestive pro magne applicando et per domum sive negotia faciendo herendo se*), he tried in the dark to rape Lisa from behind (*inter tibias*), but she "rebelled" and managed to flee.

In March, while again in the Grezani Alps bringing hay back home, he "continued to persist in his nefarious and beastly wickedness." This time, however, he finally succeeded in "penetrating the vulva" of his daughter Lisa, then thirteen years old. "Lying on her breast prostrate, with her underwear pulled up, her nudity (*nature*) and vulva exposed, her face pushed into her knees (*viso genutu*), he consummated his beastly sexual intercourse [with Lisa], his legitimate and natural daughter, breaking through her hymen, against her will." The court sentenced: "for these and many other matters which for reasons of decorum [*pro honestate*] it is best now to keep quiet" (the historian can only marvel at what could have been worse), Cardone was to be set as an example: tied to the customary ring (*ligatam faciendo cercham consuetam*), led through the territory and *castrum* of Scarperia to the place of justice, and there decapitated.[148]

Yet no matter how gruesome or striking this individual case, unlike the geographical concentrations of sex offenses in general, incest cases were evenly distributed throughout the territory of Florence. No vicariate accounts for more than four cases. Nonetheless, such prosecutions are found more in the low-lying places—the city of Pisa and the villages of the Valdarno inferiore—than in the mountains. Despite the fact that this one vivid case, told almost poetically by the notary, came from the upper Mugello, perhaps even crossing over into the jurisdictions of the Alpi fiorentine (al Frassino), the vicariate courts of the mountain districts of Romagna and the Alpi fiorentine do not register even a single case of incest.

How then do we explain the differences in the frequencies of prosecuted sex crimes across the mountainous zones of the Florentine territory? Was it because the Alpi fiorentine had been incorporated earlier into the traditional *contado* of Florence and thus had become more "civilized" over the course of the late Trecento? Certainly, the outbreak of peasant rebellion in these mountains in the early years of the fifteenth century does not suggest that these mountaineers had taken well to the lessons and rules handed down by Florentine officials. And the Romagna remained throughout this period a part of the district, retaining its own money (the Bolognese lira), its own calendar, beginning with the nativity, and many of its own gabelles and land taxes (which, as we have seen, places like the Rocca di San Casciano fought bitterly to preserve).

As suggested earlier, in the years of extraordinary military increases in state expenditures and the consequent crises of state finances charted by

Becker, Molho, Herlihy, la Roncière, and others, the Florentine patriciate refused to increase its fiscal pressure on either itself—that is, the city of Florence—or the privileged territories beyond the *contado* and within the *districtus*.[149] Instead, Florence leaned more and more heavily on its traditional *contado,* a tax policy that, by the 1390s, began to have disastrous effects on the demography and economy of the *contado,* as the mounting petitions of impoverished and indebted villages made to the *signoria* well illustrate.

Moreover, a comparative and quantitative survey of tax records from the Black Death to the beginning of the fifteenth century shows that those mountain communities, along the politically sensitive northern border with Bologna, had suffered the most. But, because of the war with Milan and the subsequent widespread and largely successful peasant and feudal uprisings of the Pistoiese, the Alpi fiorentine, the Podere Fiorentino, and the Romagna Apennines, Florentine rulers around 1402 began to change their minds and their policies toward the traditional *contado,* in terms of not only tax policy (giving rise to what I will argue is the origin of the *catasto* reforms of 1427) but also across a wide range of welfare initiatives.[150] In addition, the Florentine state appears to have refrained from interfering with the sexual mores of these mountain villagers.

At the same time, the Florentine legislators of the opening years of the fifteenth century argued that the more privileged *districtus*—the territories of the old communes of Pistoia, Arezzo, later Pisa, Cortona, and Livorno —would now have to begin to shoulder more of the tax burden, including the payment of direct taxes.[151] It is at this point, moreover, that the Florentine commune began to make serious incursions into the traditional criminal and civil jurisdictions of these territories beyond the *contado,* as Giorgio Chittolini and, more recently, Andrea Zorzi show.[152] But as Lorenzo Fabbri shows for Volterra and William Connell for Pistoia, Florentine centralization and infringement on the late medieval rights of its territorial cities and their former *contadi* were not all of a piece.[153]

As the war with Milan was scaling down and Florence was making handsome concessions to mountaineer rebels to the north, debates in the *Consulte e Pratiche* show that the Florentine state looked to expand its influence and control in the politically less volatile mountains of the lower Casentino and beyond into the territories of Chiusi, Subbiano, and Anghiari. In January 1405 these patrician interlocutors concentrated on the need to establish, or rather redraw, the boundaries of the vicariate of the

Valdarno superiore and to take power away from the numerous local *podestà* of the former Aretine *contado,* centered in Anghiari, by placing that authority directly under their own patrician rule. These discussions show the Florentine ruling elite concerned with regulating the mores of these villagers, which I now gather from the vicariates' subsequent activities meant, in large part, sexual mores.[154]

Perhaps these Casentino mountaineers really were more libidinous than those from the Alpi fiorentine or the Romagna, but here I am skeptical. Instead, as with previous tax policies within their own *contado,* so with moral and political acculturation: the Florentine ruling elite pushed and pulled at those places of least resistance, places least likely to endanger the interests of patrician landlords, whose properties lay closer to the city of Florence. At the turn of the century, as chronicled in the protests sent to Florence's highest council and in the criminal acts of the *podestà,* the *capitano del popolo,* and the vicariate courts, the hot areas of peasant revolt then threatening the state's military security were to the north, in the richer mountain valleys of the Pistoiese, the Alpi fiorentine, and the upper Casentino—and not the lower and more impoverished reaches of the Valle fiorentine and the Pratomagno.[155] And in the northern, politically hot mountain zones, prosecutions against sexual mores were light, while in the southern, politically cold mountain zones, prosecutions for sexual crimes were high (both in number and in the penalties meted out) throughout the period of relative social calm from 1406 to 1425.

In 1425, these circumstances were about to change, as war and rebellion spread southward down the spine of the Pratomagno when the Milanese troops made new incursions into the Florentine territory. As the *Consulte e Pratiche* debates and cases from the vicariate records reveal, Florence's first line of attack was military aggression and repression. But evidently the pressures of war, the resistance of mountaineers from such places as Pontenano, perhaps even collective memory and the lessons Florence had learned from 1401 to 1406, caused the Florentine government to change its tack (both at home and at its vicariate frontier outposts). By 1427, the day-to-day legislation preserved in the *provvisioni* registers shows another side of this same Florentine state. In that year alone, Florence granted tax reductions and fiscal moratoria to at least seventy-five communities in the former *contado* of Arezzo, the most ever registered in any single year. Unlike in 1402–6, the Florentine state in 1427 did not wait for the communities of Anghiari and Subbiano to present petitions asking for tax concessions. For the first time, as far as my survey of the *provvisioni* goes, Florence intervened without being petitioned, granting fiscal and administrative reductions to ease the pressure on these communities of prolonged warfare and of the competing efforts of rebels from mountain villages like Pontenano.

Once again, the Florentine ruling elite did not act in the same way everywhere throughout its territory, as insurgents from Volterra would shortly discover.[156] But, despite what the Florentine patrician Ser Tommaso may have advised in the *Consulte e Pratiche* of 1425, the Florentine state did ultimately back off, not only from destroying the insurgent zones of the Valdarno superiore and Anghiari but from further attempting to govern and control these villagers' personal mores so directly and severely, as the decline in prosecutions for sex offenses, the lowering of fines, and the near disappearance of mutilations for such offenses suggest.[157]

With the insurrections of 1425, prosecutions for sex offenses disappeared completely in the new politically hot zones of the vicariate of Anghiari, and in June 1427 even the rebels of Pontenano were forgiven and granted tax relief.[158] Thus, Pontenano was not leveled to the ground never again to be resettled, as any tourist in the Pratomagno can today attest. Indeed, as visitors enter its small piazza, past the campanile and the romanesque parish church now bearing a newly cleaned baroque facade, and as they overlook the luxuriant green mountain forests to the south, the first thing that will strike them (especially if they are avid readers of the Florentine *Consulte e Pratiche*) is a pen filled with crowing roosters and hens. As Giorgio Chittolini claims, Florence dominated its territory more thoroughly and effectively than any other Italian city-state in the early Renaissance.[159] Yet their control developed in an uneven, patchwork fashion, largely determined by the histories of these early Renaissance mountain insurrections.

7. Prosperity in the Countryside:

THE PRICE WOMEN PAID

Whether or not material conditions improved for the peasantry after the Black Death and into the fifteenth century remains controversial not only for Italy but for all Europe.[1] Historians of a Malthusian or neo-Malthusian bent have seen a golden age for the peasantry following in the wake of late fourteenth-century pestilence.[2] Other historians from radically opposed perspectives have come to similar conclusions, finding prosperity for the peasantry for at least parts of Europe and for part of the fifteenth century. Still others have argued the opposite: that the fifteenth century saw at best continued misery, not recovery.[3] Finally, in keeping with what Léopold Genicot showed in his synthetic essay of nearly thirty years ago, some have argued that similar demographic consequences across large spaces of Europe did not have uniform economic consequences.[4]

This chapter does not attempt to resolve or untangle the knots in this debate; rather, it presents data from a series of tax records comprising nineteen sample villages in the largely rural territory around Florence (its *contado*), from the Black Death through the mid-fifteenth century. The trends sketched by these records (the *estimi* and, later, the *catasti*) show a picture of growing prosperity in large swathes of the countryside during the fifteenth century, at least until the *catasto* of 1458–60.

This prosperity, however, did not derive solely from the Black Death of 1348 or even from the plagues that followed. Nor can the timing and the extent of prosperity for different sectors of this rural economy be pinned with any precision to that most impressive of exogenous variables, the plague. Instead, man-made factors—war, politics, taxation, and even class struggle—explain why 1402 and not 1348 or 1375 (as in England) was the nadir in peasant well-being and why mountaineers and not lowland peasants made the most remarkable strides in the accumulation of wealth over the course of the fifteenth century. Indeed, political factors were as crucial in determining the fortunes of rural communities in the Florentine hinterland as were the mortalities due to pestilence. This recovery and fifteenth-century prosperity, moreover, went beyond politics and depended on demographic factors, which again were not exogenous, beyond the control of individual peasants and their communities, but instead stemmed from conscious practices and family decisions. As we shall see, these practices weighed heaviest on women, from infants to elderly widows.

The trends derived from these imperfect records should be treated in the spirit of microhistory, as "clues" to a distant society, for which large expanses of everyday life, such as the weaning of peasant children and the survival of mountain widows, are shrouded in silence.[5] To be sure, the use of Florentine tax registers from the late fourteenth through the fifteenth centuries is problematic. In addition to the problems of any tax records, past and present—evasion, deceit, and missing records—changes in the rules and even the culture of taxation compound the difficulties of comparing these records over long spans of time. While the first of these records, called *capi di famiglia* (1364), differ little from earlier hearth-tax surveys common to Italian city-states dating back to the thirteenth century, by the *capi di famiglia*'s last redaction (1412–14), most aspects of the Renaissance *catasti* were firmly in place.

To make inroads into the more than a thousand surviving volumes of the *estimi* and *catasti*, I sampled eighteen rural communities and one urban neighborhood in Prato (the Porta di Santa Trinita) in the rural quarter of Santa Maria Novella. To compare communities in the plains with those in the mountains, my samples cut two geographical trajectories: one from the city walls of Florence through the rich plains of the Valdarno inferiore and Bisenzio into the city of Prato; the other from the Mugello highlands bordering the state of Bologna through the Alpi fiorentine above Firenzuola and then across the Calvana mountain range in the former *contado* of Prato, to the border of Pistoia (see map).

My first results suggest that one of the oldest and most fundamental of debates in Florentine historiography, that over tax policy and the relations between city and countryside, must be recast. Not only can it be said that no standard tax rate existed for the *contado* before the *catasto* of 1427; the inequalities between villages were extraordinary. At the extreme, one mountain village was taxed at a rate thirty-two times that of a village adja-

Map of Florentine Contado, Sample Villages

Figure 7.1

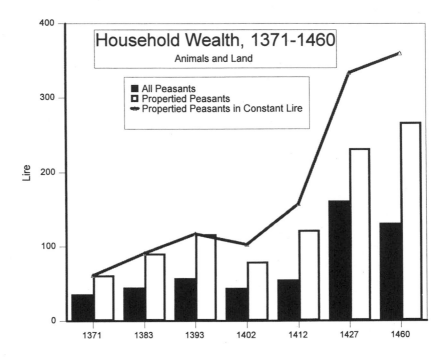

Household Wealth, 1371-1460
Animals and Land

■ All Peasants
□ Propertied Peasants
➡ Propertied Peasants in Constant Lire

cent to the city walls of Florence.[6] Of the various determinants of these tax rates, by far the most significant were geographic: distance from the city of Florence and altitude. Mountaineers and those farther from the city (often, but not always, the same) paid much higher tax rates on their property than those closer to the city and in the lowlands.[7]

In terms of tax rates, household wealth of peasants (in both mountains and plains), and perhaps most important, the tax inequalities between mountains and plains, 1401–2 was a turning point (see figures 7.1, 7.2, 7.3). The third war with Milan, heating up in the mid-1390s, brought a deepening fiscal crisis, which led the Florentine patriciate to lean even harder on its only direct taxpayers, the peasants in its traditional *contado*. Moreover, in the mosaic of unequal tax constituencies, those near the sensitive military frontiers along the northern mountain ridges of the Apennines were charged the most. In 1402 the commune of Florence demanded that the Mugello highland village of Mangona hand over 80 percent of its total wealth in direct taxes for that year alone—and that on top of other indirect taxes (gabelles) and other charges (the *podestà*'s salary, castle duty, munitions, wax for the feast of San Giovanni, etc.).

As might be expected, peasants were hard pressed to pay, and many did not. Their first means of resistance was with their feet. Many fled the tax officials by migrating not downward to greener valleys or to cities such as Florence but upward and across the border to higher villages in the *contado* of Pistoia (not liable to the *estimo*) and, more significantly, to villages in the Bolognese Apennines. Indeed, 1402 was the pinnacle of migration out of the Florentine territory and the nadir of immigration to the city of Florence (see figure 7.4).

But this exodus only meant that those who stayed were forced to pay more; Florentine taxation before the *catasto* was a zero-sum game. The period 1402 through 1406 initiated a new wave of resistance—this time, one

Figure 7.2

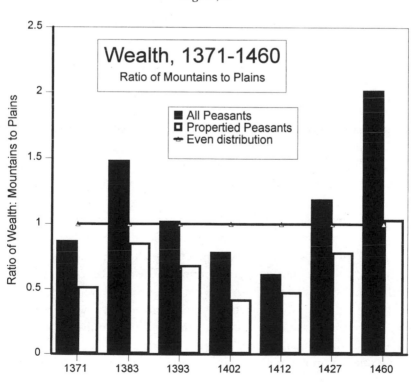

Figure 7.3

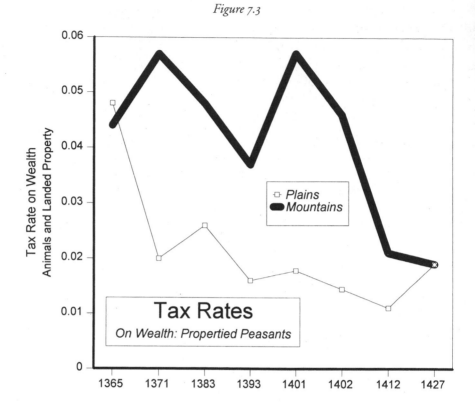

of direct confrontation. Assisted by the invading troops from Milan and rebel outposts in the Montagna Pistoiese, peasant uprisings spread across the Apennines from the Alpi fiorentine across the Romagna zones recently incorporated into the Florentine territory and down the Casentino highlands of Arezzo.

Unlike the revolt of the Ciompi a generation earlier, these peasant revolts were successful, leading to village tax immunities and privileges for individual peasants. But the consequences of the war and rebellion had deeper and longer-lasting consequences. The assessments of 1401–2 marked the watershed in community tax inequalities; afterward, not only did tax rates decline, the difference in rates from village to village narrowed progressively until the *catasto* of 1427, which instituted universal guidelines throughout the Florentine *contado*.[8] The *catasto* of 1427 did not, however, spring solely from the military and fiscal crises that followed a new wave of

Figure 7.4

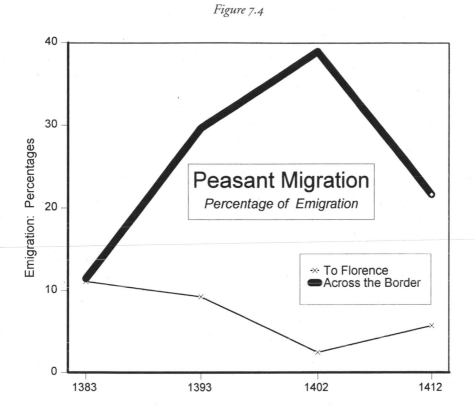

Milanese wars in 1424. Instead, the attack on unequal taxation—at least in Florence's traditional *contado*—originated with the mountain revolts of 1402–6.

The events of 1402 had other long-term consequences for Florentine peasants. As well as marking the high point in outmigration and the height of tax inequality between villages, it registered the low point in household size and population for the plains and, most noticeably, the depths of poverty for all peasants throughout the *contado,* as measured by assessments of landed property and animals. Afterward, household size increased on average from 3.6 to 5.3 members, and the population began to increase slowly, at least in the lowlands (see table 7.1 and figures 7.5, 7.6).[9]

More dramatic were the increases in family wealth, especially of landed peasants. In the space of less than sixty years the average values of their holdings more than trebled in nominal terms from 80 to 267 lire. Relative

TABLE 7.1. Population: Plains and Mountains (Six Villages), 1365–1460

	1365	1371	1383	1393	1402	1412	1427	1460
Households								
Plains	146	150	128	129	101	101	113	98
Mountains	155	190	115	120	116	78	81	60
Total	301	340	243	249	217	179	194	158
Individuals								
Plains	672	690	465	608	358	432	602	520
Mountains	694	851	411	505	440	327	399	323
Total	1366	1541	876	1113	798	759	1001	843
Family size								
Plains	4.60	4.60	3.63	4.71	3.54	4.28	5.33	5.31
Mountains	4.48	4.48	3.57	4.21	3.79	4.19	4.93	5.38
Total	4.54	4.53	3.60	4.47	3.68	4.24	5.16	5.34

Figure 7.5

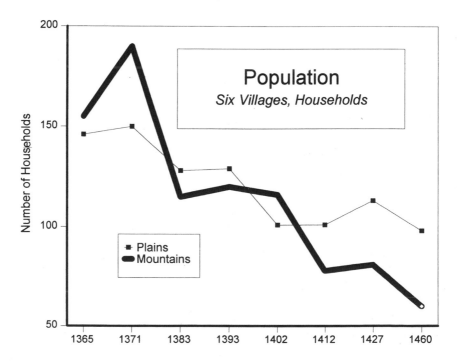

Figure 7.6

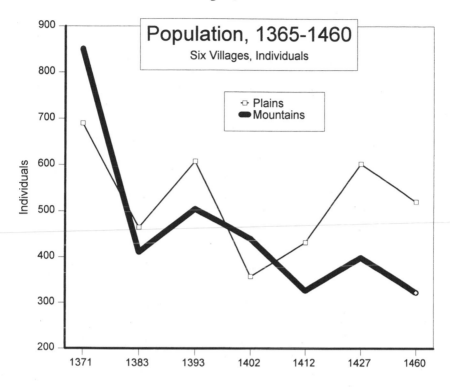

Population, 1365-1460
Six Villages, Individuals

to the price of grain, they increased still more, by three and a half times.[10] Nor was this increase simply an artifact of more careful tax accounting. The survey of 1401–2 was the first to institute the itemization of all peasant holdings, specifying land measurements and contiguous boundaries, as opposed to a single figure for the property's value. Yet, for the reasons outlined above, this date witnessed the nadir of peasant well-being between the Black Death and the early Renaissance. Nor did one of the most painstaking of tax surveys in the entire history of preindustrial Florence, the *catasto* of 1427, mark a sudden surge of peasant property values that might have resulted from more scrupulous property assessment along with the curbing of corruption on the part of tax officials.[11]

Instead, from 1402 to 1460 the average property values of at least landed peasants show a steady linear progression. If all peasants are figured in, including the propertyless (the *nullatenenti* and *miserabili,* who appear without assessments but who were usually charged a head tax), the *catasto* does show a slightly sharper increase in property values than the change between 1402 and 1412.[12] And afterward, 1427 to 1460, peasant wealth tapered, if the average for all peasants is figured. While this 1427 increase may well reflect more careful accounting and more stringent enforcement of guidelines, it may reflect also the economic benefits of rising productivity and agricultural wages in real terms and of stagnant or even falling prices for landed property. Thus, previously landless peasants and those with small plots were able to buy land, at least during the first half of the fifteenth century. By the second half of the century this trend had ended. While the holdings of landed peasants continued to increase in number and value, the number of peasants without property was once again on the rise. This reversal was strongest in the rich alluvial plains stretching from the Florentine city walls through the Bisenzio valley of Prato's former *contado,* reflecting the expansion of the *mezzadria* system (sharecropping), along with increases in urban investment in the nearby and fertile countryside.[13]

These increases in peasant property values from the turn of the century to 1460 were not, however, evenly distributed throughout the *contado;* rather, mountaineers benefited most, especially those who, in the early crisis years of the fifteenth century, were without any holdings. In 1383 peasants in the mountains were almost one-and-a-half times as wealthy as those in the plains (figure 7.2). The increase in their relative wealth since the previous tax survey (1371) may have resulted from an earlier increase of urban investment in nearby villages and the spread of the *mezzadria* system,[14] thus pushing more lowland peasants into dependency relationships with absentee landlords from the city and leaving them without taxable assets. But after 1383, the wealth of mountaineers, whether calculated for only the propertied or for all of them, declined steadily through the crisis of 1402, in absolute terms as well as relative to plainsmen.

Did these ups and downs result from climatic changes or plagues that may have destroyed people and crops more in the mountains than in the valleys? Perhaps. But it is man-made forces that emerge from the documentation: war, which ravaged the mountains, and more significantly, Florence's differential taxation, which also hit mountain communes hardest. As their taxes increased, the poverty of mountain peasants deepened both in absolute terms and relative to the more favored peasants farther down the slopes and nearer to the city of Florence (figures 7.2, 7.3).

These differentials in the timing and geographical patterns of recovery suggest that early fifteenth-century prosperity in the Florentine countryside was not simply the result of that epoch's most dramatic exogenous variable, plague. In other areas of Europe, by the 1370s the population began to recover economically from the initial shock waves and dislocation of the plague.[15] But the heavy burden of Florentine tax policy not only retarded the economic recovery of its *contado,* it led to a further emptying of the countryside, especially in the mountain districts.

After the peasant uprisings of 1401 through 1406, these patterns changed. But less harsh taxation did not improve economic conditions evenly throughout the Florentine *contado;* household wealth increased faster in the mountains than in the valleys, especially when all peasants and not only those with taxable holdings are taken into account. In 1412, the worth of mountaineers was little over half that of the valley peasants (figure 7.2). By 1460, the relations had reversed: mountaineers were twice as wealthy as valley peasants. At the same time, these figures show a steady progression in the worth of propertied peasants in the mountains. By 1460, for the first time average household wealth in the mountains surpassed that in the plains. Nor did these increases in wealth reflect merely an increase in the prices of property without any correspondence to the income or produce from the property. First, land prices remained stable throughout the first half of the fifteenth century and may have even dropped in Tuscany.[16] Second, with the *catasto* of 1427 (and probably earlier), tax officials calculated property values not from notarized prices but from estimates of the properties' annual production of grain, wine, or whatever.[17]

Along with these changes in tax policy, mountaineers prospered from other factors during the first sixty years of the fifteenth century. From the French Cévennes to the Val Demone in northeast Sicily, peasants in the highlands benefited from the relatively stable prices fetched by animal husbandry and crops other than cereals common to the lowlands, which fell precipitously through the early fifteenth century.[18] For Florence, moreover, the decline in warfare (after 1402 for the Alpi fiorentine and after 1434 for the territory as a whole) also favored the mountain zones, first and foremost, which previously had borne a disproportionate share of the damages to crops, buildings, and manpower, as notes to the tax board, desperate pleas in the *provvisioni,* and the vicariate court records of kidnapping and cattle rustling attest (see chap. 6).

Even taxes, the bane of mountaineers' existence and the reason for their emigration in the late Trecento, may have come to favor mountaineers over valley peasants after the *catasto* of 1427. While the Medici did not dismantle the system of equal tax rates throughout the Florentine *contado,* a decline in its rigor and efficiency in tax collecting, especially of liquid and mobile wealth, may well have favored the remote mountain communities—first, because of their inaccessibility, which would continue to plague the tax collector through the early modern period; and second, because a greater proportion of mountaineers' wealth relative to that of lowland peasants was invested in livestock, which were more difficult to find and to assess.[19] Thus, mountaineers may well have been prospering through the first half of the fifteenth century even more than their tax returns tell![20]

But economic and political conditions alone cannot explain the impressive recovery of fifteenth-century Florentine peasants nor the differentials in prosperity between the mountains and the valleys. If these figures on prosperity, and in particular these differentials between mountains and plains, are placed alongside population trends for households and individuals, an enigma arises. The valleys reached their population low point in 1402, stabilized afterward, and then began a slow recovery through the mid-fifteenth century (figures 7.5, 7.6). This pattern of population stability followed by slow growth is consistent with the general picture drawn by David Herlihy for Pistoia and by Herlihy and Christiane Klapisch-Zuber for the entire Florentine territory reconstructed from the *catasto* of 1427.[21] The failure of the population to respond vigorously to expanding wealth during the fifteenth century by renewed reproduction to replace lost numbers casts doubts on the Malthusian thesis, at least in its simplest form. Instead of reproducing at previously high levels, peasants throughout the territory somehow slowed their population growth once the external checks of war, famine, and pestilence had not disappeared but had eased in severity. Changes in ages at marriage—Malthus's moral constraint—may have been the most common method of population control, but it does not provide the total explanation. As Herlihy and Klapisch-Zuber argue (and about which contemporaries such as San Bernardino of Siena railed), extended periods of lactation, coitus interruptus, and heterosexual sodomy may also have been factors limiting Tuscan population growth.[22]

Yet the data from the Florentine *estimi* and *catasti* suggest darker practices of conscious family limitation that affected both ends of the age structure—infants and the elderly—and that impinged first and foremost on women. The contrast between prosperity and population change in the mountains provides another picture of at least one subpopulation within the territory of Florence not covered in Herlihy and Klapisch-Zuber's exhaustive analysis of the Florentine state in the fifteenth century. It departs even more radically from the usual Malthusian expectations of a preindustrial population: 1401–2—the worst years of war, insurrection, plague, and famine, especially for the mountains of the Florentine Alps—did not mark the end of population decline for the mountaineers as it did for those lower down the slopes and nearer the city or, indeed, in the city of Florence itself. Instead, the populations of these highland communities continued to slide through the next sixty years, even as they continued to prosper both absolutely and relative to the valley peasants. Clearly, these peasants had the wherewithal to increase their numbers but chose not to in order to preserve and even enhance their prosperity. But without war, famine, and plague, what were the mechanisms of their village and family limitation within wedlock?

In the absence of parish records, the timing and spacing of births is impossible to measure with certainty for populations other than the urban elites (who have left us family diaries, or *ricordanze*). However, an analysis of successive tax registers suggests means of population control that may be hard to accept, especially for an epoch and a city-state whose historiography has been so much associated with modernity and aesthetic sensibility. In addition to delayed marriages, sodomy, restraint, abortion, and other forms of contraception, the tax records leave the imprint of high levels of female infanticide.

In recent years, a number of essays have suggested that infanticide was not a birth control practice peculiar to Asian populations alone but a normal recourse of families, especially poor families, to control family size in various periods and places throughout Western civilization.[23] Yet these suggestions have met with biting criticism, usually aimed at deficiencies in sources. In one of the most controversial of these essays, Emily Coleman tallies a sex ratio of 135 (135 males to 100 females) among ninth-century French peasants.[24] From it, she concludes that infanticide was rife among the Carolingian peasantry, even though her source, the polyptych of Saint-Germain-des-Prés, does not include ages for any portion of the population or even the sex for most infants. (They are simply labeled *infantes.*) Her assumptions about infanticide were thus drawn not from infants or even young children but from the sex ratios of the entire population.

As we shall see from the more detailed and rigorous later documentation of the Florentine countryside, which with increasing consistency listed men and women by ages, the sex ratios were hardly randomly distributed through the age structure. While adoption and apprenticeship might account for sex imbalances in the early years of life and adolescence, migratory pressures could become more pronounced in adulthood for certain villages or entire geographical areas as Fernand Braudel and J. R. McNeill have argued for Mediterranean mountain communities in the early modern and modern periods.[25]

In the case of the polyptych of Saint-Germain-des-Prés, David Herlihy has suggested that men may have been double counted and that large numbers of women were missing from this monastic survey of its rural lands. According to Herlihy, many women, particularly those of lower status, resided in manor houses, where they worked as seamstresses, spinners, and weavers on the estates' *gynecaea,* or women's workshops, and thus would not have been included in abbot Irminon's remarkable ninth-century survey.[26] While Herlihy's point of departure is one of deep skepticism ("this ratio breaks the bounds of credibility"), he at least proceeds with an argument about the possible reasons for it, unlike those historians whose skepticism of the sources, as Klapisch-Zuber objects, is "often used to cut short further inquiry."[27]

More intensive is Herlihy and Klapisch-Zuber's critical examination of the sex imbalances in the scrupulously collected *catasto* of 1427, which shows an overall sex ratio of 119 males to 100 females. Despite questions raised about the source and its methods of registration, Herlihy and Klapisch-Zuber do not rule out the possibilities of infanticide of females as a cause of the abundance of males, and they find echoes of their hypothesis in contemporary preaching. Like San Bernardino a generation earlier, Fra Cherubino da Siena in the middle of the fifteenth century castigated his congregation for their cruel means of population control: "and indeed if they cannot abort or dispose of it, then once the creature is born, they beat it and would wish to see it dead so as to be free to go about where they want, here and there."[28]

At the same time, Herlihy and Klapisch-Zuber suggest that a general "depreciation" of the female resulted in tax officials and families underregistering girls, that late fourteenth- and fifteenth-century pestilence struck down women more than men, and that higher numbers of nuns than monks or friars (none of them listed in the *catasto*), especially among the upper classes of Florence, contributed to the *catasto's* superabundance of men.[29] Anthony Molho adds that the discrepancy in sex ratios may have also derived from "an inherent preference in the Italian language for the masculine as against the feminine gender" in naming practices: thus girls were occasionally given boys' names, such as Antonio instead of Antonia.[30]

But if women were more susceptible to plague in Tuscany (contrary to findings elsewhere), why do the *estimi* report much lower sex ratios after the virulent Trecento plagues than in the fifteenth century, when both the frequency and the mortalities of the plague were on the decline? Is there any evidence to suggest that susceptibility to plague changed in such a way as to have caused more females than males to die, as indeed did occur with different age groups? And why the differences between the plains and the mountains? Were women less hardy than men at higher altitudes, or were the plagues more deadly in the mountains? Certainly, contemporaries like the storyteller Gentile Sermini did not think so, as they left the cities for what Sermini regarded as the less "civilized" but more salubrious air of the mountains.[31] Finally, the possibility of higher female emigration from the mountains runs contrary to all recorded experience.[32]

As for possible naming practices influencing these sex ratios, would these practices have changed from one tax redaction to another? Would notaries have become more sloppy and error prone with the generally more complete and detailed *catasti* as opposed to the earlier *estimi?* And, again, would these practices have varied radically from mountains to plains to cities? There was no tax incentive in disguising a girl as a boy; indeed, the opposite was the case, since boys fourteen years old and older in 1412 (fifteen years old and older in 1427) were assessed a head tax.[33] In addition, a household filled with an abundance of young girls constituted grounds for an appeal to the tax board for lower rates, since, as household heads complained in their petitions, they had so many daughters to dower. In sum, the logic of taxation suggests that households should have overreported female and not male children.

Viewing a number of tax records instead of a single one at one point in time gives the historian a vantage point for addressing the problems and possibilities of underenumeration of girl infants. If underregistration is at the heart of these skewed ratios, these ratios would vary more or less randomly from one tax record to the next or, more likely, decline with improvements in tax surveys. If they do not, do changes in these sex ratios

TABLE 7.2. Males and Females, Total Population from Nineteen Villages, 1371–1460

	1371	1383	1393	1401	1412	1427	1460
Males	3,261	2,453	3,389	2,333	2,566	3,142	2,262
Females	2,872	2,099	3,070	2,047	2,107	2,853	2,262
total	6,133	4,552	6,459	4,380	4,673	5,995	4,524
Ratio	1.14	1.17	1.10	1.14	1.22	1.10	1.00

correlate with other demographic and economic trends? Moreover, are there distinct patterns linked to geography, such as mountains versus plains?

Without a doubt, the imbalance of girl infants does not correspond to the progressive improvement in tax reporting and collecting that characterizes the *capi di famiglia* records until the *catasto* of 1427. The *estimo* of 1371 was the first tax survey that required household heads to list the ages of their children. As might be expected, this first register is the most primitive, with the most underreporting and rounding of ages. The ages of only three-quarters of family members were listed, and most of these were for children under fifteen; fewer than 60 percent of household heads revealed their own age, and even fewer wives gave theirs (46%).[34] Moreover, when adults (those over twenty years) did report their age, nearly two-thirds rounded them to the nearest five- or ten-year multiple. Yet, the sex imbalances for this survey are not severely skewed (114 males to 100 females), a rate that the survey of 1383 exceeded (117 males to 100 females). The 1371 ratio was equaled in 1401 but exceeded again in 1412 (table 7.2). In the 1371 redaction, the villagers in the plains show even a slight imbalance in favor of infant females (95 boys to 100 girls) and even more so for infants between one and two years (91 boys to 100 girls; table 7.3).

By the next survey, 1383, the heads of households and the rural rectors who drew up the final reports had improved their skills. One might even infer a change in numerate culture at least as far as age reckoning is concerned. At any rate, for the 1383 register, household heads or the rural rectors completed a more sophisticated survey (even if it is impossible to say with absolute certainty whether their returns were any more accurate than the previous survey). Of the old and new residents combined, more than 95 percent listed their ages.[35] More remarkably, the ratios of those who ex-

TABLE 7.3. Males and Females, by Age Group, 1371–1460

	1371	1383	1393	1401	1412	1427	1460
Infant (<1)							
Plains							
Male	38	39	34	7	27	38	43
Female	40	13	33	8	24	52	31
Ratio	0.95	3.00	1.03	0.88	1.13	0.73	1.39
Mountains							
Male	75	8	48	15	3	40	29
Female	67	6	28	12	5	19	11
Ratio	1.12	1.33	1.71	1.25	0.60	2.11	2.64
Infant (<2)							
Plains							
Male	89	63	70	15	72	112	78
Female	98	27	72	12	65	91	80
Ratio	0.91	2.33	0.97	1.25	1.11	1.23	0.98
Mountains							
Male	75	13	111	31	19	88	45
Female	55	10	65	31	15	49	31
Ratio	1.36	1.30	1.17	1.00	1.27	1.80	1.45
Infant (<3)							
Plains							
Male	140	88	116	20	115	166	111
Female	138	51	109	16	96	127	108
Ratio	1.01	1.73	1.06	1.25	1.20	1.31	1.03
Mountains							
Male	136	23	161	44	25	127	61
Female	79	13	101	43	19	78	40
Ratio	1.72	1.77	1.59	1.02	1.32	1.63	1.53
Infant (<4)							
Plains							
Male	180	101	154	23	139	200	144
Female	176	57	140	19	132	167	148
Ratio	1.02	1.77	1.10	1.21	1.05	1.20	0.97
Mountains							
Male	177	31	210	56	28	156	76
Female	100	17	140	53	27	102	51
Ratio	1.77	1.82	1.50	1.06	1.04	1.53	1.49
Adults (14 to 70)							
Plains							
Male	362	505	574	186	619	684	655
Female	321	496	598	201	567	666	603
Ratio	1.13	1.02	0.96	0.93	1.09	1.03	1.09

(continued)

TABLE 7.3. (continued)

Mountains							
Male	283	216	603	457	403	493	365
Female	155	219	722	478	290	483	340
Ratio	1.83	0.99	0.84	0.96	1.39	1.02	1.07
Elderly (>60)							
Plains							
Male	68	144	173	55	165	217	139
Female	50	94	124	46	118	193	88
Ratio	1.36	1.53	1.40	1.20	1.40	1.12	1.58
Moutains							
Male	48	71	207	163	111	161	88
Female	17	55	156	124	60	168	63
Ratio	2.82	1.29	1.33	1.31	1.85	0.96	1.40

Figure 7.7

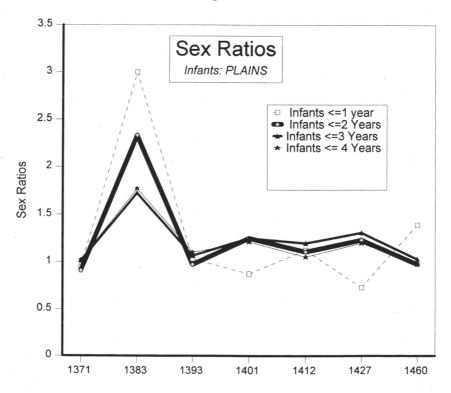

Figure 7.8

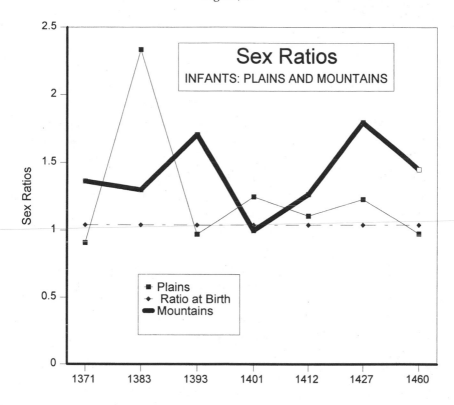

pressed their ages as rounded figures dropped from two-thirds to less than one-third of all adults, a rate that remained more or less constant in these surveys through the fifteenth century.[36] Yet the global sex ratio of males to females in these nineteen villages did not decline, but increased. More astoundingly, in 1383 the sex ratios for infants (two years and younger) in the plains soared to the highest level for any subpopulation found in these samples over this 90-year time span: 233 boys to 100 girls, or 7 boy babies for every 3 girls (figures 7.7, 7.8).

Nor did the famous *catasto* of 1427 record a significant decline in the overall sex ratios for these villages (110 males to 100 females); rather, this ratio was the same as found in the *estimo* of 1393. Moreover, the less rigorous *catasto* of 1460 (at least in terms of recording rural mobile wealth) records the least skewed overall sex ratios in this documentation; in that year, the sexes reached exact parity in their numbers; that is, the number of girls exceeded the biological rate at birth of 104 boys for every 100 girls.[37] More gripping, the *catasto* of 1427 records the second highest infant sex imbalance found in these documents and the highest registered by mountain people at any time, an extraordinary 180 males to 100 females (figures 7.8, 7.9). Thus, the lack of any correspondence between the skewness of the sex ratios and the exactitude and sophistication with which these various tax records were gathered and reported strongly suggests that the absence of girl babies cannot so easily be dismissed as simply a deficiency in registration.

Can differences in sex ratios between the plains and mountains be explained by documentary deficiencies or differences in the numerate cultures across the Florentine *contado,* the logic being that less numerate cultures would be less precise about other matters, such as listing all their family members and the female ones in particular? Except for the remarkable sex imbalance in favor of boy infants in the plains in 1383, the mountaineers consistently show higher infant sex ratios than the valley peasants. This differential becomes more pronounced after the crisis of 1401–2, reaching its pinnacle in the year of the *catasto* of 1427. According to the hospital records of the Misericordia in Prato, the years immediately preceding the redaction of the *catasto* of 1427 brought that hospital to a crisis in its search for wet nurses for the expanding numbers of abandoned babies, who were predominantly female (and who were born mainly in the countryside surrounding Prato).[38]

Do these differentials reflect a relative sophistication among valley peasants in reckoning their ages, along with keeping more tidy and precise records? Actually, the opposite pattern is reflected, confounding yet another generalization about mountain people assumed by historians such as Fernand Braudel and Giovanni Cherubini and taken from storytellers such as the early-fifteenth century Gentile Sermini, who describes the mountain people south of Siena as "brute animals": "zotichi, grossi e materiali, rustici e villani e sconoscenti, ingrati, senza alcuna umanità o discrezione."[39] Mountaineers, in fact, reckoned their ages with slightly more sophistication than plains peasants, rounding their ages in 53.5 percent of the cases of adults twenty years and older (6,873 reported ages) as opposed to 56.3 percent (6,363) in the valleys. Even more surprising, the mountaineers rounded their ages less than merchants, artisans, and workers who lived in the city quarter of Santa Trinita of Prato.[40]

Finally, the patterns of sex imbalances for infants do not show a random variation over time but instead suggest a logic not usually associated with

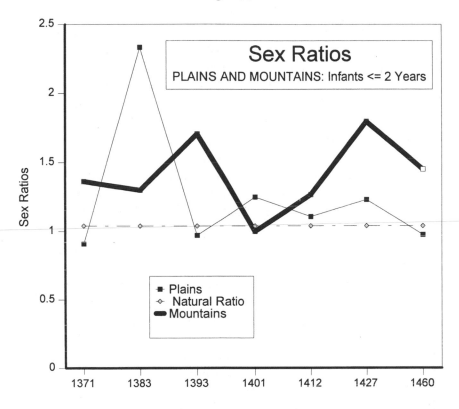

Figure 7.9

infanticide or with abandonment (which often led to death).[41] These extreme forms of family limitation are most often associated with the poor and with periods of crisis, when families as a last resort found it necessary for the survival of the family as a whole to smother or abandon unwanted newborns.[42] Yet these data do not reflect such a relationship between poverty and infanticide. Only 41 percent of the babies two years old and younger belonged to families with no taxable property (the *nullatenenti* and *miserabili*); the sex ratios of these babies, however, are nearly identical to those with property (124 males to 100 females, as compared to 122 to 100).[43] Indeed, the richest peasants—those with more than 250 lire of assessed wealth, or the top decile of the peasantry in the eighteen rural parishes and communes sampled for this study—were the ones whose male infants (two years old and younger) most outnumbered female infants (130 to 100).[44] Similarly, Herlihy and Klapisch-Zuber find a positive correlation between wealth and male babies for the Florentine territory in 1427 but refrain from drawing conclusions from this observation.[45]

More suggestive, however, are the variations of these infant sex ratios over time. These variations are not randomly distributed, nor do they point to a pattern of infanticide or the abandonment of girl babies as an act of last resort. Instead, at least as far as the mountaineers are concerned, infanticide was a rational, premeditated act of family planning. First, in the tax surveys of 1371–83, the infant sex ratios (babies two years old or younger) among the mountaineers remained relatively stable and at near parity in the years of plague and military disruption (figures 7.8, 7.9).

In 1366 the Florentine government intensified its offensive against the Ubaldini feudatories, whose unofficial rule extended through the hills and mountainous zones of the upper Mugello and into the Romagna Apennines. In 1373, Florence declared its war "of extermination" against the Ubaldini, apportioning the then massive sum of thirty thousand florins to wage the war—almost double that collected in a year of direct taxes from the entire *contado* of Florence.[46] This war, accompanied by plagues in 1374 and 1383, deeply scarred the demographic face of the upper Mugello. Villages near enemy castles like Mangona and Montecarelli, once the size of Sesto, were decimated, their populations never to return to their pre-1370s levels.[47] By contrast, the survey of 1393 came in a period of peace, between Florence's feudal war and just before resumption of war with Milan in the mid-1390s, when the upper Mugello once again became Florence's principal battlefield. Yet it was in the period of social and military peace that the infant sex ratios in the mountain hamlets of the Mugello suddenly soared to their second highest point in these samples (171 to 100), or three boy babies for every two girls.

In the year 1402, when the four horsemen of the apocalypse converged on the mountains of the upper Mugello with a vengeance (Mangona's population in 1393 was almost halved from the previous tax redaction),[48] the infant sex ratios in the mountains reached their lowest point. For the first and only time in these tax surveys, the ratio of boy to girl babies was at parity—under the normal biological rate of 100 to 104. In dire material and psychological crises, such as those of the 1370s and again in 1402, it appears that mountain families struggled as best they could to preserve their fragile numbers and did not limit their families through killing or abandoning girl babies. Evidently, in periods of severe crisis and massive mortality, even a female heir was thought to be better than no heir at all.

In 1402, population and average family size turned sharply downward.[49] In the quarter of Santa Maria Novella, the infant population reached its nadir, according to these samples. Perhaps mothers and fathers killed or abandoned their babies without any consideration for sex; or else, as Cavalcanti's history of the Casentino migrations in the 1430s suggests, mothers fled with both male and female children.[50] However, given the strong patrilineal prejudices of Florentine society, more likely it was plague, warfare, and famine and not mountain mothers and fathers that limited families in these moments of crisis.[51]

With the recovery of these mountain populations after the cessation of Milanese incursions over the Bolognese borders, widespread plunder, peasant revolution, and Florentine reactions, the infant sex ratios began to become unbalanced: 127 males to 100 females in 1412 and 180 to 100 in the year of the *catasto,* 1427. In 1460, these ratios evened out but still persisted at 145 to 100. If only newborns are considered (those of one year or less, the majority of whom are listed by months in the 1460 *catasto*), 1460 shows the continuing rise of abandonment or murder of infant girls. The sex ratio in that year soared to an unprecedented 264 to 100; that is, infant boys may have outnumbered infant girls by two to three times.

As we have already seen, the years following 1402 saw lower taxes and increases in economic wealth generally for the rural communities to the north of Florence (the quarter of Santa Maria Novella) but especially for the mountaineers, whose average taxable wealth had doubled that of the lowland peasants by the end of our analysis, the *catasto* of 1460. Moreover, these were years of relative peace—if not everywhere in the Florentine territory, at least throughout the mountains of the upper Mugello. For the later waves of warfare in 1404–6, 1412–14, 1424–27, and 1433–34, other areas took the place of the Mugello as the principal battlefield of the Florentine republic: the Chianti mountains along the borders of Siena, the Valdinievole, Pisa and its former *contado,* the Val di Chiana, the Casentino, and points further east.[52]

At least as far as abandonment is concerned, these trends in the sex ratios of infants, plotted over time and by geography, are corroborated on the receiving side: the records of the orphan hospitals of San Gallo (founded in the thirteenth century), of la Scala (founded in 1389), and of the Innocenti (whose first admissions were in 1445). Richard Trexler shows a decline in abandoned babies brought to San Gallo during the crisis years 1396–1404.[53] The numbers rise between 1404 and 1413—that is, during the years of economic improvement, declining taxation, and relative peace for the northwest corner of Florence's *contado*. During these years, 61.2 percent of the babies brought to or collected by the hospice were female.[54] The numbers of *gittatelli*, or abandoned babies, increased through the fifteenth century, leading in 1419 to the commune's decision to build a third hospice, which opened its doors to increasing numbers of infants in 1445.[55]

Most remarkable is the dominance of the Mugello in these statistics: eleven of thirty-nine abandoned babies in the entire territory of Florence (including the city of Florence) came from this hilly and mountainous zone north of the city.[56] Tomoko Takahashi's map of abandoned babies matches the geographical distribution of wet nurses, who Klapisch-Zuber and Lucia Sandri tell us often abandoned their own children to increase their salaries—the highest of any domestics—by nursing the children of the Florentine patriciate.[57] Indeed, the salaries of wet nurses climbed steadily over the course of the fifteenth century, especially until 1460.[58] And these geographical patterns of abandonment and of the origins of wet nurses would persist through the sixteenth century.[59] Nonetheless, it would be instructive to analyze Takahashi's figures with an eye to altitude, to determine the proportion of babies who came from villages in the mountainous zones of the Mugello or the Valdarno superiore and Casentino (which would fill the registers of the Ospedale degli Innocenti in the second half of the fifteenth century and the sixteenth century). But for the moment, it must suffice to say that Takahashi's figures from the orphan hospitals of Florence corroborate those from other sources, such as family *ricordanze*, on the salaries of wet nurses and their origins as well as the differentials in the sex ratios shown by the *estimi* and *catasti* of the late Trecento and early Quattrocento.

Infant girls were not the only females to pay a price for the countryside's and, most strikingly, the mountaineers' prosperity after the crisis of 1402. When we turn to adults—those between fourteen and seventy years, defined by the tax law as early as 1412 as accountable for the head tax if male—the sex ratios do not show a wide imbalance in favor of males. Instead, in the years before the crisis of 1402, women slightly outnumbered men, especially in the mountains (figure 7.10). With increasing taxation

Figure 7.10

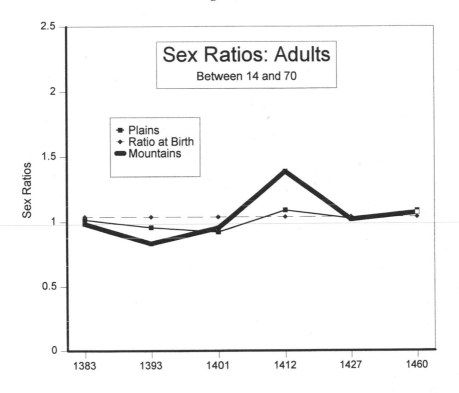

and poverty, the mountains may have been experiencing migratory patterns that would later characterize mountain civilization throughout the Mediterranean, what J. R. McNeill calls the "feminization" of agriculture.[60] As men left the mountains to seek higher pay in the valleys and cities as day laborers, skilled artisans, thieves, and mercenaries, women were left behind to till the fields, reversing the gender imbalance but eventually leading to underpopulation and undercultivation of ecologically sensitive terraces. In 1393 the sex ratio of these mountain communities had fallen to 84 males to 100 females. According to Herlihy and Klapisch-Zuber's computerized maps of variations in the sex ratios through the territory of Tuscany, such patterns persisted in the poorer mountains of the southern Chianti and the eastern Casentino through 1427 and most likely thereafter.[61] Indeed, Braudel sees this pattern of male outmigration as characteristic of the Mediterranean mountains during the early modern period, reaching as far back as biblical times.[62]

But after 1402, the pattern was reversed in the Florentine Alps of the upper Mugello. In 1412 the sex ratio even jumped momentarily to 100 males to 139 females, but afterward the ratio hovered around the biological rate at birth, 104, in the valleys and the mountains alike. Perhaps the general period of relative peace also contributed to this equality in sex ratios; without wars, the demand for highland mercenaries would have tapered. But, more significantly, these ratios conform with the trends observed earlier. A decline in the outmigration of families matched the economic recovery and expansion of landed and animal wealth in the mountains after the crisis of 1402. Although young men would have still migrated, as is implied by the change in sex ratios, from the abundance of males in their early years, prosperity evidently meant that more men stayed home on the farm than before, at least after adolescence.

Yet these sex ratios do not persist throughout the life cycle of Florentine peasants in the early fifteenth century. At the other end of the age structure—the elderly—the sex ratios again diverge, and again it was women, this time older women, who disappear from the households of both mountain and valley communities. Did these differentials result from sexual differences in longevity? Probably not, since women once past the period of childbearing outlived men, at least as far as the age pyramids in the *catasto* of 1427 reveal. Rather, the answer is more likely a matter of migration. Older men and widowers stayed with their families and persisted as the heads of households; as Klapisch-Zuber points out, the structure of rural households was gerontocracy.[63] Rarely did younger men take over as *capi di famiglia* before the death of a father or uncle. Of 7,630 household heads found in my samples taken from the five *estimi* redacted between 1371 to 1412, children supplanted their fathers as household heads in only seven families.[64]

The same respect for age did not, however, hold for older women. Often, when widowed mothers continued to reside with married sons or other male relatives they were the last to be listed in the household, which otherwise followed an order based on age. Tax officials and rural rectors rarely recognized as household heads even those widows who lived with very young sons, sometimes as young as five or six.[65] To be a household head in the countryside, a widow either lived alone or with only younger women. The sex ratios for the elderly suggest that many of these women left their farms for charitable institutions and domestic service in the city. Indeed, the *usciti* ledgers of the *estimi* are filled with single women, mostly

Figure 7.11

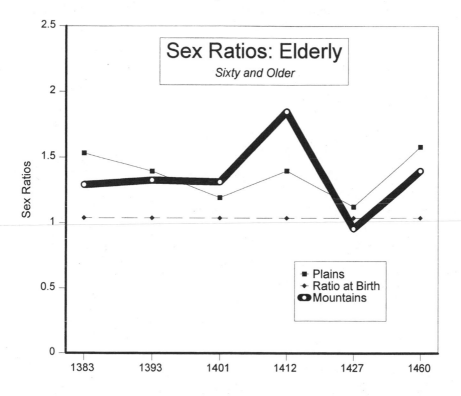

widows, who immediately after the death of their husbands are said to have left the village for Prato or Pistoia or, most often, Florence as *fante,* or domestic servants.

Yet, unlike the patterns of infanticide or infant abandonment, population control by the outmigration of elderly women was practiced as much in the plains as in the highlands. Indeed, in the last decades of the Trecento, before the crisis of 1402, when valley peasants were favored over mountaineers in the *estimo*'s mosaic of unequal taxation and when their wealth outstripped that of the highlanders, widows and elderly women either escaped or were pushed out of their rural homelands in the valleys more than in the mountains. In 1383 the sex ratios of the elderly in the plains exceeded 150 males to 100 females. For every three men over fifty-nine years, only two women in that age group remained on the farm (figure 7.11). Like infanticide, these rates fell with the crisis of 1402, but returned to the high levels of the precrisis period by the end of this analysis in 1460, when the injurious levels of rural taxation had subsided and the wealth of landed peasants had reached its pinnacle. In that tax year, the sex ratios for the elderly (sixty years and older) peaked in the plains (158 males to 100 females) and were only sightly less in the mountains (140 to 100). Again, the absence of women in these rural hamlets is coupled more with good times than with the bad.

These migratory practices are corroborated again at the receiving end. Klapisch-Zuber finds from the *ricordanze* of the Florentine patriciate that domestic servants had a golden age beginning with the opening of the fifteenth century. Increasingly, women replaced both men and slaves as domestic servants in the merchant palaces of urban Florence, even as salaries continued to advance.[66] Moreover, those who profited the most from these improvements in salaries and working conditions were not young girls in search of dowries and a household apprenticeship but the elderly. As Klapisch-Zuber puts it: "If the Quattrocento was a golden age for female servants, it was above all the category of older women that benefited."[67] Similarly, Richard Trexler argues that Florence's Orbatello, founded in the 1370s for the care of elderly women, was "the only island in Europe where a female community preserved family units and prepared new ones."[68] By Trexler's account, these women, who came largely from the rural territory of Florence, were well treated and able to exercise considerable self-rule.

Here, pull factors—higher salaries and improved contracts and an array of charitable institutions—may well have been more operative than push factors—the possible desires on the part of younger men to oust elderly mothers and aunts from the household, whom they may have found disruptive or simply less productive for the rural household economy. Indeed, the consequences for older women do not seem as dire as for female infants, especially during the fifteenth century, when wages and working conditions appear to have improved. And in its attitudes and actions against widows and old women, Florence never approached those of late sixteenth- and seventeenth-century northern Europe, with its witch hunts directed principally against older women and widows.[69] The vicariate criminal court records for the Florentine territory between 1398 and 1434 present only a smattering of cases directed against old women for supposed "incantations," which were usually aimed at breaking the love relations of other men and women.[70] But, as Klapisch-Zuber has suggested, the plight of widows may have been worse in the countryside than in the cities.[71] The attraction of high wages and a more comfortable life in an urban *palazzo* may not have altered the fact that back home on the farm younger men sought to evict their older female relatives in order to break these women's hold on the property's usufruct.

Whether older women were pushed out of their homesteads or they left of their own volition to take up domestic servitude in the cities or to be assisted by urban institutions for the care of the poor, the consequences for the rural economy were the same. Their departure helped to control population increase and, in particular, led to a decline in the dependency ratio—that is, the number of older and younger persons in the household who had to be supported by restricted parcels of land, animals, and the labor power of men and women in their prime.

In conclusion, more than the usually considered demographic parameters—fertility and mortality from plagues, war, and famine—other factors conditioned fifteenth-century prosperity in the Florentine countryside. Elimination through selective migration and selective infant abandonment and infanticide played their role in policies of family limitation. According to the records of the late Trecento *estimi* and the *catasti* of the fifteenth century—some of the earliest records in Western civilization to list all family members with ages—these practices were more pronounced in the mountains than in the lowlands near the city of Florence. In the mountains, moreover, household wealth increased most rapidly after the fiscally and militarily induced economic and demographic nadir of 1402, but the population did not recover accordingly, or even stagnate, but continued to fall. With migration from their rural homesteads and with their lives, females at both ends of the age spectrum paid the price for the prosperity of these male-governed Renaissance households.

Notes

1. The Social History of Women in the Renaissance

1. Burckhardt, *Civilization of the Renaissance*, 389. For a recent criticism of this optimistic view of women in the Renaissance, see Grieco, *Ange ou diablesse*, 14–15.

2. Vasari, *Le vite;* Baron, *Crisis of the Early Italian Renaissance.* For Vasari as a historian, see Rubin, *Giorgio Vasari,* esp. chaps. 3–5. Burckhardt, *Civilization of the Renaissance,* also sees Florence as the most thoroughly Renaissance city of Italy.

3. See my comments and the texts cited in Cohn, *Death and Property,* 198–99; for the intellectual history of baroque Europe, see Maclean, *Renaissance Notion of Woman.*

4. See Klapisch-Zuber's criticism of recent historians' distinction between private and public: "Including Women," 4; "Il pubblico, il privato." See also Martines, *Italian Renaissance Sextet,* 234: "public and private were one in Renaissance Italy."

5. For a useful guide to recent research across subdisciplines on women in the Renaissance, see King, *Women of the Renaissance.* The literature on, and examples of, the narrative history approach is now legend. Stone coined the term in "Revival of Narrative." See also the critique by Hobsbawn, "Revival of Narrative: Some Comments." For examples of this historiography, see Le Roy Ladurie, *Montaillou;* Ginzburg, *Il formaggio e i vermi;* Darnton, *Great Cat Massacre;* Davis, *Return of Martin Guerre,* and *Fiction in the Archives;* Brucker, *Giovanni and Lusanna;* Muir and Ruggiero, *Microhistory,* and *History from Crime;* and Raggio, *Faide e parentelle.* Curiously, Cipolla, *Cristofano and the Plague,* is rarely listed in lists of this new genre, but it appears to me that Cipolla, before Le Roy Ladurie, led the rush of economic and social historians to tell stories based on the biographies of those previously lost to history.

6. For an excellent essay on this approach and its philosophical underpinnings, see Muir, "Introduction: Observing Trifles." The term was coined by an American historian, George R. Stewart, but was first appropriated for a new wave of Italian historiography by Grendi, "Micro-analisi e storia sociale." See Ginzburg, "Microstoria." As Revel points out, two historical approaches lie behind the Italian school of *microstoria.* One relies on reestablishing all the possible networks of an individual or a small place, such as the attempt by Levi, *L'eredità immateriale;* this approach is spelled out in Ginzburg and Poni, "Name and the Game." The other approach abandons the dream of *histoire totale* on the small scale to reproduce fragments, or case studies. My remarks are aimed at this second strand of microhistory. See Revel, "Microanalisi."

7. Grendi, "Micro-analisi"; also see Revel's criticisms, "Microanalisi."

8. Kelly, "Did Women Have a Renaissance?"

9. Such claims are found most often in popular general surveys, such as Servadio, *La donna nel Renascimento.*

10. Nor is Burckhardt the only nineteenth-century historian whose theses offer points of departure for recent essays on the social history of late medieval and Renaissance women. Karl Bücher (1883) argued that late medieval women in Germany gained power in the workforce because of their alleged increase in numbers relative to men. His conclusions have recently been placed in doubt; see Herlihy, *Opera Muliebria,* 178–79; Opitz, "Life in the Late Middle Ages." The point of departure for Chojnacki's "Patrician Women" is again that of a late nineteenth-century historian. He attacks Bartolomeo Cecchetti's (1886) view not of female equality or power but of the weakness of women and argues instead that Venetian women "contributed a good deal to the relative intra-class harmony and stability that constituted one of the hallmarks of the Venetian patriciate during the Renaissance" (177).

11. Goldthwaite, *Private Wealth in Renaissance Florence,* 263–65; Goldthwaite, "Florentine Palace," esp. 1010–12. For an earlier Burckhardtian interpretation of women in Renaissance Florence, see Del Lungo, *La donna fiorentina.* For a review of Burckhardtian strands in recent Renaissance historiography, see Cohn, *Cult of Remembrance,* 21–22; Cohn, "Burckhardt Revisited."

12. Hughes, "Regulating Women's Fashion," 156; Herlihy, "Did Women Have a Renaissance?" For a view of women's clothing and sumptuary laws similar to Hughes's, see Chojnacki, "Power of Love," 131: "Yet the wearing of sumptuous clothing may also have been a way for women with wealth but few opportunities for productive economic (let alone political) outlets to make a gesture of self-assertion."

13. Herlihy and Klapisch-Zuber, *Les Toscans;* F. W. Kent, *Household and Lineage;* D. V. Kent, *Rise of the Medici;* Kent and Kent, *Neighbours and Neighbourhood.* For the numerous essays of Molho and Kirshner on the Monti delle doti, see Molho, *Marriage Alliance,* 440 and 441–42.

14. Martines, "A Way of Looking at Women," esp. 28.

15. Kelly, *Leon Battista Alberti,* and "Did Women Have a Renaissance?" 40–43.

16. Kelly, "Did Women Have a Renaissance?" 44. For a less sanguine view of the power of ladies in the chanson de geste tradition, see Duby, "Courtly Model," who argues that fine amour was "a game controlled by men" (251) and was "first and foremost a criterion of distinction within masculine society" (256). For a recent criticism of Kelly's "literal reading" of texts, see Benson, *Invention of the Renaissance Woman,* 3–4.

17. Kelly, "Did Women Have a Renaissance?" 20. On Kelly's failure to address such questions with socioeconomic research, see the perceptive remarks of Brown, "Woman's Place Was in the Home."

18. Kelly, "Did Women Have a Renaissance?" 20.

19. See King, *Women of the Renaissance.* As suggested above, Italian historians such as Gabriella Zarri pursue their research outside both Burckhardt's and Kelly's paradigms. Rather, Zarri seeks to resolve other questions, such as the relationship

between the political rule of princely courts and the rise of women saints and other charismatic women in the late fifteenth through seventeenth centuries. For further comments on the work of Zarri, see chap. 5; for that of Maria Serena Mazzi, another prominent Italian historian of women in the later Middle Ages and Renaissance, see chap. 6.

20. Stone, "Revival of Narrative," 3.

21. See Muir, "Introduction: Observing Trifles"; Ruggiero, *Binding Passions.*

22. See Kuehn, *Law, Family and Women,* chap. 7, this volume.

23. See, for instance, Grieco, *Ange ou diablesse,* and "Body, Appearance, and Sexuality." Most contributions to Davis and Farge, *Renaissance and Enlightenment Paradoxes,* focus on how women were represented; of these, see in particular, Thomasset, "Nature of Woman"; Hughes, "Regulating Women's Fashion"; Frugoni, "Imagined Woman." In addition, see Hughes, "Representing the Family," and "Distinguishing Signs"; Cropper, "Beauty of Women"; Scaraffia and Zarri, *Donne e fede;* Finucci, *Lady Vanishes;* la Roncière, "Regards sur la femme." From the perspective of intellectual history, see Maclean, *Renaissance Notion of Woman.*

24. See the work of Zarri, Sensi, and Papi.

25. See Zarri, *Le sante vive,* chap. 1, "Istituzioni dell'educazione femminile," and "Monasteri femminili e città." Kristeller, "Learned Women"; King, "Booklined Cells," and *Women of the Renaissance,* esp. chap. 3, temper the view that woman made strides in the world of learning during the Renaissance. On women writers in the late Renaissance and the Counter-Reformation, see Weaver, "Le Muse in Convento"; work in progress by K. J. P. Lowe on women monastic writers.

26. Zarri, *Le sante vive,* 32–39. For a different view, see Benson, *Invention of the Renaissance Woman,* 31: "Those who came after found the *De Mulieribus Claris* weak in modern lives, and this is where the most extensive development took place."

27. Zarri, *Le sante vive,* 87-163; Zarri, "Les prophètes," and *Finizione e santità.*

28. In confronting Kelly's question, Herlihy, "Did Women Have a Renaissance?" turns from the economic and demographic materials that inform his *Opera Muliebria* and focuses on women's "alternate route," that of charisma represented in saints' lives. He charges that Kelly "ignores the alternate route to personal fulfillment and social leadership, that through charisma," maintaining that such an account "cannot make sense of a Saint Catherine of Siena or a Joan of Arc . . . individuals in the true meaning of the word" (16). Yet, for Italy this model of sainthood was short-lived and spread only exceptionally into the fifteenth century; see Cohn, *Death and Property,* 72–83; Opitz, "Life in the Late Middle Ages," 316: "As the middle ages drew to a close . . . criticism of the cult of sainthood reduced women's influence in religion. Scholarly knowledge replaced piety."

29. Trexler's works: "Infanticide in Florence," "Foundlings of Florence," "Le célibat à la fin du Moyen Age," "La prostitution florentine," and "Widow's Asylum of the Renaissance" have been recently reprinted in *Dependence.* I treat them in greater depth in chaps. 2, 5, 6, and 7.

30. Herlihy, *Opera Muliebria,* and "Women's Work." Also see Opitz, "Life in

the Late Middle Ages," 303; the introductory remarks by Stuart, *Women in Medieval Society,* 5; Muzzarelli et al., *Donne e lavoro nell'Italia medievale;* 10; Galetti, "La donna contadina," 41–54; Wiesner, "Spinsters and Seamstresses," 205: "The Renaissance brought a much sharper division and a harsher devaluation of women's labor."

31. Chabot, "La reconnaissance du travail."

32. Franceschi, *Oltre il "Tumulto,"* 132.

33. See Cohn, *Laboring Classes,* chap. 4.

34. Golberg, *Women, Work, and Life Cycle,* 86.

35. Brown, "A Woman's Place Was in the Home." See also Brown and Goodman, "Women and Industry in Florence."

36. Brown and Goodman, "Women and Industry in Florence," 211.

37. Ibid., 214: "In the late Renaissance . . . when both wool and silk production shifted to cheaper, coarser, and simpler cloths, women formed the majority of weavers in the two industries." See Braverman, *Labor and Monopoly Capital,* for a more general history of such sexual divisions of labor and their relation to technological change.

38. See Pinto, "Personale, le balie e i salariati"; and the essays of Klapisch-Zuber on domestic servitude in *Women, Family, and Ritual.*

39. See Lombardi and Reggiani, "Da assistita a serva," 304: "Erano infatti proprio le ragazze piú mature e piú abili nei lavori tessili ad essere maggiormente richieste per serve e la loro assenza interrompeva il processo di trasmissione del sapere."

40. Molho, *Marriage Alliance.*

41. Kirshner and Pluss, "Two Fourteenth-Century Opinions"; Kirshner, "Materials for a Gilded Cage." Kirshner also shows that the rights of widowers over their wives' dowries was particularly strong in fourteenth-century Florence, in contrast to other cities in Tuscany. Only in Florence could widowers with no surviving children retain the whole dowry. See Kirshner, "Maritus Lucretur Dotem."

42. Bellomo, *Ricerche sui rapporti patrimoniali tra coniugi.*

43. Kirshner, "Wives' Claims against Insolvent Husbands," 302.

44. Kuehn, *Law, Family, and Women,* chap. 9, esp. 235. Rosenthal, "Position of Women," goes further. From the business of a single notary (Ser Matteo Mazzetti), Rosenthal asserts that almost 17 percent of women acted without a *mundualdus,* and thus this "shatters our present view of female behaviour and prerogatives" (378).

45. Kuehn, *Law, Family, and Women,* chap. 10. Quotation on 254.

46. Strocchia, "Remembering the Family," attempts to show the power of elite women in Renaissance Florence and their room for maneuver within the system of patrilineal descent; but similar to Kuehn, Strocchia fails to investigate such changes over time. Also see Rosenthal, "Position of Women."

47. Molho, *Marriage Alliance,* 217–18. From even a larger database of marriages, Padgett, "Marriage and Elite Structure," 11, supports Molho's argument.

48. See the following works by Hughes: "From Brideprice to Dowry," "Urban

Growth," "Domestic Ideals," and "Struttura familiare." If one puts together different works of Herlihy, just the opposite trajectory appears for Renaissance Florence. While Herlihy's *Opera Muliebria* charts the loss of occupational opportunities for artisan and working women in the late Middle Ages, his earlier essay, "Growing Old in the Quattrocento," 107, argues that the patrician "wife was thus in a position to exert stronger influence upon their [her children's] cultural formation than could her older, occupied, and, frequently, absent husband. . . . Strong feminine influence does seem apparent in a new consciousness of childhood and in the development of new ideas concerning child rearing and education."

49. Hughes, "Urban Growth," 15.

50. Hughes, "Domestic Ideals," 139.

51. Hughes, "Urban Growth," 21.

52. Hughes, "Domestic Ideals," 140.

53. Ibid., 142.

54. Hughes, "Urban Growth," 23.

55. From very different sources, Ruggiero, *Boundaries of Eros*, 66–68, sees advances in Venetian women's power after the 1360s: "only slight inequality in penalties for women is a surprising indicator of female status in patriarchal Venice" (68).

56. Chojnacki, "Patrician Women," "Dowries and Kinsmen," "Power of Love," "Kinship Ties and Young Patricians," and "Marriage Legislation." Chojnacki, "Most Serious Duty" brings together these various aspects of women's power in Venice. These essays have done for Venice what Herlihy suggests Klapisch-Zuber has not done for Renaissance Florence: "But have we not somewhat exaggerated the predominance of the lineage over and against other forms of kin organization, which persisted?" Herlihy, foreword to Klapisch-Zuber, *Women, Family, and Ritual*, ix. Kuehn, *Law, Family, and Women*, 6, attacks Klapisch-Zuber for the same reasons: "It also must be acknowledged that law institutionalized and protected rights in and through women. . . . In any case, I do not think that the picture regarding women was quite as neat as Klapisch-Zuber's analysis would make it seem."

57. Chojnacki, "Patrician Women," 188–89, 193.

58. Ibid., 195–96; also see Chojnacki, "Power of Love," 129, 139.

59. Chojnacki, "Marriage Legislation," 173. Molho, *Marriage Alliance*, questions the conclusions drawn by Herlihy and Klapisch-Zuber, *Les Toscans*, 344, on women's downward marriage.

60. Chojnacki, "Kinship Ties and Young Patricians," 241, 260.

61. Chojnacki, "Patrician Women," 200–201.

62. Ibid., 202.

63. Ibid.

64. One might ask the same questions of the rise of mid-thirteenth-century Florentine women, such as Umiliana dei Cerchi, who as "lineage outsiders" reacted against the general trends of patrilineal descent within the ranks of the patriciate. See Lansing's provocative analysis of Umiliana's *Vita* in *Florentine Magnates*, chaps. 6, 7.

65. See also Klapisch-Zuber, "Le 'zane' della sposa."

66. Klapisch-Zuber, "Cruel Mother," 123, 130. Also see Calvi, *Il contratto morale,* 47–49; and the criticism of Klapisch-Zuber's "bleak assessment" by Diefendorf, "Family Culture, Renaissance Culture," 673ff.

67. See Calvi, *Il contratto morale,* 20–25; Calvi, "Diritti e legami."

68. Klapisch-Zuber, "Griselda Complex," 224.

69. On this theme, also see Klapisch-Zuber, "Le 'zane' della sposa."

70. Klapisch-Zuber, "Griselda Complex," 240–41; Klapisch-Zuber, "Ethnology of the Marriage." On the marriage ritual, see as well Klapisch-Zuber, "Zacharias; or, the Ousted Father."

71. Klapisch-Zuber, "Name 'Remade,'" 305–7. Klapisch-Zuber builds on these themes in essays reprinted in *La maison et le nom:* "L'invention du passé familial," "Le travail généalogique," "Parrains et filleuls," and "Compérage et clientélisme."

72. Klapisch-Zuber, "Blood Parents and Milk Parents," "Female Celibacy," "Women Servants."

73. Klapisch-Zuber, "Women Servants," 68.

74. Klapisch-Zuber, "Blood Parents and Milk Parents," 141. See, also, Sandri, *L'ospedale di S. Maria della Scala,* chap. 5; Sandri, "Baliatico mercenario," 102: "Allattamento mercenario e abbandono dei bambini alle istituzioni assistenziali sono, infine, lo ripetiamo nuovamente, due fenomeni indissociabili da punto di vista congiunturale ed economico." For Venice, see Romano, "Regulation of Domestic Service."

75. Klapisch-Zuber, "Holy Dolls." For the effects of farming baby boys out to wet nurses in Renaissance Florence, see the provocative thesis by Pitkin, *Fortune Is a Woman,* 229: "Yet the material of this chapter suggests that in a way—in terms of infantile experience—the typical Florentine boy of Machiavelli's day may well have been 'orphaned' at the age of two from the family of his *balia.*"

76. Klapisch-Zuber, "Les femmes dans les rituels," 19.

77. Herlihy, foreword to Klapisch-Zuber, *Women, Family, and Ritual,* xiii–xiv.

78. Davis and Farge, *Renaissance and Enlightenment Paradoxes,* 4.

79. Ibid., x.

2. Women in the Streets, Women in the Courts, In Early Renaissance Florence

1. On the class structure of Sant'Ambrogio parish and other parishes on the periphery of Florence, see Cohn, *Laboring Classes,* chap. 5; Stella, *La révolte des Ciompi,* 125–43. According to contemporary chroniclers, men and women from the parish of Sant'Ambrogio often sparked insurrection, which spread to other neighborhoods. This was one of the four or five neighborhoods singled out as principal hotbeds of Ciompi insurgents; see, for instance, Molho and Sznura, *Alle bocche della piazza,* 35, 46.

2. AP, 2769, 13v.: "dominam Filippam Macthey populi Sancti Ambroxij de Florentia contra quam per modum et viam accusationis processimus coram nobis et

nostre curie producta per Pierum Cianchini, populi Sancti Simonis de Florentia in eo, de eo, et super eo quod loco et tempore in dicta accusatione continet cum dicebatur pluribus vicibus dississe et pertulisse contra dictum Pierum et plura verba iniuriosa dicendo: 'Sozo, traditore, landronciello' et tunc dictus Pierus dicitur dissisie eidem: 'Si tu esses homo, prout es femina, tu non diceres michi hec verba,' et ipse dicitur respondisse: 'Si ego sum femina facerem tibi omne dedecus,' ac etiam post predicta dicebatur pluribus vicibus blasfemine nomen domini nostri Yesu Cristi et sue gloriose matris senper virginis Marie, dicendo, ut dicebatur: 'Festu l'abbia Deo e la madre che in questo mundo te fece nassiere, che me darebbe il core d'avere più homini ad farie occidere che no avereste ad de cenare teco.' Et constat nobis et nostre curia predictam dominam Filippam non esse culpabilem nec punibilem de predictis."

3. Boccaccio, *Decameron*, 498–501. Heißler, *Frauen der italischen Renaissance*, 102–3, singles out this story as evidence that contemporaries believed women to have been oversexed. However, what strikes me as remarkable about this story is Boccaccio's invented legal principle that the courts presumed that men and women were equal before the law and that for laws to be valid they had to have the consent of their constituencies, both male and female.

4. Lesnick, "Insults and Threats," argues from the 1275–80 criminal records of Todi that slanderers consistently accused males of being thieves and females of sexual infidelity; Poos, "Sex, Lies, and the Church Courts," 592, makes similar claims for late medieval England. On insults, also see Madero, *Manos violentas*. While Filippa's words begin with the standard curses and accusations, her threats go beyond the usual for these criminal cases.

5. I wish to thank my former colleague Cathy Newbury (formerly of the government department at Wesleyan University) for information regarding the dining habits of the Tembo in Zaire; also see Le Roy Ladurie, *Montaillou*, 38.

6. For a recent essay charting changes in approach and attitudes toward the historical treatment of medieval and early modern criminal records, see Dean and Lowe, "Writing the History of Crime." For a discussion of these approaches—and in particular the validity and limitations of the case-study approach—see chap. 6.

7. Burckhardt, *Civilization of the Renaissance*, 240, 241.

8. Ibid., 245: "Pandolfini [Alberti] finds at his villa a peace and happiness, for an account of which the reader must hear him speak himself."

9. Alberti, *I libri della famiglia*, 207–8.

10. Ibid., 228–29.

11. Burckhardt, *Civilization of the Renaissance*, 240–43.

12. Del Lungo, *La donna fiorentina*, 109–47.

13. Goldthwaite, *Private Wealth*: "One aspect of this new sentiment was the liberation of women both from the obscurity of medieval life and from the idealism of medieval poetry . . . Perhaps the finest document testifying to the new status of women and the developed sentiments of familial affection is the collection of letters of Alessandra Strozzi to and from her sons, which is one of the most appealing social documents of the era" (263–64).

14. Martines, "Way of Looking at Women," 15, 16. Ibid., 17-18: "the question arises, what type of source or document lends itself best to the study of 'feminine' perceptions? And the answer is surely letters—personal correspondence." On the layers of the Florentine ruling class, see, most recently, Molho, *Marriage Alliance,* which indeed takes its model from Martines's studies on the Florentine oligarchy. The letters of Alessandra Strozzi continue to stimulate interest among a younger generation of historians; see Tomas, *"Positive Novelty"*; Gregory, "Daughters, Dowries, and the Family"; Crabb, "How Typical Was Alessandra Macinghi Strozzi?" For an earlier interest in these sources, see Gutkind, *Frauenbriefe.*

15. Trexler, "Le célibat," and "Widow's Asylum." For the end of the Renaissance and early modern period, see S. Cohen, *Evolution of Women's Asylums.* See also Trexler, "La prostitution florentine"; the criticisms of Mazzi in "Il mondo della prostituzione" and *Prostitute e lenoni;* Herlihy, "Some Psychological and Social Roots of Violence," 140; Molho and Kirshner, "Dowry Fund"; Molho, *Marriage Alliance;* Chojnacki, "Patrician Women." Also see chap. 1, this volume.

16. For recent literature on women in the workplace, see Herlihy, *Opera Muliebria,* 178-79; Opitz, "Life in the Late Middle Ages"; Chabot, "La reconnaissance du travail."

17. Cohn, *Laboring Classes.*

18. While the records for these tribunals survive only from 1343, the institutions reach back to the central Middle Ages. The *podestà* was created at the end of the twelfth century, the *capitano del popolo* in 1250, and the *esecutore degli ordinamenti di giustizia* in 1307. For a history of these institutions, see Davidsohn, *Storia di Firenze,* 1:1032-36 and 2:410-13; Waley, *Italian City-Republics,* 40-45. For an introduction to Florentine criminal procedure, see Kohler and degli Azzi, *Das Florentiner Strafrecht;* and Dorini, *Il diritto penale.* The tribunal of the executor of the ordinances of justice was abolished immediately after the return of the Medici from exile in 1434, but even before that date its annual business had dwindled to include only deliberations and cases regulating the corruption of public officers. On the later history of the *otto,* see Antonelli, "La magistratura"; most recently, Brackett, *Criminal Justice.*

19. On changes in the Florentine population, see Herlihy and Klapisch-Zuber, *Les Toscans,* 173-77, and table 16. Between the *catasto* of 1427 and that of 1458-89, the city population of Florence as recorded in these tax registers had increased by only 225, from 37,144 to 37,369.

20. A recent study of the *otto di guardia* and criminal jurisprudence in the fourteenth and fifteenth centuries, Stern, "Inquisition Procedure," suggests that the *otto* began to make deep inroads into the business of the traditional medieval courts only after the rise of the Medici. But given the sparsity of surviving documents from the *otto di guardia* of the pre-1460s, this proposition is difficult to prove. Also, see Stern, *Criminal Law System,* chap. 7, which expands her argument.

21. Brucker, *Florentine Politics,* 108, 110.

22. See ibid., chap. 5.

23. See Cohn, *Laboring Classes,* chaps. 6, 7; Brucker, *Florentine Politics.* There was an abortive insurrection in Prato against Florentine taxation; see Brucker, *Florentine Politics,* 292.

24. Stefani, *Cronaca fiorentina,* 289–90.

25. Goldthwaite, "I Prezzi," 33; la Roncière, *Prix et Salaires à Florence,* 118, 260–62, corroborates the trend discovered by Goldthwaite by extending the analysis of prices to cover a variety of goods and services.

26. Cohn, *Laboring Classes,* 184–85. In addition to the *otto di guardia,* the commune of Florence created another four summary courts during the first part of the fifteenth century—the *onestà* (1403), which dealt with cases of prostitution; the *conservatori dell'onestà dei monasteri* (1421); the *conservatori delle leggi* (1429), which dealt largely with the abuse and corruption of office; and the *ufficiali di notte* (1432), which adjudicated mostly crimes of sodomy. On these tribunals, see Zorzi, *L'amministrazione,* 46ff.

In the surviving records of the *ufficiali di notte,* none of the cases involved women; see ASF, *ufficiali di notte,* 9. The other tribunal, the *onestà,* adjudicated cases concerning public prostitution. Trexler, "La prostitution florentine," calculated that in its eighty-three-year history, it tried 1,092 cases, or 13.6 cases per annum. These cases are not treated in this analysis. Like the *ufficiali di notte,* the *onestà* opened a new area of penal justice hardly dealt with earlier by the medieval tribunals—control over prostitution. Brackett, "Florentine Onestà," concerns largely the administrative history of this tribunal.

27. Cohn, *Laboring Classes,* 185.

28. ASF, Otto di guardia (della Repubblica), 11 (May–August 1460).

29. On the lay chaplains, see Cohn, *Laboring Classes,* 198–99; Manikowska, "Accorr'uomo." Surprisingly little work has been done of this communitarian, late-medieval form of law enforcement in Italy; see Zorzi, "Judicial System," 40; Stern, "Inquisition Procedure."

30. Cohn, *Laboring Classes,* 199. Zorzi, "Judicial System," 45–46, speculates that these community bodies declined in most places in Europe during the late fourteenth century.

31. Cohn, *Laboring Classes,* 187.

32. Z-score = 1.85, which is insignificant at the critical level 0.05; where P = observed proportion, π = the hypothesized proportion, and N = sample size. To calculate Z, the two sample years, 1344–45 and 1374–75, were considered as subsets of a single population, and the hypothesized proportion (π) was computed as the mean proportion of the two sample years. Thus π = .195; P = .22; and N = 862.

33. According to a standard error of proportion test, the difference is significant at a 0.05 level of confidence: Z = 2.81; P = .17; π = .14; and N = 1,056.

34. I use the total number of cases involving women in this *filza* of the *otto,* since the *otto* never made clear the residence of the injured party.

35. Cohn, *Laboring Classes,* 187–88.

36. On the class nature of assault cases, see ibid., 189–91.

37. Unlike the earlier published statutes of 1322–25, the Florentine statutes of

1415 included an entire section of laws regulating agricultural laborers, ranging from stiff penalties for abandoning work to ceilings on their wages; see *Statuta popoli et communis Florentiae* 2:393–404.

38. These similarities and differences were computed using the frequency that women were involved in a certain type of crime, such as assault and battery, expressed as a percentage of the total number of cases involving women in a given period. By a chi-square test, the differences between the 1344–45 and the 1374–75 categories of crime are insignificant at 0.05: chi-square = 7.92 at seven degrees of freedom (*df*). On the other hand, the differences between the 1374–75 and the 1455–66 patterns of female crime are significant at 0.05: *df* = 7; chi-square = 16.04.

39. For cases of assault and battery in which women were sentenced in defense of their children and husbands, see AP, 116, f. 192v, 207v; and AP, 127, f. 173r.

40. For the possibilities and problems of Florentine family names in demarcating elite status, see Molho, *Marriage Alliance,* 280–84. The percentage of those possessing a family name in marriage records increases from 12 percent of the spouses during the second half of the fourteenth to 19 percent during the latter half of the fifteenth century (see Cohn, *Laboring Classes,* 45). This change, however, is negligible in comparison to the shift in prosecutors shown in these criminal cases.

41. On these changes, see Cohn, *Laboring Classes,* chap. 10; Zorzi, *L'amministrazione,* and "Judicial System"; Stern, "Inquisition Procedure."

42. On the *mundualdus* and Lombard law, see Kuehn, *Law, Family, and Women,* 212–37; Giardina, "Advocatus e mundualdus."

43. See Cohn, *Cult of Remembrance,* chap. 6; Kirshner, "Materials for a Gilded Cage."

44. *Statuta populi et communis florentiae (1415),* 1:118, bk. 2, rub. 9, "Quod nulla mulier debeat per se, sed procuratorem agere in causa civili." Earlier, in the statutes of the *podestà* (1321), a woman could draw up contracts with the consent of her husband and needed a *mundualdus* only if not married; see ASF, Statuti della repubblica fiorentina, 2:116, bk. 2, rub. 39; 2:141, bk. 2, rub. 70; 2:142, bk. 2, rub. 71.

45. See Cockburn, "Nature and Incidence of Crime," 57; Lundsgaarde, *Murder in Space City,* 10.

46. See Stone, "Interpersonal Violence"; Gurr, "Historical Trends in Violent Crime." Unlike the present, homicides by family members were less frequent than those by friends and neighbors, although in absolute terms the decline in infrafamilial murder may not have changed (at least in England). According to Spierenburg, "Faces of Violence," the decline in homicides parallels a decline in spontaneous, emotive action more generally.

47. See Hammer, "Patterns of Homicide," 20; Hanawalt, "Peasant Family and Crime," 297, 320; Hunniset, *Medieval Coroner,* 31. From the experience of contemporary U.S. cities, Lundsgaarde, *Murder in Space City,* concludes: "The violent behavior that ultimately leads to injury and death is, therefore, quite similar, al-

though in principle the victim's condition—whether dead or alive—conveniently and legally serves to categorize the offense" (156). In Stone's words ("Interpersonal Violence," 24–25), "homicide is only an aggravated, and often accidental, type of assault."

48. See for instance Bongi and Del Prete, *Statutum Lucani*, 147, bk. 3, rub. 17: "De eo quod percussus et vulneratus, et post dictam percussionem mortuus infra viginti dies continuos, presumatur propterea mortuus."

49. See Lundsgaarde, *Murder in Space City*.

50. In all three periods of our study, the plaintiff in these crimes was almost exclusively a male or the state (the *podestà*, the *capitano*, or a lay chaplain of the parish).

51. Ruggiero, *Boundaries of Eros*, 25, finds a similar pattern in fifteenth-century Venice: while cases of heterosexual rape adjudicated by the Council of Forty declined dramatically, concern for homosexuality increased; see 25ff and chap. 6: "Sodom and Venice."

52. See Rocke, "Il controllo dell'omosessualità," "Sodomites in Fifteenth-Century Tuscany," and *Friendly Affections, Nefarious Vices*. I wish to thank him for allowing me to glance through his book before publication.

53. ASF, Ufficiali di notte, 9, 17r. In this case, Domenico di Giovanni Lunghi from Modena, a vendor of sweets in the Mercato vecchio of Florence, lured with sweets the boy Agnolino to his apartment for sex.

54. Ibid., 2r, 3v, 4r, 4v, 6v, 14r, 19r. Also, see Rocke, *Friendly Affections*.

55. Trexler, "Ritual in Florence."

56. Brownmiller, *Against Our Will*, 190–91.

57. Herlihy, *Opera Muliebria*, 178–79; Herlihy, "Women's Work"; Chabot, "La reconnaissance du travail."

58. E. Cohen, "Honor and Gender," finds that a similar "gender division of labor" characterized the ideals of Roman "street" society in the mid-sixteenth century.

59. Dean and Lowe, "Writing the History of Crime" (13) are right: "The element of 'social justice' in barn-burning, for example, is often absent in the sources and is conjectured by the historian." Yet, from the laconic texts of the criminal inquisitions and sentences, which rarely divulge the motives for crimes (as the authors note, 5–6), to assume that these acts were simply accidental would be as problematic if not more so.

60. For such groups or even gangs of women, see AP, 116, f. 185v; and AP, 127, f. 297v, f. 400r.

61. These figures contrast with the picture of female crime that Hanawalt, "Female Felon," has drawn from the criminal records of fourteenth-century England, where only one woman to every nine men was charged with a criminal offense and where crimes of physical aggression perpetrated by women were much rarer than that found for fourteenth-century Florence.

62. See da Certaldo, *Libro di buoni costumi*; Sacchetti, *Trecentonovelle*, 85: 172–74: "Uno fiorentino toglie per moglie una vedova stata disonestissima di sua

persona, e con poca fatica la gastiga sì, ch'ella diviene onesta" and ibid., 86:174–78: "Oh quanti sono li dolorosi mariti che fanno cattive mogli." See also Boccaccio, *Decameron,* day 9, story 9: "Due giovani domandan consiglio a Salamone," 831– 37.

63. See Di Simplicio, "La criminalità a Siena," "Perpetuas"; S. Cohen, *Evolution of Women's Asylums.*

64. Machiavelli, *Mandragola, Clizia,* 128: "Questa favola si chiama 'Clizia,' per- ché così ha nome la fanciulla, che si combatte. Non aspettate di vederla, perché Sofronia, che l'ha allevata, non vuole per onestà che la venga fuora."

65. See Dean, "Criminal Justice"; Stern, "Inquisition Procedure," 299–301; and Stern, *Criminal Law System,* chap. 2. In addition to changes in how cases were brought to trial in the traditional medieval courts, the courts of the *otto,* the *on- està,* the *ufficiali di notte,* and the vicariate in the countryside relied either exclu- sively or predominantly on inquisitions from the court police and judges, as op- posed to personal accusations. On the vicariate courts, see chap. 6.

66. Weissman, *Ritual Brotherhood.* In the period 1370–99 there were 136 women of a total membership of 360; see ASF, Archivi delle Compagnie Soppresse, San Frediano 5, vol. 25. On neighborhood confraternities and San Frediano, see Hen- derson, *Piety and Charity,* 111–12.

67. Trexler, *Public Life,* 224–41: "We emerge from a period of unconsecrated cel- ebrations, staged first on May Day and later during Carnival, and enter a sacred cycle of civic feasts dedicated to Zanobi, Barnabas, and finally to the Baptist him- self. We leave behind a group of celebrations in which women and youth, groups outside the political body, had played a role, and enter one in which the partici- pants are mostly mature males" (240).

68. In a comparison between the demographic growth of Verona and Florence, Herlihy ("Deaths, Marriages, Births, and the Tuscan Economy") shows that, while the population of Florence increased during the late fifteenth and early sixteenth centuries, the number of households remained almost constant. In contrast to the more dynamic economy and demography of Verona, the stagnation in the num- ber of households in Florence reflects the city's loss of prominence in financial and industrial development.

69. See Molho, "Florentine Oligarchy," and "Politics and the Ruling Class"; Cohn, *Laboring Classes,* chap. 3 and conclusion.

70. See Herlihy, "Mapping Households," "Santa Caterina and San Bernar- dino," and "Family Solidarity," 180; Goldthwaite, *Private Wealth,* 268–69; Cohn, *Death and Property,* 72–94; Kuehn, *Law, Family, and Women,* 157–75.

71. Kuehn, *Emancipation,* 78ff.

72. Thus far, the work of Herlihy and Klapisch-Zuber, *Les Toscans,* has gone the furthest in these directions. For Genoa, see the excellent study by Hughes, "Urban Growth," which contrasts artisan and patrician women's property rights during the later Middle Ages. For France, see Gauvard, "*De Grace especial.*"

3. Last Wills

A version of this chapter was presented at the conference "Renaissance Families: Ideology and Social Practice," sponsored by the Renaissance Studies Program, Brown University, 16 March 1991.

1. See for instance Goody, Thirsk, and Thompson, *Family and Inheritance.*

2. Vovelle, *Piété baroque;* and *La mort et l'occident;* Ariès, *Western Attitudes,* and *Hour of Our Death;* Chaunu, *La mort à Paris;* Chiffoleau, *La comptabilité de l'au-dela,* and "Perchè cambia la morte." Historians such as Croix, *Bretagne;* Hoffman, *Church and Community;* and Norberg, *Rich and Poor in Grenoble* look more closely at the mix of pious choices but do not place their findings in the full context of testamentary bequests, both pious and nonpious, or within traditions of property descent. For a discussion of the historiography on death, mentality, and testaments, see Le Roy Ladurie, "Chaunu, Lebrun, Vovelle"; Cohn, *Death and Property,* 2–5.

3. Kuehn has criticized me for believing that last wills and testaments were "self-executing" instruments and that they were not subject to future conflict, repudiation, or litigation (review of Cohn, *Death and Property, Law, Family, and Women,* 2, 15; and "Law, Death, and Heirs"). Such criticism reflects an unfair and inattentive reading of my two books on last wills and testaments, where I stress that the will was a social act embedded in the frameworks of religious and notarial practices and conditioned by the immediate demands of kin and clergy at the bedside. By analyzing changes in conditional pacts and contingency clauses, I emphasize how wills in Siena changed through the fifteenth century, as testators entered a more litigious culture and attempted to circumvent future conflicts and repudiations by heirs and charitable institutions. My intention was not to trace inheritance patterns but to chronicle changes in the collective (not the individual) mentality through reading large numbers of testaments.

4. Of these, 3,226 were complete last wills and testaments. Selected from numerous state and ecclesiastical archives, they extend in time from some of the earliest notarized specimens of the twelfth century until 1425. Except for Florence, my samples comprise the bulk of the surviving testaments. Only for Florence could I have easily gathered more testaments from archival collections, but these additional wills would have come principally from the diplomatic archives of such institutions as the hospital of Santa Maria Nuova and would have biased the Florentine data more toward the wealthy and powerful than in the other five city-states. Thus I limited my selection from these sources so that the Florentine sample would remain commensurate with the other city-state samples. For a further discussion of my sampling techniques and decisions, see the more technical and detailed discussion in *Cult of Remembrance,* app. A, 289–94.

5. For a more detailed discussion of "mendicant piety," see Cohn, *Death and Property,* chaps. 4, 5.

6. Florence, Arezzo, and Perugia look more alike with, respectively, twenty-three, twenty, and eighteen alienation clauses per thousand legacies (pious and

nonpious). On the other hand, the other three city-states, Assisi, Pisa, and Siena, recorded, respectively, only seven, six, and five restrictive clauses per thousand legacies.

7. Cohn, *Death and Property,* 146–58.

8. This merchant must have been the brother of the famous penitential Umiliana dei Cerchi (who died in 1264). Her *Vita,* in Vito, *Acta Sanctorum,* 385–418, refers to her brothers and blood kin without naming them, "et vexationibus a patre, fratribus et consanguineis aliis" (388). According to her *Vita* she was "defrauded" of her dowry by her father and ruthlessly tormented by her brothers for refusing to remarry or to leave the family palace, where she led a life of rigorous asceticism, parceling out family belongings to the poor. On her life and antipatrilineal ideology, see Benvenuti Papi, "Umiliana dei Cerchi"; Lansing, *Florentine Magnates,* chap. 6. Perhaps Umiliana's fame and success with her female kin and the neighboring Franciscans of Santa Croce conditioned the remarkable intensity of this will's patrilineal and antifeminine orientation even a generation after her death. In addition, it is striking, especially for wills of the late Dugento, that of twenty pious legacies not a single bequest was left to Santa Croce or any other mendicant order. To my knowledge, this testament has not been published nor has it been commented on in the vast literature on Umiliana dei Cerchi and on the Florentine civil strife at the end of the century sparked by the controversy between the Cerchi and Donati families.

9. ASF, Dipl., Arch. gen. 1291.viii.30. For other early testaments of similar complexity that routed properties down specific generational tracks, see the will of the nobleman dominus Schiatta f.q. domini Bocche f.q. domini Rayneri Rustici from the Abbati family (ASF, Dipl., S. M. Novella 1300.ii.9); Solius f.q. Martini de Tedaldis (ASF, Dipl., Arch. gen. 1313.ii.6). On the Abbati testament, see Lansing, *Florentine Magnates,* 40, 179–80.

10. ASF, Not. antecos. 13364, 7v, 1300.i.4.

11. Ibid., 205, 28r–29v, 1364.vii.20. For a will with similar directives of entail, see the testament of Alamannus's nephew, Tolosinus, redacted on the same day; ibid., 29v–31r, 1364.vii.20.

12. ASF, Dipl., Arch. gen. 1416.10.13.

13. Ibid., 1368. viii. 24; Sacchetti, *Trecentonovelle,* story 63, 122–23.

14. The case of Alexio's inheritance from his father was a cause celebre, involving a complex and extended litigation between Santa Maria Novella and the Strozzi family. According to Orlandi, *"Necrologio,"* 1:131, 623–47, this estate was extraordinarily rich—valued at 20,000 florins. At age fourteen, the boy entered the Dominican order at Santa Maria Novella and, according to the boy's uncles, was held there "not for reasons of devotional zeal, but for greed and avarice." To free the boy from this alleged captivity, his uncles utilized their connection with the bishop of Città di Castello and the archbishop of Ravenna and appealed directly to Pope Urban V, who ordered that Alexio be placed in an apartment belonging to the archbishop of Florence. Thus protected from pressures from the friars and his relatives, the boy was to decide for himself whether he would remain a friar or re-

turn to lay existence. The case was resolved in favor of Santa Maria Novella, and Alexio flourished as a scholar of philosophy, dying at the early age of thirty-three. His body is still preserved intact in the *cappelleta* under the steps of the chapel of Saint Thomas Aquinas.

15. ASF, Dipl., S. M. Novella 1377.vii.21. Ten years later, another woman from the Florentine elite, domina Francesca, the widow of a man from the Guidalotti family and the daughter of Nardus Juncte from the Rucellai family, directed her landed properties through generations of the male line; ibid., 1386.i.23.

16. Ibid., S. M. Nuova 1313.vi.23. For similar examples, see ibid., 1340.x.14. In Arch. Gen. 1346.iii.16, the testator demanded that his nephew be "obedient, reverent, loving, and attentive" to his uncle, who was given the authority to manage his nephew's affairs while he was "in his adolescent years." In Dipl. S. M. Novella 1396.vi.24, a Florentine merchant working in Paris, Iacobus de Iuochis, left his illegitimate daughter under the "protection" and "discipline" of his wife.

17. ASF, Not. antecos. 13364, 7v, 1300.i.14.

18. ASF, Dipl., S. M. Nuova 1319.ii.10.

19. Ibid., S. M. Novella 1351.iv.2.

20. Ibid., 1396.vi.24.

21. ASF, Not. antecos. 4417, 133v–134r, 1406.iii.25.

22. ASF, Dipl., S. M. Nuova 1390.5.4.

23. Ibid., Arch. gen. 1407.viii.31.

24. Arch. S. Lorenzo 841, 1370.iii.8.

25. ASF, Not. antecos. 5891, 196v–197v, 1362.viii.18.

26. Arch. dei Laici 726, 1374.iii.26.

27. Ibid., 61v, 1375.10.31.

28. ASF, Not. antecos. 9523, 30v–42v, 1412.viii.5.

29. Ibid. 992, 152v–54v, 1334.xii.8; and ibid. 990, n.p.

30. Arch. dei Laici 726, 51r–52r, 1374.5.23.

31. ASF, Not. antecos 9982, 33r–34v, 1415.ii.25.

32. Arch. dei Laici 726, 60r–61r, 1374.vi.2.

33. ASF, Not. antecos. 9982, 16r, 1411.viii.1.

34. Ibid. 9981, 38v–42v, 1416.viii.5.

35. Arch. Capitolare, Arezzo 57, 39r–42r, 1340.vi.24.

36. ASF, Dipl., Misericordia 1363.vi.30.

37. ASF, Not. antecos. 5885, 231r–v, 1363.vi.22.

38. ASPr, Perg., Mt. Morcino 202, 1383.xi.5.

39. Ibid., S. Domenico 177, 1421.xi.19.

40. Ibid., Not. bast. 10, 28v–29v, 1389.ii.26.

41. Ibid., Not. prot. 7, 84r–v, 1393.v.26.

42. Ibid., Not. bast. 11, 94v–96r, 1390.viii.15.

43. Ibid., Perg., Monteluce 365, 1417.iv.7.

44. Ibid., Mt. Morcino 78, 1362.iii.23.

45. Ibid., 202, 1383.xi.5.

46. Cohn, *Death and Property*, chap. 6.

47. In times past, writers such as Fustel de Coulanges, *La cité antique,* and Maine, *Dissertations on Early Law and Custom,* found this same opposition between the property rights of women and the strength of the patrilineal devolution of property. More recently, anthropologists such as Goody, *Death, Property, and the Ancestors,* and the historian Guichard, *Structures sociales,* stress the same relationship but go further in relating other rites and customs to the systems of property devolution.

48. Goody, "Inheritance, Property, and Women," 10. Herlihy, *Opera Muliebria,* claims that women in the earlier Middle Ages, before the thirteenth century, inherited equally with their brothers. Afterward, aristocratic families favored male offspring and reserved "resources primarily for the support of its sons, often only the eldest son" (63). Unfortunately, no note or statistics underlie this claim. Patterns of primogeniture do not emerge in any of the towns examined in my study. In Siena, traces of primogeniture arise only in the sixteenth century.

49. Goody, "Inheritance, Property, and Women," 10.

50. The difference before and after the 1362–63 plague is highly significant at .01, p = .5172, π = .4184, N = 631, Z = 5.04.

51. In Perugia, the choice of daughters as universal heirs over more distant kinsmen was equal to that in Florence: 36 percent (45 of 126). Assisi, Arezzo, and Siena lay between Florence and Pisa: 45 percent (23 of 51), 50 percent (55 of 110), and 51 percent (38 of 74), respectively.

52. Riemer, "Women, Dowries, and Capital Investment," 72; her conclusions are based on a sample of only twenty-four testaments, drawn between 1283 and 1307.

53. In Perugia, in forty-nine cases of ninety-three, women named their husbands as universal heirs. Seven of nineteen such wills by Florentine women named their husbands as universal heirs.

54. ASPi, Osp. di S. Chiara 2078, 80r, 1311.1.6.

55. On the fifteen-lire customary gift, see Bonaini, *Constituta,* 41:786–87: "De his que a viro in uxorem dantur vel relinquuntur."

56. On the *mundualdus;* see Cortese, "Per la storia"; Bellomo, *La condizione giuridica,* 26–28; Giardina, "'Advocatus' e 'mundualdus.'" Kuehn, "Cum consensu mundualdi," 309, argues that "the appointment of a *mundualdus* for a woman was decidely quotidian," and, from sampling one notarial chartulary of 1422–30, finds 179 women participating in notarized contracts with the consent of such a male protector. Unfortunately, Kuehn fails to report the number of women who drafted notarized documents without a *mundualdus.* On the other hand, Rosenthal, "Position of Women," argues forcefully that, against the dictates of communal legislation, most patrician women from Quattrocento Florence drew up contracts without the consent of a male protector; the *mundualdus* appears in only 17 percent of the notarized contracts involving the women she examines. From this evidence, she questions the harsher picture of women drawn by Klapisch-Zuber and claims that this evidence on the *mundualdus* "shatters our present view of female behavior and prerogatives" showing "the independence of women." Rosenthal's

study, however, shows the pitfalls of an examination of a single place without comparative perspectives. As Kuehn points out from an examination of the communal statutes of Pisa and Siena—and as the testaments drawn for my comparative study illustrate—Florence and the towns subject to its law were unusual in their preservation of these Lombard laws restricting the contractual independence of women.

57. As the wide variety of options practiced by husbands in each of these towns indicates, these differences in widows' property settlements were matters of custom and practice rather than dictates established through communal statutes. On the widow's rights to the property of her deceased husband, see Pertile, *Storia del diritto privato;* Bellomo, *La condizione giuridica,* 26–28; Bellomo, *Ricerche sui rapporti patrimoniali;* Klapisch-Zuber, "Griselda Complex," "Le 'zane' della sposa," and "Cruel Mother." On the succession of the dowry, see Bonaini, *Constituta,* 23:742–45: "De exactione dotis," 748–50: rub. 25 "De sacramento manifestationis bonorum quondam mariti ab eius uxore prestando," 750–51: rub. 26 "Quibus mulieribus permissum sit dotem et donamenta suo sacramento probare," 752: rub. 28 "Quo casu pater de dote filio prestita in solidum teneatur," 752–54: rub. 29 "De donatione propter nunptias," 754–756: rub. 30 "Quid mariti ex morte uxoris sine pacto lucrantur." Camerani, *Statuto di Arezzo (1327),* bk. 3, rub. 63, 173–74: "De dotium et donationum propter nuptias restitutione, et qualiter ius reddatur." *Statuta populi e communis Florentiae (1415),* I., bk. 2, rub. 61, 156–59: "De dote, et donatione restituendis, et exigendi modo." Azzi, *Statuti di Perugia dell'anno MCCCXLII,* bk. 2, rub. 35, 334–36: "De le dote e le dotate fenmene." Zdekauer, *Il constituto del comune di Siena dell'anno 1262,* dist. 2, 35, 214–15: "Quod mater possit habere expensas a filiis suis, donec steterit cum eis."

58. Husbands provided their to-be widows these property arrangements in 19 of 115 cases in Assisi; 38 of 254 in Arezzo; 41 of 227 in Perugia; 40 of 176 in Siena; and 84 of 217 in Pisa. In addition, husbands in all six cities would sometimes use their testaments to add an *ultra dos* or *augumentum,* a supplement to her dowry, which usually would travel with her regardless of her future behavior or remarriage.

59. Kirshner, "Materials for a Gilded Cage"; Ercole, "L'istituto dotale," 197–211.

60. In Florence, 46 of 247 husbands with surviving wives left their wives with this choice; next in importance but only half as frequent (24 cases) came the standard formula found for the other cities, in which the widow was granted rights to the usufruct of her husband's property provided she remained chaste and never remarried. For the social and psychological ramifications of this system of widowhood, see Klapisch-Zuber, "Cruel Mother." To my knowledge, the communal statutes do not encode this dilemma for the wife, where she would lose the rights to her dowry if she chose the usufruct of her husband's property. Nor does Ercole, "L'istituto dotale," 222–57, mention such a settlement in surveying "the restitution of the dowry to widows" in communal statutes across the Italian peninsula. He instead insists that "la restitutione della dote contro gli eredi del marito è infatti universalmente riconosciuta e protetta; tutti gli statuti non potrebbero essere più espliciti in questo senso" (223).

61. In Perugia, 22 of 227 husbands with surviving wives, and in Arezzo 27 of

254, made this arrangement. These practices ran beneath the arrangements set by statutory law and cannot be interpreted from a comparison of the published city statutes of the Trecento for the six cities.

62. See, for instance, Rosenthal, "Position of Women."

63. On Lombard vs. Roman, see Cohn, *Cult of Remembrance*, chap. 8: unlike Tuscany, which fell under Lombard control in the seventh century, the Duchy of Perugia (which included Assisi) remained under Byzantine suzerainty and thus retained Roman law. The possibilities of these other variables as keys for understanding the differences in the patterns of piety among these cities is discussed more fully in ibid.

64. Burckhardt, *Civilization of the Renaissance*.

65. Greenblatt, *Renaissance Self-Fashioning*, 3.

4. Women and the Counter Reformation in Siena

A short version of this chapter was presented at the hundredth session of the American Historical Association (28 December 1985) and at the Social History Workshop of New York University. The themes of this essay were later incorporated into Cohn, *Death and Property in Siena*.

1. Stone, *Family, Sex, and Marriage*, 145–56.

2. Ibid. This is also the impression given by Walzer, *Revolution of the Saints*, 193–96. On the other hand, Stone appears to have changed his mind on the fate of women under Protestantism and Counter-Reformation Catholicism. While his earlier *Crisis of the Aristocracy*, 271–80, contrasts sharply the affective ties of the Puritan marriage to the patriarchal one that structured Catholic and High Anglican couples, *Family, Sex, and Marriage*, instead, asserts that women's power declined within the family throughout the sixteenth century both in Calvinist and in Counter-Reformed families. In this later book, chronology counted more than religion in distinguishing family ambiences. The transition of the patriarchal to the companionate marriage occurred toward the end of the seventeenth century, a century after the spread of gentry Puritanism and the modeling of the more egalitarian marriage described in Stone's *Crisis of the Aristocracy*. Stone and Stone, *Open Elite?* returns to the chronology of the companionate family implicit in *Crisis of the Aristocracy*.

3. Cohn, *Death and Property*, 1–2, discusses more fully the biases of the source, the constraints placed on individual testators, and the principles by which I selected my sample of testaments. For the sixteenth and seventeenth centuries, the majority of these acts were redacted by notaries from the city of Siena and concern Sienese testators. I gathered all the testaments in the notarial protocols for at least four different notaries, selected at random for each decade before the archival reforms instituted by Francesco II in 1585. After this date, the grand duke of Tuscany required Sienese notaries to bind together all their testaments and codicils in separate volumes instead of mixing these acts with other notarial business as had been generally the custom. I selected between thirty and forty testaments for the

decades after 1585, from at least three different city notaries. These urban notaries, however, did not work exclusively within the city limits of Siena. In the sixteenth and seventeenth centuries, about 10 percent of their clients resided in the countryside.

4. AA, Sinodi 3, 1r.

5. The model came from Carlo Borromeo's visitation to the archdiocese of Milan in 1572.

6. For the Counter-Reformation impact on social classes from the aristocracy to artisans and the differences between the city and the countryside, see Cohn, *Death and Property,* 188–98.

7. This discussion is treated in detail in ibid., pt 2.

8. See, for example, Nardi, "Aspetti della vita dei religiosi," and "Matteo Guerra." Guerra was an illiterate peasant, who in the atmosphere of the Counter Reformation was able to enter into the old strongholds of the Sienese nobility, such as the confraternity of the hospital of Santa Maria della Scala and the parish of San Giorgio, where he guided a reform movement often in direct opposition to the old exponents of the highest elite families.

9. For a change in the direction of the Counter Reformation in seventeenth-century Siena, see Cohn, *Death and Property,* chap. 11.

10. This visitation did uncover violations, and the visitors made recommendations. The violations, however, were considerably fewer than those a generation earlier. Those at the end of the century occurred mostly within rural parishes, whose properties still suffered from the damages of the war of 1555. It would be misleading to assume that the more muted tones of the second visitation resulted from the disposition of a more lenient taskmaster. As the following years of his office of archbishop would demonstrate, the moralistic and inquisitional zeal for reform drove Tarugi as much as any of the early Tridentine episcopal reformers. The archbishop's court of the early Seicento prosecuted with increased fervor the misdeeds of parish priests and parishioners. Tarugi was particularly severe with regard to the reform of the clergy. They were to be "the mirrors of virtue" for the faithful—"santi vivi." In 1600, Tarugi established a special inquisition to scrutinize the behavior of clerics; indeed, not all of them matched up to the suprahuman standards of this post-Tridentine zealot. Nardi, "Aspetti della vita dei religiosi," has studied the episcopal court records through the first half of the Seicento, finding examples of sexual scandals involving the clergy. It is worth noting, however, that not a single example provided by Nardi involved a parish priest from the city of Siena. Without a doubt, urban curates visited prostitutes and were involved in other scandals, but the major source of infractions still came from the poorer parishes of the countryside. Milan presents a comparable picture of the changes in piety wrought by the visitations of 1570. According to Wright, *Counter-Reformation,* 218, the visitations of Carlo Borromeo's cousin Federigo show a laity from 1595 to 1631 "faithful to the sacraments, but not always fulfilling the terms of pious bequests of their ancestors; attentive to the catechetical Schools of Christian Doctrine, in the urban centres, but not always so in rural areas."

11. In his introduction, Oblelkevich, *Religion and the People,* 8, expresses the common view of the Counter Reformation as "essentially an elite pattern of religion, inaugurating an era of one-way religious pressure from the top down and equally an era of increasing resistance and partial conformity from below." For similar positions from historians of "the new social history," see Delumeau, *La peur en Occident,* and *Le pèché et la peur;* Ginzburg, *I benandanti,* and *Il formaggio e i vermi.*

12. AA, Sinodi 3. Bossi's court prosecuted most severely those from the priesthood and the nobility. In sexual scandals the penalties were unequal; often, peasants and artisans were slapped on the wrists, while noble men and women received stiffer sentences, even exile from the territory of Siena. For the populist appeal of Carlo Borromeo in the diocese of Milan, see Chabod, *Per la storia religiosa,* 272–77.

13. See Marrara, *Riseduti e Nobilità,* 59–60. For Lyon, Hoffman, *Church and Community,* 41, finds a different social pattern in the acceptance of Counter-Reform piety. There the elites led the way, while "artisans and common people clearly did not follow the elites and rush to embrace Tridentine Catholicism."

14. See Bendiscoli, *Dalla Riforma alla Controriforma,* 128; Mols, "Saint Charles Borromée," 717; Zancan, "La donna," 811. Women and men were separated in church, and women were required to keep their heads veiled in church and in religious processions.

15. Historians have begun to look more favorably on the ambience of Counter-Reformation Catholicism for women. See, for instance, Davis, "City Women," 65–96; Hoffman, "Wills and Statistics," and *Church and Community;* Norberg, *Rich and Poor;* Martin, "Out of the Shadow." These historians compare the piety and devotion of Catholic women relative to men in the second half of the sixteenth and seventeenth centuries, or they compare Catholic and Protestant women in this period, but they do not investigate changes in piety and women's rights, power, and property relations in Catholic societies before and after the Council of Trent.

16. French historiography sees the percentage of women who redacted their own wills as a progressive linear development paralleling the inexorable forces of modernity: see Vovelle, *Piété baroque,* 320. In Provence, before the eighteenth century, women redacted testaments only two-thirds as frequently as men.

17. Parenti, *Prezzi,* 27.

18. On the apathy of men in Lyon to the charitable causes of Trent, see Hoffman, "Wills and Statistics," 830.

19. See membership roles, such as those for the confraternity of Santa Trinità, Biblioteca Comunale, A.II.1; and the numerous new companies for women, which appear in the visitations of Tarugi, AA, Visite 27. Also see Rusconi, "Confraternite, compagnie e devozioni," 496–97.

20. For a discussion of Counter-Reformed congregations for women, see S. Cohen, *Evolution of Women's Asylums.*

21. For the condition of nunneries at the time of Bossi's visitation, see Catoni, "Interni di conventi senesi del Cinquecento," 187–94.

22. Nardi, "Matteo Guerra," 36–37; and S. Cohen, *Evolution of Women's Asylums.*

23. In Siena, the war against Florence in 1552–55 compounded the economic and social crisis of the mid-Cinquecento. Although the disastrous consequences of this prolonged war and the Sienese patriotic zeal may have sparked charitable assistance (see Nardi, "Matteo Guerra," 17–18), new institutions to rehabilitate the poor did not receive significant funding and recognition until well after this military and demographic crisis.

24. For the repressive character of these institutions, see Foucault, *Folie et déraison,* 54–96; Norberg, *Rich and Poor,* 297.

25. In addition to evidence in these testaments, see Trexler, "Death and Testament," 34ff.

26. Based on the following sample sizes for women's testaments: thirty, twenty-six, sixty-one, and fifty.

27. The struggle between the church and prestigious lineages over sacred space in churches is of long duration in Western civilization. See P. Brown, *Cult of the Saints.* In the visitations of 1575–76, Bossi demanded that members of several of Siena's most prominent families exhume their ancestral bones from places that, according to new Tridentine specification, were too near high altars and other sacred places.

28. It might be argued that these statistical changes resulted from the demographic, social, and economic dislocations created by the war with Florence, 1552–55. The historian would then need to explain the reason for a time lag of twenty-five to fifty years. To borrow Robert Lopez's phrase, "I doubt the paternity of children who were born . . . years after the death of their fathers" ("Hard Times and Investment in Culture," in *The Renaissance* [New York, 1962], 43). Second, though the occurrence of pestilence may have affected pious bequests and the differentials between men and women in charitable giving in the short term, they do not register in Siena as a force that fundamentally altered trends for the seventeenth century. For the short-term effect of plague on testament writing, see Pastore, "Testamenti in tempo di Peste."

29. No doubt the notary was in some measure responsible for the drafting of these personal expressions, but these remarks were not formulaic; they were not automatically replicated either from notary to notary or within the testaments drafted by a particular notary. In addition, these phrases often contain bits of variable information, such as the length of time the husband and wife "have lived together with sincere love," or more simply put in other wills, "per essere insieme habitati." See *Not. postcos.* 423, 134, 6r, 1605.iv.4; and 532, 9r–v, 1601.ix.7; 1786, 16, 31r–33r, 1644.vi.12; and 20, 38r–39v, 1645.viii.27.

30. ASS, Not. antecos. 2684, 64, 1551.viii.12.

31. ASS, Not. postcos. 3625, fasc. 1, 168, 1575.i.2, "Conoscendo l'amore et benevolentia inverso di essa portata da donna Margarita d'Andrea detto Bresia da Pretra arata sua dilettissima consorte et quanto si sia affadigata et si affadighi del continuo a servitio di detto Andrea et in mantenerli li suoi beni et essi accrescerli et augumentarli volendola riconoscere et rimeritarla di tante sue fadighe, et acciò che

essa dopo la sua morte non sia scacciata dalli infrascripti suoi heredi, onde essa potesse per alcun' modo patire di farne la medissima donna Margarita per suo certo sper et non per forza o per inganno alcuno ma spontaneamente et in ogni miglior modo lassò donna madonna et usufruttuaria et libera et generale amminstratrice di tutti li suoi beni." Similar statements of respect and affection or gratitude for a wife's *fadighe et industrie* are found in numerous documents from the late sixteenth and seventeenth centuries; for instance, Not. antecos. 3130, 21v–23r, 1563.ii.11; 2265, 11r–12v, 1583.ix.13; Not. postcos. 184, 4r, 1594.ix.24; 23r–25v, 1595.vi.21; 532, 9r–v, 1601.ix.7; 423, 6r, 1605.iv.54; 1164, 31, 35v, 1613,viii.17; 971, 50, 63v–64v, 1610.xii.20; 52, 65v–66r, 1611.x.24; 1762, 34, 68r–69r, 1641.vii.16; 2479, 6, 9r–10r, 1664.xii.13.

32. Stone, *Family, Sex, and Marriage,* 136–45, 217–53. The hasty historian might suppose that the difference between these two documents reflects differences between artisan and peasant marriages. However, their dating is the essential difference. The testament of Andrea di Giovanni is the first in my sample to suggest the mutual affection and toil of years of matrimonial partnership. Later, particularly during the seventeenth century, such sentiments are found more often among urban artisans.

33. During the period of the Grand Duchy, the only change in legislation that affected the property rights of women was promulgated in 1620. Cosimo II extended the rights of succession to parts of the inheritance to the female kin of those who died without a notarized testament. Cantini, *Legislazione Toscana,* t. 15, 153–63, Riformatio rub. 130, bk. 2, Statuti Florentini de Mulierum Successione ab in testato.

34. On these practices, see Tamassia, *La famiglia italiana,* 325.

35. Not. postcos. 170, 34r, 1590.iii.7, "In omnibus . . . suam heredem universalem instituit . . . dominam Virginam . . . eius uxorem, cum hac tamen conditione . . . , quod teneatur ipsa domina Virginia per unum annum post hobitum dicti testatoris vitam vidualem et honestam servare."

36. Not. postcos. 170, 34v, 1590.iii.10.

37. In 1501–50, ten of twenty-seven cases; 1551–75, nine of twenty-nine; 1576–1600, nine of twenty-seven. For 1601–50, twelve of thirty-seven. In the second half of the Seicento, it was nineteen of thirty-three cases, which constitutes a significant increase over the percentages of the Cinquecento; $p = .5758$; $\pi = .4526$; $n = 118$; $z = 2.69$. Demographic factors may have conditioned these increases in the proportion of wives as universal heirs, particularly in consequence of the crisis of the seventeenth century. For the aristocracy in Siena, see Cohn and Di Simplicio "Alcuni aspetti," 313–30. From the wills, it is possible to calculate the percentages of those men who left surviving wives but no sons to inherit the patrimony. These figures do not, however, correlate with changes in the percentages of widows as universal heirs. In 1401–1500, 43.5 percent of husbands left no surviving sons (wives were universal heirs in 12 percent of the relevant cases): in 1501–50 the percentage of surviving sons increased to 54.3 percent, along with the increases cited above in wives as universal heirs. During 1551–75, the proportion of husbands

without sons to survive them fell to 34.5 percent but with no corresponding rise in wives as universal heirs; then in the last quarter of the Cinquecento, most likely as a consequence of the war, husbands without sons to succeed them rose to its highest point, 73.1 percent, but again without any correspondence for wives as heirs. The percentage of husbands without surviving sons declined slightly during the first half of the Seicento to 67.6 percent; then in the second half of the century, the rate returned to its late Renaissance level of 45.5 percent at the very time when the percentage of wives as the universal heirs to their husbands' estates almost doubled. Another demographic factor that might have conditioned these changes could have been the variance in the ages at marriage, particularly for women. According to Hajnal, "European Marriage Patterns," 101–43, the ages at marriage for women across Western Europe began to rise during the Seicento. It might be argued that women received more favorable settlements from their husbands because they had become their husbands' equals in terms of age. Unfortunately, statistics on ages of men and women at marriage are not yet available for Siena. Herlihy and Klapisch-Zuber, *Les Toscans,* show that in Florence by the end of the fifteenth century the ages at marriage for women had begun to drift upward—that is, during the very period when property conditions for women in Siena were worsening.

38. Customarily, wives were to grant their husbands only a third of their dowries, if no children survived from the marriage. Zdekauer, *Il constituto del Comune di Siena,* vol. 2, rub. 33, 214.

39. Not. postcos. 1762, 41, 75r–76r, 1642.vi.4.

40. Ibid. 1051, 52, 65v–66r, 1611.x.24, "E perchè fra di loro è stato sempre, et è reciproco amore, e benevolenza, et in oltre haver da lei ricevuto buona e fedel servitù, e governo nelli suoi bisogni di malattie, et altre infinite amorevolezze, e buona compagnia fattali." In addition, see the will of the saddle maker, ibid. 184, 180, 23r–25v, 1595.vi.21.

41. Ibid. 2479, 1, 2r–3r, 1663.x.9.

42. Ibid.: "In tutti . . . suoi heredi universali institutui . . . Francesco e Maria Anna suoi e di detta donna Maddalena figli, volendo anco che la medissima sia coherede delli medessima di dover tenere, e stare con detti suoi figli fino a' che essa viverà o viveranno respettivamente et educarli nel Santo timore di dio, e tutto perchè confida nella sua bontà, et integrità, e lassa la medissima donna e madonna e non solo usufruttaria, ma' volse ancora, che in caso di necessità per souvenire detti suoi figli, o' altra, possi venderle, o' impegnare di casa quello che gli piacerà, senza che da nessuno gli possi esser tenuto conto di quello, che essa facesse, che intende, e vuole fino che essa viverà che detti figli stieno appresso la medesima e sia padrona assoluta di fare quel tanto che gli piacerà essendo certo che essa terrà conto di detti suoi figli come ha' fatto per il passato però glieli raccomanda per l'Amor di Dio, e quando sarà in età nubile detta Maria Anna sua figliola a' maritarla secondo le sue forse comporteranno."

43. Ibid. 2730, 95, 1678.viii.26.

44. Ibid. 115, 56r–59r, 1680.iv.4.

45. See Klapisch-Zuber, "Cruel Mother"; Calvi, *Il contratto morale*, 47–49.

46. Ibid. 3124, 3.

47. Cooper, "Patterns of Inheritance," 192–327, describes the inheritance only for the "great landowners" and does not concentrate on the possible transformations in these patterns over the long period of his study.

48. Not. postcos. 1164, 27, 31r–32r, 1612.ix.13: "In tutti . . . esser volse suoi heredi universali l'infrascritti suoi figliuoli, tanto masti, quanto femine, per equal portione, cioè Filippo. Ferdinando. Petro. Portia. Verginia. Livia. Caterina. et Aurelia: con espressa proibitione e protestatione, ch'in tale sua heredità, al detto Signor Bernardo suo Consorte, e lor Padre non s'acquisti ragione alcuna d'usofrutto, o' d'altro, che per ragione . . . ch'i suoi beni liberamente pienamente et immediatamente tanto per ragione di proprietà e quanto d'usofrutto, e di possesso appartenghino ad essi suoi figliuoli, di maniera che ne anco detto lor Padre n'habbia l'amministratione: e perciò dispose, e volse che l'attioni a lei competenti come sopra sieno a benefitio de medessimi esercitate et intenate dalla sopradetta Signora Margarita sua Madre, o da qualunque pure constituito da lei, facendola esecutrice della presente sua ultima voluntà, di maniera, che l'effetto sia, che i detti suoi figliuoli ne sentino l'utile, e commodo, et a lei appartenga il peso, e l'autorità di fare tutte le riscossioni, e mettere quanto prima insieme, et al netto tutte le sue facultà, acciò che quanto prima li detti suoi figliuoli possino a goderle e specialmente le femmine, che n'hanno maggior necessità; rendendosi sicura, che il detto suo Consorte sia per approvare questa sua dispositione e commendarla, conoscendo non esser fatta per far'a lui alcun torto, ma benefitio alla Fameglia, così richiendolo lo stato disagioso di lui." Similar concern for the well-being of the family, meaning the immediate future of the testator's children as opposed to the lineage, is expressed in the will of the hatmaker Julius f.q. Quirichi of Siena, ASS, Not. antecos., 2265, 8v–9v, 1581.v.16.

49. Not. postcos., 114, 8v–10v, 1662.viii.25.

50. Ibid. 3110, 150, 7v–9r, 1690.iii.10, "Tutte le figlie femmine legitime e naturali, tanto nate quanto che avvienisse nascere della detta Chiara Papari . . . e ciascuna di esse figlie equalmente . . . esclusi sempre et in qualsi voglia caso e tempo per maggior cautela, . . . li figli maschi mentre però vi siano figlie femmine."

51. See, for instance, Borromeo, *Ammaestramenti*, 25, "Da loro avete la carne ed il sangue per cui siete loro parenti; questo li spinge, questo cercano e di qua proviene tutto il danno. Ma bisogna staccarsene, bisogna licenziarli. . . . Con questo divina risposta, dilettissime, dovete dar bando ai parenti, troncare le visite, chiudere i parlatorii, e allontanare da voi tutti questi impedimenti."

52. At the end of the sixteenth century, women were optimal targets for ecclesiatic designs and opportunities. Because of the lineage strategies of the Cinquecento, dowries, especially those of noble families, may have inflated more than any other commodity in early modern European economies. See Cooper, "Patterns of Inheritance"; Cohn and Di Simplicio, "Alcuni aspetti." This meant that women on their deathbeds often were left in control of patrimonies far grander than those of their mothers and grandmothers.

53. See Lazzareschi, "Una mistica senese," 22:419–33 and 23:3–46.

54. Di Simplicio, *Peccato penitenza*, 242–311, shows through a detailed examination of ecclesiastical court records that wife rape and wife beating persisted through the early modern period.

55. Nardi, "Aspetti della vita dei religiosi," 219, argues that "manifestations of (sexual) violence tolerated in previous periods became entirely unacceptable" under the tighter and more severe scrutiny of ecclesiastical authority by the early Seicento.

56. ASS, Not. postcos. 2742, 4, 1580.viii.30, "Et per la medissima ragione et legato lassò a Laura sua figlia et moglie di Pace Coiaio l'usufrutto d'una sua bottiguccia nel T. di Camollia presso alla fonte d'ovile sotto casa Paliti fincella . . . si possa aitare et sovvenire a suoi bisogni, atteso ch'essa è povara et abbandonata dal marito et non ha donde possa vivere se no con le sue fatighe."

57. ASS, Not. postcos. 532, 20v–21v, 1602.iv.27.

58. Ibid. 1568, 48, 73v–76r, 1642.vi.27, "Al quale disse havere molti obligati per la fadighe durante, e spese fatte nell' occasioni delle sue adversità passate, e nominatamente nell' occasione delle liti, e per recuperare le sue doti in fiorenza e fino che le recuperò, e così per lo spatio di cinque anni, e li vantaggi ha fatto le spese à essa, e suoi fighioli all'hora piccoli del proprio in numero di quattro figli e poi sempre trattatela bene."

5. Nuns and Dowry Funds

A version of this chapter was presented at a conference on nuns in early modern Europe organized by Alice Kelikian and Olwen Hufton at the European University, Fiesole, Italy.

1. Cohn, *Death and Property,* chap. 10; and chap. 4 in this volume.

2. For a recent book on several of these new institutions, see S. Cohen, *Evolution of Women's Asylums.*

3. These wills are filled with long, monotonous lists of paltry sums to numerous, individually itemized, pious beneficiaries, which in one instance—the 1337 testament of Count Donoratico, ruler of Pisa—enumerated as many as 148 separate religious institutions and pious causes. ASPi, Osp. di S. Chiara 2071, 23r–25v, 1285.5.5; Cohn, *Cult of Remembrance,* 112–14.

4. See Cohn, *Cult of Remembrance,* chaps. 5, 6, 7.

5. Ibid., chaps. 4, 5.

6. For the fifteenth century, Carmichael, *Plague and the Poor,* argues that the plague did behave with a class bias, striking the poor neighborhoods of the city of Florence with disproportionate severity. By then the wealthier classes had made a general practice of what had been for the band of noblemen and ladies of Boccaccio's *Decameron* a new experiment—escape to villas in the surrounding hills during the summer months of pestilence. More recently, Livi-Bacci, *Population and Nutrition,* argues vigorously that there was no relationship between poverty or nutrition and susceptibility to the plague.

7. See G. Casagrande, "Forme di vita religiosa femminile," 156.

8. Testators and their notaries estimated the values of landed properties—the most valuable legacies—less often than other legacies. Because testators tended to liquidate their properties less frequently after the second strike of pestilence than before, calculations of the total values of legacies may understate the values of bequests for the late Trecento and early Quattrocento in comparison with the pre-Black Death periods. These figures, however, should not introduce any bias in regard to comparisons of different types of bequests, such as between nunneries and dowry funds.

9. The median bequest for nuns in this period was 0.93 florins.

10. ASPr, Not. bast. 39, 30r–31v, 1348.vi.21.

11. The median bequest for nuns at Perugia in 1348 was a mere 1.6 florins, half the median value of all Perugian pious legacies for the same period.

12. See Cohn, *Cult of Remembrance*, 74.

13. For Milan, see Sebastiani, "Monasteri femminili milanesi," 6: "Per quello che riguarda la città non mi sembra che per lo Stato di Milano si possa ritrovare quel fenomeno di aumento del numero di monasteri e di effettive presenze di monache segnalato da Trexler per Firenze." For Bologna, see Zarri, "I monasteri femminili a Bologna." Zarri, "I monasteri femminili benedettini," 338. "Nel corso del Trecento, attraverso un complesso intreccio di soppressioni e unioni, i monasteri benedettini si riducono di 8 unità . . . nel quattrocento si ha un'ulteriore contrazione delle istituzioni benedettine che contano ora soltanto sei communità . . . Certo la decadenza dei monasteri nel Trecento non è fenomeno che riguardi solo l'ordine benedettino." For Borgo San Sepolcro, see Banker, *Death in the Community*, 15, 26–31. In addition to a general papal attempt to move women from houses of spontaneous devotions to recognized monasteries in the second half of the thirteenth century, "a wave of reformed Benedictinism" passed through central Italy in the late thirteenth century, "transforming nunneries in Borgo San Sepolcro." Banker describes the plethora of nunneries in Borgo at the beginning of the fourteenth century and the disappearance of groups such as the "carcerate" later in the century.

14. Zarri, "I monasteri femminili a Bologna."

15. While Trexler considered the conclusions of this pathbreaking article as "entirely provisional," scholars continue to accept his conclusions on the rapid growth of nuns and nunneries from the early fourteenth century through the sixteenth century without question or modification; see Bizzocchi, *Chiesa e potere*, 31; Lowe, "Female Strategies for Success," 212; Ross, "Middle-Class Child," 205–6; Chabot, "La reconnaissance du travail," 570: "Dans les stratégies familiales, le couvent a toujours eu pour fonction d'absorber une partie des excédents féminins exlus du marché matrimonial. Au cours du xve siècle, on commence cependant à assister à un phénomène bien connu qui ne fait que s'amplifier pour aboutir à la veille du Concile de Trente à la saturation presque totale des monastères féminins."

Although failing to cite Trexler, Gregory, "Daughters, Dowries, and the Family," 236, assumes the same: because of the high price of dowries in the fifteenth century "the convent . . . was thus an essential component of patrician society." Finally, Brown, "Monache a Firenze," 122, repeats the same logic found above but shows that at the time of the first *catasto* of religious institutions (1428) the number of nuns in Florence's largest convent, San Jacopo Ripoli, remained depressed (120) and that the period of "maximum expansion" for the convent of Le Murate was not until the end of the sixteenth century.

16. From the vast resources of the *monte delle doti* archives, Molho, *Marriage Alliance*, 218, 300–304; and Molho, "*Tamquam vere mortua*," challenges Trexler's claims for the late fifteenth century. Molho's analysis shows that neither dowry prices nor the enrollment of nuns increased markedly within the Florentine elites until the last years of the fifteenth century. Indeed, from the 1430s through the 1470s the percentage of girls whose fathers made investments in the *monte delle doti* and who entered nunneries remained at a low level (1.81%), and the sharp increases in enrollments did not begin until the 1530s. See also Villani, *Nuova Cronica*, vol. 2, bk. 11 cap. 94; Trexler, "Le célibat," table 6. On the difficulties of calculating the numbers of religious women, especially those from the third orders, in the *catasto* reocrds of 1429, see Herlihy and Klapisch-Zuber, *Les Toscans*, 152–59. Also, see their modification of Trexler's numbers, 155 and 157. They find that slightly more than half the monastic establishments in 1429 were male houses.

17. Power, *English Medieval Nunneries;* Trexler, "Le célibat," 1346–47. Schen, "Charity in London," 37–38, 51, confirms Power's conclusions based on testamentary bequests on the eve of the Reformation.

18. Florence's dowry market was unique or nearly unique in one regard. It was the only city, with the possible exception of Genoa, to establish a *monte delle doti,* a funded debt based on dowry investments made soon after a daughter's birth. See Herlihy, "Deaths, Marriages, Births." Curiously, Molho, *Marriage Alliance*, does not mention the Genoese fund. But it is not clear whether dowry prices as a result rose more sharply in Florence than elsewhere in Italy. Indeed, Molho shows that dowry prices among the elites of Florence remained relatively stable until the last decades of the fifteenth and the early years of the sixteenth centuries, when wealth and social status in Florence, similar to Siena, began to polarize (chap. 7, esp., 300–304). Molho's statistics contradict both the belief of contemporaries such as Antonio Strozzi (who commented in 1450 that "in truth there are few good prospects here, and big dowries are becoming the custom, the reason being this convenience of the dowry fund") and the views that historians derived from them (see Gregory, "Daughters, Dowries, and the Family," 218–19).

19. According to Chojnacki, "Dowries and Kinsmen," 571–72, it was between 650 and 3,000 ducats. See also Chojnacki, "Marriage Legislation." Chojnacki is uncertain whether these nominal increases represent increases in real terms and argues that a comparative price series would be impossible to assemble for Renaissance Venice. Yet he is convinced that dowries did increase and also that they comprised an increasing portion of Venetian patrimonies, giving increasing power to wives and daughters in patrician households—a consistent theme through Chojnacki's essays; see, for instance, Chojnacki, "Power of Love," 139.

20. Cohn and Di Simplicio, "Alcuni aspetti."

21. Catoni, "Interni di conventi." I know of no work that attempts to trace the demographics of nuns and nunneries for late medieval and early modern Siena.

22. See Banker, *Death in the Community,* chap. 3; Henderson, *Piety and Charity,* 109ff.

23. G. Casagrande, "Il fenomeno della reclusione," 477.

24. Sensi, "Incarcerate," 112.

25. ASF, Dipl., Cistercensi 18.ii.1278; *Testi fiorentini,* 235–43.

26. Banker, *Death in the Community,* 15, 30–31; C. Davis, "Ubertino da Casale"; Benvenuti Papi, "Le forme comunitarie," 445ff; Rusconi, "Discorso conclusivo." For early initiatives by a bishop to regulate the expansion of "domine, sorores, mulieres religiose, encarcerate, recluse e così via" on the local level, see G. Casagrande, "Forme di vita religiosa femminile," 156–57.

27. For Milan, see Sebastiani, "Monasteri femminili milanesi." For Bologna, see Zarri, "I monasteri femminili benedettini," 336–37: "Il XIII secolo favorisce il sorgere in Bologna di un grande numero di nuove istituzioni religiose femminili. . . . I romitori femminili, del resto, non ebbero mai lunga durata e la loro esistenza fu spesso contrastata sia per motivi di sicurezza sia per motivi disciplinari." For Padua, see Rigon, "I laici nella chiesa." For Borgo San Sepolcro, see Banker, *Death in the Community,* 26–31. For Città di Castello, G. Casagrande, "Forme di vita religiosa," 156–57: "Il secolo XIII è un secolo anche di donne e di donne religiose nel caso specifico." For Rome, see Oliger, "Regula Reclusorum"; G. Casagrande, "Il fenomeno della reclusione," 489. For Perugia, see G. Casagrande, "Penitenti." For Pisa, Ronzani, "Penitenti." For Tuscany, Benvenuti Papi, "Le forme comunitarie," 446: "La 'rivoluzione' religiosa femminile del Dugento morente nel Trecento e riattivata sia pure relativamente nella regolarizzazione osservante del Quattrocento." For Umbria, see G. Casagrande, "Il fenomeno della reclusione," 489ff; Sensi, "Incarcerate," and "La monacazione." For Lazio, see Brentano, "Il movimento religioso," and *New World in a Small Place,* 302ff.

28. Lowe, "Female Strategies for Success," 209–21.

29. Cohn, *Cult of Remembrance,* 81; Ronzani, "Penitenti," 741.

30. Cohn, *Cult of Remembrance,* 43–60.

31. The earliest dowry funds were of the same general character as the handouts to the "poor of Christ." Instead of comprising entire dowries for a select number of nubile girls, bequests such as that of Severinus f.q. Jacobi, citizen of Florence (ASF, Dipl. S. Croce 1279.iv.5), gave small dowry portions to numerous girls without specifying the mechanisms for selection. His dowry fund "pro mulieribus pauperibus maritandis" specified that "either 40 soldi or 60 soldi" be given until 100 lire had been spent, thus dowering between thirty-three and fifty girls. In Florentine testaments of the late fourteenth and early fifteenth centuries, 100 lire would have been earmarked to dower no more than four girls.

32. In the year of the Black Death, these bequests reached 174 florins per dowry foundation. But in this critical year, only ten dowry funds listed the sums to be granted, and their value was inflated greatly by a single bequest—that of the Are-

tine aristocratic ruler Tarlatus of the Tarlati family, whose 4,000-lire fund to dower forty virgins selected from the city of Arezzo and small villages through the Casentino was the largest dowry fund and the second largest pious bequest, for any cause, found in these samples. Arch. dei Laici, reg. 726, 48v–50v, 1348.ix.27. The median dowry fund of that year was a more modest sum of 46.5 florins.

33. Cohn, *Cult of Remembrance*, 65–71.

34. As I make clear in *Death and Property*, and *Cult of Remembrance*, 39, 67–71, this change in mentality was not accompanied by a fall in the number or value of bequests to the mendicant orders. Instead, as institutional histories have shown for a long time, the orders themselves were changing, softening their views on issues such as poverty as their foundations became more bureaucratic and wealthy.

35. This evidence comes from the Florentine *provvisioni* or the decrees promulgated by Florence's highest council, the Tre Maggiori. The earliest tax incentives to attract foreign laborers into the Florentine *contado* or into its larger *districtus* were not passed immediately after the demographic catastrophe of 1348; they appeared only after the second strike of plague, in 1364 (ASF, Provv. reg. 52, 34v), and then recurred with increasing regularity only in the last two decades of the Trecento, when Florentine lawmakers added to the incentives granted to foreign rural laborers similar tax breaks and moratoria on debts for Florentine peasants who had earlier evaded taxation by migrating across the border.

36. See my comparisons between Saint Catherine of Siena and San Bernardino in Cohn, *Death and Property*, chap. 5.

37. Molho, *Marriage Alliance*, 28.

38. On the *monte delle doti,* see Molho and Kirshner, "Dowry Fund"; Molho, *Marriage Alliance,* esp. chap. 2. On *tamquam vere mortua,* see Molho, *Marriage Alliance*, 30, 35; Molho, "*Tamquam vere mortua.*"

39. For a summary of the early fourteenth-century famines and its vast bibliography, see Livi-Bacci, *Population and Nutrition.*

40. This ratio was calculated by comparing the total value of itemized gifts, both pious and nonpious, for men and women. These figures, of course, do not include the residuary properties left to the "universal heirs," which almost invariably were left without estimated values.

41. Schen, "Charity in London," 40, finds that men and women in Reformation London, 1500–1620, gave to pious causes in equal amounts. Given the large discrepancies in wealth by sex, women must have bequeathed far greater proportions of their wealth than men to the church and charity (63, 66).

42. Martines, "Way of Looking at Women," 24.

43. Davis and Farge, "Horizons of Everyday Life," 13.

44. For such an expectation, see Riemer, "Women in the Medieval City," and "Women, Dowries, and Capital." On the other hand, Schen, "Charity in London," shows that women made more bequests to women than to men only after 1580. Both Hughes, "Struttura familiare," and Chojnacki, "Kinship Ties," show that women were more free than men to dispose of their wealth to blood relatives and affines, but this did not necessarily mean that women consistently gave more

to women than to men. Chojnacki further argues, however, that increasingly from the fourteenth through the fifteenth centuries, as dowries rose in Venice, the legacies of patrician women comprised larger portions of daughters' and other kin's dowries.

45. Cohn, *Death and Property in Siena*, 198–202; Henderson, *Piety and Charity*, 33–47.

46. The same pattern appears with the gender differences in the sponsoring of religious confraternities.

47. Of these women, three were from the city of Pisa, one was from Arezzo, and one was from Florence.

48. ASF, Not. antecos. 205, 1363.vi.21.

49. Notaries rarely specified professions in these documents, especially before the Black Death of 1348, and comparing proportions of those bearing family names is risky, since naming practices differed over time and place. As a consequence, I divide the testators into two groups based on medium wealth, calculated from the total of all monetized pious and nonpious bequests for any given period.

50. Before 1348, testators in the bottom half of wealth (median = thirty-six florins) bequeathed 12.46 percent of their 3,418 legacies to nunneries and a scant 0.09 percent to dowry funds; the upper half bequeathed 18.30 percent of 7,191 legacies to nunneries and 0.45 percent to dowry funds (sample size = 1,084 testators). From 1348 to 1425, the bottom half (median = forty-six florins) bequeathed 6.99 percent of 3,546 legacies to nunneries and 1.33 percent to dowry funds, and the wealthier, 9.10 percent of 7,428 legacies to nunneries and 2.77 percent to dowry funds (sample size = 2,301 testators). In 1362–63, the bottom half (median = ninety-eight florins) bequeathed 4.70 percent of 553 legacies to nunneries and 1.08 percent to dowry funds; the wealthier, of 917 legacies, bequeathed 13.09 percent and 1.20 percent, respectively (sample size = 241 testators).

51. For such practices in Quattrocento Florence, see Lowe, "Female Strategies for Success," 219.

52. See "Canzone delle monache," cited by Ross, "Middle-Class Child," 206. For the sixteenth and seventeenth centuries, see Weaver, "Le Muse in Convento," 269–70. See also Gill's evocative "Open Monasteries."

53. Chojnacki, "Marriage Legislation," 164.

54. Catoni, "Interni di conventi," 171.

55. Gill, "Open Monasteries," 33–35; for a similar view, see Chabot, "La reconnaissance du travail," 570, who claims that the early fourteenth century was a period of success for Franciscan and Dominican third orders. In a later essay, "Women and the Production of Religious Literature," Gill does not draw such a stark divide in women's creativity between those belonging to third orders and those cloistered in traditional nunneries.

56. Benvenuti Papi, "Umiliana dei Cerchi," 117, suggests that these third orders were the repositories of the more radical spiritualist ideology. Thus, as a result, they may have preserved longer than the other mendicant orders a distrust of tes-

tamentary legacies. Diefendorf, "Family Culture, Renaissance Culture," 675, questions Klapisch-Zuber's charge that the dowry system robbed women of their inheritance. Diefendorf speculates that the dowry system delivered what the law promised—a separate but equal form of dispensation. The evidence from wills, however, suggests that this was not the case: on their deathbeds, women possessed less than half the value of property held by their brothers. Moreover, the bias in these records suggests that women probably possessed an even smaller proportion of wealth relative to men, since men gave relatively fewer bequests and tended to channel a greater proportion of their estates to their universal heirs (a sum that was rarely stated in monetary terms).

57. Zarri, *Le sante vive*, esp. chap. 1; Weaver, "Le Muse in Convento" and "Suor Maria Clemente Ruoti"; Lowe, "Female Strategies for Success."

58. J. Brown, "Monache a Firenze," 117–52; and Heißler, *Frauen*. See chap. 6, this volume, for a critical view of the relation of these stories to social realities.

59. Lowe, "Female Strategies for Success," 209. Also see Weaver, "Le Muse in Convento," 257–58.

60. See, in particular, chaps. 2, 3, 4.

61. See Benvenuti Papi, "Umiliana dei Cerchi," 87–117; Lansing, *Florentine Magnates*, chap. 6; and chap. 3 of these essays.

62. Lansing, *Florentine Magnates*, 132.

63. For a poignant statement of this prioritization, see Catherine of Siena's letter to Monna Giovanna in *I, Catherine*, 132–33. These attitudes revitalized a general clerical view of the superiority of the virginal state for women. Also see C. Casagrande, "Protected Woman," 81: "The virginal state is the highest and safest step, the married state the lowest and most dangerous. Widowhood is halfway, dragged downward by the gravity of past contamination . . . a virgin's chastity was worth more than double a widow's and more than triple a wife's."

64. C. Casagrande, "Protected Woman," 103.

65. According to Binion, "Fiction as Social Fantasy," a general disgust with the family, at least in literature, swept across Europe only in the late nineteenth century.

66. See Cohn, *Cult of Remembrance*, 286–88; Cohn, "Burckhardt Revisited from Social History."

67. Kirshner, "Materials for a Gilded Cage"; Cohn, *Cult of Remembrance*, 195–201; and chap. 3, this volume.

68. On the broad changes from the more conjugally oriented family of the early Middle Ages to one based on the male lineage, see Hughes's seminal essay, "From Brideprice to Dowry."

69. Such was the case of the Florentine wool carder who in 1368 channeled his possessions down his male line and left candle holders to the Florentine hospital of Santa Maria Nuova to advertise his newly invented family coat of arms, even though he did not even yet possess a family name; ASF, Dipl., S. M. Nuova, 1368.viii.24.

70. Cohn, *Death and Property*, 151–55, 205; Klapisch-Zuber, "Name 'Remade.'"

71. For Genoa, Hughes, "Urban Growth," argues that the trends in women's

property rights, family structure, and ideology were not the same for artisans and patricians and that the gap widened in the attitudes and structures of these two classes during the late Middle Ages and the Renaissance. See chap. 1, this volume.

72. See chaps. 1 and 3, this volume; Klapisch-Zuber, "La femme et le lignage," and "Griselda Complex"; Kirshner, "Materials for a Gilded Cage"; Molho, *Marriage Alliance*.

6. Sex and Violence on the Periphery

1. On the early appellate court, see Davidsohn, *Storia di Firenze*, 163–67. On the history and jurisdiction of the vicariates, see Pinto, "Controllo politico"; Guidi, *Il Governo*, 2:187–89, 3:193–213. The earliest vicariate was the Valdinievole founded in 1340; later, that of San Miniato (or the Valdarno inferiore), founded in 1370. The earliest criminal cases go back to 1346; See ASF, Giudice 89. Vicariates such as the Mugello, the Chianti, and the Valdelsa, were not established until 1415, but *fasciolae* of criminal acts from their *podestà* are bound together in the criminal acts from the "*extrinseci*" series of these Giudice records as far back as 1407 and 1403, respectively.

2. Wickham, *Mountains*, chap. 12.

3. Salviati, *Cronica*.

4. In at least two instances from the early fifteenth century, personal reflections of *vicarii* survive in *ricordanze*. See Salviati, *Cronica;* Pitti, *Ricordi;* Zorzi, "Giusdicenti e operatori." Moreover, as I argue below, the stories of Sacchetti hinge on his experiences as *podestà* and *vicarius* in places such as the Valdarno inferiore.

5. For salaries, see Zorzi, "Giusdicenti e operatori," 529–30. Also see Salviati, *Cronica;* Zorzi, "I fiorentini e gli uffici pubblici." In 1429 the Florentine government created a new tribunal, the *conservatori delle leggi,* in an attempt to curb the excesses of Florentine officials. Also, see Sacchetti, *Trecentonovelle*, story 77, 149–51: "Due hanno una quisitione dinánzi a certi officiali, el'uno ha dato all'un di loro un bue e l'altro gli ha dato una vacca; e l'uno e l'altro s'ha perduta la spesa."

6. In rare instances, the cases contained in these volumes extended to the outer reaches of the Florentine suburban ring (that is, within the *pieve* of San Giovanni)—places such as San Martino a Campi to the east (ASF, Giudice 101, 2, 93v, 1422.vii.14) and San Piero a Ponte a Ema in Bagno a Ripoli just south of the city of Florence (ASF, Giudice 101, 2, 68r, 1422.vii.4).

7. The volume for 1426–27 has been miscataloged as part of the *intrinseci* series (76).

8. I also collected, in addition to sex crimes, blasphemy and the destruction of sacred images. These form a small portion of the acts and do not come into discussion in this chapter. Along with gambling games, blasphemy fell under the jurisdiction of a new court, the *conservatori delle leggi* in 1429; see Zorzi, *L'amministrazione*, 62. Criminal cases labeled as "rebellion" or "conspiracy" against the "Magnificent Commune of Florence" comprise all but 10 percent of the cases (eight of seventy-seven) I selected as political cases. The others consist principally of peasant attacks on officers of the Florentine state.

9. See, for instance, Muir, "Introduction: Observing Trifles"; Revel, "Microanalisi." Some historians assume that the two approaches are mutually exclusive; see Grendi, "Premessa"; and Ginzburg, "Microstoria."

10. See Brucker's magistral *Civic World;* and his *Society of Renaissance Florence.*

11. Walter, "Infanticidio a Ponte Bocci."

12. These cases can be found in Mazzi's lengthy article on Florentine sex crimes in 1427, "Cronache di periferia," and in Mazzi, *Prostitute e lenoni.* For a similar approach to criminal records and the "exemplification" of their microhistories, see Cohen and Cohen, *Words and Deeds;* and E. Cohen, "Camilla the Go-Between."

13. ASF, Giudice 98, 29r–31v, 1406.iii.13.

14. Ibid., 100, 1:355r, 1390.vi.28.

15. When two samples of criminal cases from the Florentine *contado,* found in the *podestà* records, are added (1400–1402, 288 cases, and 1410–15, 277 cases), the ratio increases to five male babies in eight cases of infanticide. See ASF, AP 4261, 1r–v, 1411.i.27.

16. A woman from Senni in the *podesteria* of Scarperia abandoned her male baby in a ditch within her lover's parish, Santa Maria a Fagna. The baby was found, revived, taken to the woman, and she confessed to the abandonment. She was fined sixty lire; ASF, Giudice 101, 1:72r–v, 1419.vii.31. In the one case that I found of infanticide in two samples taken from the *podestà* records (565 cases from the Florentine *contado* and district), the mother of the dead child was sentenced to be buried alive, a condemnation otherwise reserved for the commune of Florence's most dreaded rebels.

17. For a contemporary story of a women made pregnant during an illicit affair—in this case, with her brother-in-law—in which the woman successfully disguised her pregnancy as illness, see Sercambi, *Novelle,* vol. 1, story 60, "De dishonesto adulterio et bono consilio," 265–72.

18. The bed was located in a part of the house called the "common place" (*vulgariter dicto "eluogho comune"*).

19. ASF, Giudice 102, 2:201v–202r, 1433.vii.9. This must have been a form of *pitture infamanti* but unlike the accustomed ones painted for public viewing on the walls of the Bargello. See Edgerton, *Pictures and Punishment.*

20. Ibid. 99, 3:144v–45r, 1415.xii.2.

21. Ibid., (miscatalogued as *intrinseci*) 76, 282r–3v, 1426.iii.3.

22. For contemporary language for female genitalia as mouth and throat, see Sacchetti, *Trecentonovelle,* story 208, 489–92, where he makes a pun about the mouth of the crab and Mauro pescatore da Civitanuova's wife's "bocca senza denti." Sercambi, *Novelle,* 1:310–12, uses the same expression.

23. ASF, Giudice 99, 2:48v–49r, 1415.v.ult.

24. According to Du Cauge, *Glossarium,* 5:180, *pelles* were the hides of wild animals.

25. His sister, however, was not absolved; she was fined a hundred lire and sentenced to three years in the prison of San Miniato.

26. On the events of the Carnival of 1511 and its obsessions with animal sym-

bolism, see Muir, *Mad Blood Stirring,* chap. 5; for Muir's contrast between the Friulan vendetta and Renaissance civility, see 252–62, 282.

27. Burckhardt, *Civilization of the Renaissance.*

28. Salviati, *Cronica,* 214, 284. In his memoirs on his experience as captain of Pistoia in 1406, Salviati recollects: "Fecivi parecchie esecuzioni personali; ciò fu impiccare uno, tagliare il piè a un altro, et un altro condannai a stare in prigione x. anni per manigoldo di Pistoia, et un altro feci scopare. Altro caso non v'avvenne nel mio tempo, che sia degno di memoria" (261).

29. For a contemporary story that jokes about the genitals as the direct cause of libidinous evil, see Sacchetti, *Trecentonovelle,* story 116: "Prete Juccio della Marca è accusato allo Inquisitore per le sue cose lascive," 258–59.

30. ASF, Giudice 99, 105r–6v, 1413.vi.28. In addition, Muccino was fined the hefty sum of 500 lire. On 13 August, the court, however, canceled this fine and possibly the mutilations (although the marginal note does not make this clear), since Muccino had paid the treasury 200 lire and had paid the sums to provide Angela with food and clothing (21 lire and 5 soldi) for ten years, according to the deliberations made in her behalf by the *abate* and priors of Anghiari. In addition, he provided a 200-lire dowry for her future husband, Johanni Vici Maxini, from the same village, whom she married less than a month before (17 July). For whippings as a commonplace in penalties of sexual misconduct, see Boccaccio, *Decameron,* day 5, story 7.

31. Curiously, the notary records the boy's age as 100, but through the court cases his age can be reconstructed.

32. See for instance the case involving the "publicum et famosum sodomitum hominem Checchum Johannis Bocci de florentie habitum pisis," who was accused of multiple homosexual assaults; ASF, Giudice 101, pt. 2, 349r–52r.

33. See Molho, *Marriage Alliance,* 244–50, for reasons for misalliances among the Florentine elite.

34. Although denounced by the vicariate's inquest, it must have been her parents who initiated the criminal proceedings.

35. ASF, Giudice 99, 3:104r–5v, 1415.xi.9.

36. For 1427, I found 14 sex crimes of 590 criminal cases, or 2.27 percent; for the entire Giudice volume (76, which covers most of 1426, 1427 and one month of 1428), there are 30 sex cases of 1,034 cases, or 2.9 percent.

37. In 1624, infanticide was made a "new offense" in England and thereafter was investigated and prosecuted with new levels of surveillance. See Sharpe, *Crime in Early Modern England,* 60. In my sample of 2,599 cases from the courts of Florence, I did not record a single case of infanticide; see Cohn, *Laboring Classes,* apps. H.1–H.3. For the rarity of infanticide cases in general, see Opitz, "Life in the Late Middle Ages." Hanawalt, "Female Felon," 260, believes that the low number of infanticide cases reflects social realties, but the seventeenth-century change in English law, the enforcement of this law, and the immediate soaring of cases of infanticide speaks against her assumption.

38. See Mazzi, "Cronache di periferia," 611; Mazzi, *Prostitute e lenoni,* 88: "Se

non si possono apprezzare quantitativamente i fenomeni, si può però ugualmente procedere a una lettera che esemplifichi casi, motivi, e circostanze"; Grendi, "Premessa"; Pastore, *Crimine e giustizia,* and my review of it, where I assert that terms like "thick description" mask a return to the old anecdotal social histories of the late nineteenth century. Moreover, Lenman, Parker, and Gatrell maintain that criminal statistics have no value before late Victorian and Edwardian police surveillance and record keeping at the end of the nineteenth century, but these scholars do not propose that historians of the premodern past return to explications of individual case studies. See Lenman and Parker, introduction to "State, the Community"; and Gatrell, "Decline of Theft."

While Ruggiero, *Boundaries of Eros,* does not shun the counting of criminal cases and constructs a rank ordering of penalties, he lends more credence to "the language of crime," often running the risk of investing formulaic legal phrases with a historical specificity they do not possess. Such is his interpretation of the formulaic motive for evil, "spiritu diabolico," which he ascribes as relating specifically to sex crimes in Venice during the fourteenth century (23). Instead, the term was widely used throughout medieval and early modern court cases across Europe and was used for various crimes, not only sexual offenses. For a cautious but more reasoned view of the role and possibilities of quantitative treatment of early modern criminal statistics, see Sharpe's excellent survey, *Crime in Early Modern England.*

See also Grendi, "Micro-analisi, and criticisms of it"; Revel, "Microanalisi"; Sbriccoli, "Fonti giudiziarie," esp. 495; and Grendi's response, "Sulla 'storia criminale,'" which, in my reading, begs the question: how does one judge what is and is not "exemplary"? What is the "normale"? And how does one discover it? Or what cases are the real exceptions as opposed to the "eccezionale normale"?

39. See Sharpe, *Crime in Early Modern England,* 3: "This extensive documentation makes it possible to treat crime as something more than an aspect of an undemanding and subsidiary area of history, capable of and deserving only anecdotal treatment."

40. See Trexler, "Infanticide in Florence."

41. Trexler, "Foundlings of Florence"; Hunecke, "Intensità e fluttuazioni"; Sandri, "Modalità dell'abbandono," and *L'ospedale di S. Maria della Scala;* Takahashi, "I bambini abbandonati," and "I bambini e i genitori."

42. Unfortunately, these cases rarely trace the routes by which these cases came to trial. None were denounced by individuals but instead were brought to trial by the vicariate's inquisition. Only scattered remains of inquisitions survive for the vicariate courts (ASF, Giudice 96). For the ways criminal cases came to trial, see Dean, "Criminal Justice," 17ff.

43. This pattern of heavy penalties for infanticide cases and low numbers of indictments was common throughout late medieval and early modern Europe.

44. For a recent work siding with the value of literary impressions over that of statistics on wages, see Hatcher, "England in the Aftermath of the Black Death." For late medieval Florence, see Molho, *Marriage Alliance,* where every statistical

finding is coupled with supporting testimony from contemporary Florentines; or at a further extreme, see Mazzi, *Prostitute e lenoni,* 134, and Heißler, *Frauen der italienischen Renaissance,* 85–86, who take stories such as that of Masetto da Lamporecchio as indicative of the "comfortable" lives of nuns and of their "actual" sexual behavior.

45. See Sercambi's adaptation of day 3, story 1, in *Novelle,* story 100, 236–40: "De Malitia Hominis: In Firenze era uno monastero di donne," and his own twist, in story 31, on the same theme of nuns' lust: "De libidine: Del monasterio dell'Olmo d'Arezzo e della badessa," 144–47. See also the remarks of Martines, *Italian Renaissance Sextet,* 159–60: "All the Italian city-states reported scandalous cases of convents which routinely violated their own rules governing claustration, and the religious houses of some nuns seemed little better than clandestine brothels."

46. On the juridical significance of this cry, see Davidsohn, *Storia di Firenze,* 5: 295–96; Manikowska, "Accorr'uomo." For contemporary stories that revolve around such cries, see Sacchetti, *Trecentonovelle,* story 53, 109–12, and story 102, 208–10.

47. ASF, Giudice 99, 71v, 1413.v.ult.

48. Ibid. 100, 2:126r–v, 1417.vii.1.

49. Ibid. 101, 23r–v, 8.vi.1419.

50. Ibid. 2:154r–55r, 1422.vii.13.

51. Ibid., 155r–v, sd.

52. Ibid., 155v–56r, sd. The court's insouciance regarding whether a sexual offense was committed by violence or consent seems to be a quirk of these peculiar offenses. The median fine for sexual offenses with consenting partners was half of that meted out to rapists, 50 lire versus 100 lire. The means, however, were about the same: 206 lire for consent, 202 lire for rape. The fines for consent were skewed by one case in which a Florentine man living in Pisa prostituted his wife, with her consent, on a number of occasions in 1418. He was fined 1,000 florins—the largest fine I found in the documents for any offense—and was imprisoned for two years; she was whipped, and one of her clients was fined 500 lire. See ibid., 2:412r–14v, 1417.xi.13. Yet those involved in consensual sex crimes were more likely to be sentenced to death than rapists: 24 percemt (18 cases), as opposed to 16 percent (36 cases). (By a chi-square test, this difference is not significant; Pearson chi-square at one degree of freedom = 2.50.) Moreover, consenting partners were fourteen times more likely to be given sentences involving mutilation, torture, or whipping than were rapists, and these differences are significant: 5.8 percent (11 of 74 cases) versus 0.89 percent (1 of 111 cases); Pearson chi-square = 6.11, which is significant at a confidence level of .013.

53. On the "wall" and the relations between cloistered nuns and the outlying community, see Weaver, "Convent Wall."

54. ASF, *Giudice* 101, 2:162v–63r, 1422.viii.17.

55. See, for instance, Brown, *Immodest Act.* Little has been written on the ecclesiastical courts in Renaissance Tuscany; but see Brucker, *Giovanni and Lusanna;* Stern, *Criminal Law System,* 40–43.

56. ASF, Giudice 100, 1:114r–v, 1416.v.30.

57. There are three stories if that of "Alibech, who becames a hermit" (day 3, story 10, 321–31) is counted.

58. On the interaction between nunneries and the outside world, see Lowe, "Female Strategies for Success" and for the post-Tridentine period, Weaver, "Convent Wall."

59. In some areas of central Italy, the penalty for raping a nun outweighed what society deemed just in the rape of other women (virgin girls, married women, and widows). In the late medieval statutes of Foligno, for instance, those who violated married women or recluses "dedicated to God" were fined five hundred lire, while the rape of widows and young virgins "from good families" brought penalties of three hundred lire. However, if a man raped a nun cloistered in one of the principal nunneries of the city, he was fined a thousand lire; if the fine was not paid in fifteen days, he was to be decapitated; Messini and Baldaccini, *Statuta communis Fulginei*, 142, 2nd part, rub. 43.

60. ASF, Giudice 98, 54r–55v, 1404.vii.12.

61. Ibid. 100, 2:83r–v, 1417.v.15.

62. Ibid., 102, 2:77v–78v, 1432.ii.20.

63. I do not know of a single Florentine story or even chronicle of the late Middle Ages or early Renaissance that features a priest as a revolutionary. Yet, in the political cases found in these documents, they appear as ringleaders or accomplices in at least seven cases of conspiracy and rebellion against the Florentine state. These cases may have been even more prevalent, since court notaries do not always distinguish whether a "Ser" was the village priest or a notary.

64. According to Stern, *Criminal Law System,* 42, based on the 1415 Statutes of Florence (bk. 3, rub. 43), "a cleric was automatically disqualified from clerical status by committing certain crimes, such as homicide, theft, rape, arson, or any other enormity." This does not, however, seem to have been the practice during the first thirty-five years of the fifteenth century, at least in the territory of Florence beyond the city.

65. ASF, Giudice 100, 1:100v–1r, 13.viii.1416. Perhaps, the priest was dead, and the notary wrote *quodam* when he meant *quondam* ("una cum quodam Ser Currado de pede montium presbitero et rectore ecclesie sancti laurentii de Montegusone").

66. For the web of patron-client relations that accounted for clerical appointments, favors, and protection throughout the Florentine territorial state of the fifteenth century, see Bizzocchi, *Chiesa e potere.*

67. These included Niccolò da Uzzano, Messer Bartolomeo Popoleschi, Bartolomeo Valori, and Gino Capponi.

68. Pitti, *Ricordi,* 442ff.

69. On tax fraud, see ASF, Giudice 98, 14v–45r, 1405.viii.29; 99, 199r–202r, 1414.xi.2; 250r–v, 1414.v.22; 76, 479–57r, 1427.ix.27.

70. Ibid., 127r–29r, 1406.viii.30. For a similar ruse in Boccaccio's *Decameron,* but involving a fooled prelate and a widow, see day 8, story 4; and Sercambi's

adaptation of the same story in *Novelle,* story 33. For a closer parallel in a later story, see Firenzuola, *I Ragionamenti,* day 1, story 4, 162–71, "Don Giovanni ama la Tonia."

Another case of a man holding a political office in the territory of Florence found guilty of sexual abuse concerned the notary and chancellor (*cancellarius*) of Terranuova in the Valdarno superiori, who raped his "beautiful" eight-year-old servant girl (*puella formosa*) in his stable while she was attending his mule, "destroying and ripping apart her vulva with a great effusion of blood." Although he denied the charges, he was found guilty and fined three hundred lire, which he paid; ibid. 76, 25v–6r, 1426.vii.23. More than judges or officers of the court, soldiers, as might be expected, were the ones more often charged with rape or attempted rape.

71. For such spiritually incestuous affairs between clerics and their baptismal relatives, see Boccaccio, *Decameron,* day 7, story 3.

72. ASF, Giudice 101, 1:54r–v, 1419.viii.16.

73. For such an incestuous affair in Boccaccio's *Decameron,* see day 7, story 3, 599–605, "Frate Rinaldo si giace colla comare"; Sacchetti, *Trecentonovelle,* story 111, 225–26.

74. In Sacchetti, *Trecentonovelle,* story 25, 49–50, "Messer Dolcibene per sentenzia del Capitano di Forlì castra con nuovo ordine uno prete, a poi vende li testicoli lire 24 di bolognesi," a priest is tried and castrated by the secular court; and in story 116, 234–35, "Prete Juccio della Marca è accusato allo Inquisitore per le sue cose lascive," before making his appeal, a priest receives the same sentence from the ecclesiastical tribunal.

75. ASF, Giudice 101, 2:68r–v, 1422.vi.20.

76. Ibid. 102, 1:256r–7r, 1430.iv.3.

77. *Letteratura italiana,* 2:1558–59. For Sacchetti's stories, which deal with rural rectors, *podestà,* and courtroom dilemmas, see Sacchetti, *Trecentonovelle,* stories 77, 109, and 141.

78. Le Roy Ladurie, *Montaillou;* see also the stories culled from the criminal tribunals of Venice by Ruggiero, *Binding Passions,* and "Abbot's Concubine."

79. Far fewer of Sacchetti's *novelle* revolved around sexual desire or marital infidelity than those of the *Decameron;* of ten such stories (25, 28, 84, 86, 116, 131, 156, 190, 206, 207), four turn on the libidinous ways of clerics (25, 28, 116, 207).

80. See Mazzi, "Incanti amorosi," 494; Molho, *Marriage Alliance,* 137–43.

81. Molho, *Marriage Alliance,* 139–40.

82. However, Boccaccio's vilification of the Corbaccio is less about her as a widow than about her as an unfaithful wife. See Boccaccio, *Il Corbaccio.*

83. Mazzi, "Incanti amorosi," 507. See also the more tempered comments of Martines, *Italian Renaissance Sextet,* 33: "We gather from the *novellieri* . . . that good-looking widows—presumably skilled in, but now denied, the enjoyments of sex—were particularly singled out and courted by men; but they were also the ones most spied upon, most vulnerable to rumor and gossip." For prescriptive literature of the late fourteenth and fifteenth centuries that continued to produce

such images of "the morally and socially dangerous" widow, see Zarri, *Le sante vive*, 32–37.

84. This preponderance of married women as the objects of, and participants in, sexual crime concurs *grosso modo* with Comba's findings that between 1350 and 1450, 44 percent of the women in sex crimes were married ("Appetitus libidinis coherceatur"); and with Dubuis's findings of 66 percent for the Alps of the Valle di Susa ("Comportamenti sessuali").

85. ASF, Giudice 102, 2:230r–v, 1433.x.5; ibid., intrinseci 76, 72v–73r, 1426.viii.ult.

86. See the case of the man (ironically) from Corneto in the maritime province of Gherardesca, the former *contado* of Pisa, who on more than one occasion ("propter gelosiam") beat his wife, dragged her by the hair, and cracked her skull, causing a great effusion of blood; ibid. 100, 2:271r–2r, 1417.xi.13. Also see Molho, *Marriage Alliance;* Sacchetti, *Trecentonovelle;* story 85: "Uno fiorentino toglie per moglie una vedova stata disonestissima di sua persona, e con poca fatica la gastiga sì, ch'ella diviene onesta," 172–74; and his story 86: "Oh quanti sono li dolorosi mariti che fanno cattive mogli," 174–78; Boccaccio, *Decameron,* day 9, story 9: "Due giovani domandan consiglio a Salamone," 831–37. Savio, *Statuti comunali di Villanova d'Asti,* 85, cap. 59, gave husbands the right to beat, "with restraint," inobedient wives and to whip ("atrociter") those guilty of adultery. Similar communal statutes can be found elsewhere in northern Italy. See also the case of the woman from Montetopoli who, with another married woman from Certaldo, schemed to poison her husband; ASF, Giudice 98, 79r–80r, 1404.ii.24: "Io non posso con questo mio marito perché spesso mi batte et dammi di male battitute et per certo io debo vedere modo di seperarmi da lui et conviene ch'io m'uccida o io uccida lui" (f. 79r.).

87. Ibid. 2:42v–3v, 1405.xii.17.

88. In nine of nineteen cases, the accused was charged with more than one affair. One such "publicum et famosum sodomitum," Checcho di Giovanni di Bocci, a Florentine living in Pisa, received thirteen separate charges of sodomy. His affairs with men and boys cut across social classes, from state employees of Pisa and men with family names to a cobbler and a shop apprentice ("ragazzo"). His love affairs stretched across Tuscany—Pisa, Livorno, Lucca, Florence, Montevarchi; Ibid. 101, 2:349r–52r 1422.xi.9.

89. Twenty-four of 187 cases.

90. ASF, Giudice 99, 2:71r–3v, 1414.v.26.

91. See, for instance, the charges against Ser Andream Jacobi of Massa Marittima, who lived in Castel Fiorentino, of raping several women whose names the court refused to reveal. His crime was considered an insult to the vicariate of the Valdarno inferiore and the state of Florence: "contra formam juris statutorum et ordinamentorum comunis florentie et dicti vicariatus. Et contra honorem Magnifici et Excelsi populi et comunis florentie et partis guelforum propter que poterat oriri rumor et scandalam in dicto vicariatu." ASF, Giudice 100, 2:139r–v, 1417.viii.17.

92. Ibid. 98, 2:2r–v, 1405.xii.17; 2:259r–v, 1407.viii.6; 101, 1:80v, 1419.viii.5.

93. Ibid., 100, 332r.

94. Ibid. 102, 2:370r–v, 1433.iii.15.

95. Chabot, "Sola, donna"; Klapisch-Zuber, "Cruel Mother."

96. Klapisch-Zuber, "Cruel Mother," 118.

97. Ibid., 120.

98. See the critical assertions of Kuehn, *Law, Family, and Women,* 4–6. On the symbols of the widow's divorce from her affines at her husband's death, see Chabot, "La sposa in nero."

99. If incest cases are subtracted, the proportion of unmarried girls falls to less than a quarter: 46 girls, 134 married women, and 7 widows. (Of course, demographically, given the early marriage age for women, these ratios may not be so surprising.)

100. ASF, Giudice 100, 2:211v, 1417.iii.24.

101. Ibid. 101, 1:32r–v, 1419.vii.10.

102. Ibid., 2:7r–v, 1422.v.25.

103. Ibid. 102, 1:47r–v, 1429.ix.9.

104. Ibid. 76, 444r–v, 1427.viii.3. According to E. Cohen, "Honor and Gender," 621, "Chatting at doorways and gates was often a prelude to a love affair" in early modern Rome.

105. Mazzi, "Incanti amorosi," 494.

106. The term is Sharpe's, *Crime in Early Modern England,* 44–48.

107. See Kuehn, *Law, Family, and Women,* chap. 1.

108. ASF, Statuti delle comunità 624, Palazzuolo and the Podere fiorentino, 1406, 54v–55r; and ibid., 317, Firenzuola, 33r. Moreover, in the commune of Santa Maria a Monte (in the vicariate of San Miniato, the rapist's fine of two hundred lire could be commuted into a two-hundred-lire dowry for his unmarried victim but only on the condition that she consented to the marriage; Casini, *Statuto del Comune di S. Maria a Monte (1391),* 100–101, bk. 1, rub. 55. By the statutes of the Florentine *podestà,* a postfactum marriage agreement could reduce (but not cancel) the penalties; see Cagesse, *Statuti della repubblica fiorentina,* 2:229, bk. 3, rub. 69. Despite inflation over the century, the same penalties and options continued through the early fifteenth century; *Statuta populi et communis Florentiae (1415),* 1:318, bk. 3, rub. 112.

109. See *Statuta populi et communis Florentiae (1415),* 1:318, bk. 3, rub. 112: "De poena raptus mulierum, adulterii, et stupri, et petentis uxorem, vel virum, non apparente instrumento matrimonii." Also see Balletto, *Statuta Antiquissima Saone,* 14, cap. 9; Lamboglia, *Gli antichi statuti di Apricale,* 95; Gianfranceschi, *Gli statuti di Sarzana,* bk. 2, 110–11; Ruggiero, *Boundaries of Eros,* chapt. 2, "Fornication and Then Marriage," esp. 43–44.

110. ASF, Giudice 99, 3:258v–59v, 1416.iv.6; Johannes Tofani of Nassa in the curia of Monte Aguto, the *podesteria* of Castel Focognano in the vicariate of Anghiari, pulled a ten-year virgin girl off her donkey as she was riding through the village of Nassa and raped her. For his sentence, he was given the choice of paying a three-

hundred-lire fine and having both testicles cut off or marrying his victim when she reached "the legitimate age," bringing her a fifty-lire dowry, and paying the vicariate of Anghiari a hundred lire.

111. Ricciardo Cancellieri's insurrection was certainly not at first a peasant revolt but arose from factional warfare among the aristocratic elites of the city of Pistoia. See Chittolini's brief reference in "Ricerche sull'ordinamento territoriale," 325.

112. See Cohn, "Inventing Braudel's Mountains."

113. These acts did not come immediately after the Black Death of 1348, nor were they extended to artisans to emigrate to the city of Florence and other cities in the district.

114. Guasti, *I capitoli,* 1:109, 354; n. 19: "Che quegli uomini possano esigere i pedagii, salvo dai cittadini, contadini e distrettuali di Firenze, o per le loro mercanzie e per robe che fossero del C. di Firenze."

115. ASF, Giudice 97, 28r–29v.

116. On the *marzocco* and its symbolism in early Renaissance Florence, see Johnson, "Lion on the Piazza." The lion was the symbol of the Angevins, who were Florentine allies in the early fourteenth century and the leaders of the international Guelf alliance. It first entered the company of Florentine civic symbols, however, only after the Ciompi, when in 1382 a statue of the *marzocco* was erected in the Piazza Signoria. Moreover, it does not appear to have spread to the countryside or to Florence's subject villages and towns in the *districtus* until the 1420s. At any rate, in the wave of peasant insurrections between 1401 and 1406, the *marzocco* never appears as an object of resentment.

117. ASF, Giudice 76, 574v–6v, 1427.i.24.

118. In addition to the vicariate court records, see ASF, Provv. reg. 118, 67r–8r, where the commune of Campogialli petitioned for tax relief on 27 October 1427. In addition to describing damages to property and men incurred through war with the Milanese, the commune complained to the *signoria* that it had been "coerced" into rebellion against Florentine dominion by its "enemies" from the village of Pontenano.

119. ASF, Giudice 76, 574v–6v, 1427.i.19: "Ma eglino fugiranno come puttane."

120. Ibid., 517v–19r, 1427.xi.17.

121. See the numerous sessions of the *Consulte e Pratiche* in which Florentine patricians (1401 through 1403) anxiously debated how to handle the uprising of Pistoia, which had spread through its district of the Montagna: Conti, ed., *Le "Consulte e Pratiche" (1401);* and ASF, Consulte e Pratiche 35, 61r, 66r, 69r, 71r–76v, 122r; 36, 49v, 56v; 37, 4r.

122. ASF, Consulte e Pratiche 46, 180v, 31.vii.1426: "Sed si dominationi videretur ob honorem comunis aliquod faciendum esse ad id poterit providere videtur eis quod oppidum illud deleatur in totum et quod petra supra petram non remaneat et per modum quod ibi non cantet gallus vel gallina ut alibi habitetur et bona confiscentur comuni et ecclesia fiat censuaria comunis et per alios non occupetur." I wish to thank Arthur Field for bringing this text to my attention.

123. On this key moment in the development of republican thought, see Baron,

Crisis of the Early Italian Renaissance; Skinner, *Renaissance;* Pocock, *Machiavellian Moment.*

124. Grendi, "Premessa," 699; Bailey, "Reato, giustizia penale e autorità"; Pastore, *Crimine e giustizia.*

125. See Cohn, *Laboring Classes,* chap. 10; and Bailey's summary of the literature on the history of crime in England, "Reato, giustizia penale e autorità."

126. See Lenman and Parker, "State, the Community, and the Criminal Law," (46): "As we have argued above, even dramatic fluctuations [crime rates] may well reflect nothing more than changes in prosecution policy."

127. The second period was not, however, free of external hostilities. Foreign campaigns continued against villages on the Florentine periphery, such as the incursions of Ladislao of Naples in the 1410s, when towns such as Foiano, formerly in the *contado* of Arezzo, were leveled. Nor was this period of relative social peace free of fiscal crisis, as Molho, *Florentine Public Finances,* chaps. 2, 3, shows from the Monte records and as hundreds of desperate peasant petitions for tax breaks testify. The archives of ASF Giudice degli Appelli e nullità, lack a modern inventory. As mentioned, the *extrinseci* records covering the years 1426 to 1428 are miscatalogued as *intrinseci.* Moreover, volume 96 contains several *fasciolae* that overlap the *extrinseci* volumes from 1398 to 1415, but most of these records are of the inquisitions of cases instead of their sentences. Among the sentences, I found two cases of adultery (1398 and 1408) and one of rebellion (1398). These records have not been tallied among the statistics compiled from the *extrinseci* series.

128. A perfect inverse correlation would be −1.00. This figure was calculated by assigning attempted rape and consensual sex offenses a value of 1 and rape a value of 2 and, commensurably, assigning political crimes not stated explicitly as acts of rebellion a value of 1 and acts of rebellion, 2.

129. I wish to thank John Shearman for this insight.

130. On such informal means of control and pressure in late medieval English rural life, see Poos, "Sex, Lies, and the Church Courts."

131. See Cohn, *Laboring Classes,* chap. 10 and apps. H.1–H.3. Sex offenses for both city and *contado* comprised only 1.5 percent of cases in 1344–45 (25 of 1,628); 1.6 percent in 1374–75 (7 of 440); but nearly doubled by the mid-fifteenth century, 2.6 percent (14 of 531). In addition, I have compiled two samples of criminal sentences in the *contado* and district of Florence found in the records of the *podestà;* the first comes from the insurrectionary years, 1401–2, 288 cases; the second from the quieter years of 1410–15, 277 cases. In the first sample, the *podestà* tried only 4 sexual offenses (1.39%). Of these, 1 was also a case of murder (ASF, AP 3762, 35r–v, 1400.x.12), and all but 1 were cases of housebreaking and rape (ibid. 3822, 80r–v; 3782, n.p.). In the period of social quiescence, similar to the vicariate court cases, the percentage of sex offenses adjudicated by the *podestà* increased but remained below the levels recorded in the vicariate courts (6 cases, or 02.17%). All of these were violent crimes involving armed housebreaking, robbery, and in one case murder (infanticide).

132. Camerani, *Statuto di Arezzo (1327),* 212, bk. 3, rub. 30. De pena adulterii:

"Et de nullo adulterio, strupo vel incestu possit inquiri nec aliter procedi, nisi accusatio per patrem vel ipsam mulierem, virum, fratrem vel filium mulieris fuerit instituta"; and Bongi and Del Prete, *Statutum Lucani,* 136, bk. 3, rub 4.

133. Casini, *Statuto del comune di S. Maria a Monte,* 101: "Et delle predette cose il podestà della detta terra possa concoscere et procedere per via d'achusa facta per tale vergine, monaca, vedova overo maritata overo d'essa maritata marito overo d'esse vergine, monaca, vedova overo maritata padre o fratelli overo per altri loro congiunti in fine in terzo grado per la linea del padre."

134. See Ninci, *La "Consulte e Pratiche" (1404),* 25–26, for the *Consulte e Pratiche* debates of 8 January 1404, in which the *onestà* (control over prostitutes), the *otto di guardia,* and the new vicariate for the Valdarno superiore are discussed in the same sitting.

135. Elias, "On Transformation of Aggressiveness"; Prevenier, "Violence against Women."

136. For the three periods (each of which comprises eight years of surviving criminal sentences, despite the differences in actual chronologies), the number of rape trials varies from four to thirty-three to fifteen. Of course, the relationship of rape trials to the actual incidence of rape is highly problematic; see chap. 2.

137. For a similar pattern in mid-fifteenth-century Venice (though for an urban population), see Ruggiero, *Boundaries of Eros,* 43ff.

138. ASF, Not. antecos., P 91 (1442–64), now 16091; P 91 (1462–84), now 16093; L 57 (1464–73), now 11431.

139. See Rocke, "Il controllo dell'omosessualità," 705–6; Rocke, *Friendly Affections;* Dean and Lowe, "Writing the History of Crime," 13; Dean, "Criminal Justice," 30.

140. See the stimulating survey by Lenman and Parker, "State, the Community, and the Criminal Law," 12–14, which stands on its head Durkheim's distinction between punitive versus restitutive systems (*Division of Labor,* 1893). However, Zorzi, "Judicial System," 54–57; and Dean, "Criminal Justice," argue that for Renaissance Florence and Bologna the harshness of penalties declined, and in Bologna, mutilations disappeared almost altogether as the state became more efficient in its surveillance, control, and adjudication of criminality. "Against greater leniency in punishment was greater rigor in prosecuting crime" (Dean, "Criminal Justice," 30). See also Rocke, *Friendly Affections.* The use of torture for pretrial confessions, on the other hand, may have been on the increase during the fifteenth century; see Stern, *Criminal Law System,* 39–40; Chambers and Dean, *Clean Hands and Rough Justice.*

141. ASF, Giudice 101, 2:68r–v, 20.vi.1422; 181v–2r, 1422.viii.22; 102, 2:111r–v, 1432.xi.26. Sentences of mutilation increased from only two in the first period (6%), to seventeen (10.56%) in the second, and then fell to four in the third (6%). While these numbers are small, they are suggestive, given the changing severity of fines. On the other hand, the death penalty shows a steady decline for sex cases, from 29 to 21 to 14 percent. But this progression is somewhat misleading in that the cases were composed largely of violent rape in the first period, whereas con-

sensual sex and attempted rape predominated in the middle period. Interestingly, in the third period the vicariate courts did not condemn a single sex offender to death. Would this change with the rise of the Medici?

142. I found only three sentences of live burials, all in the years between 1406 and 1425 and all reserved for political offenders: ASF, Giudice 99, 191r–2v, 1413.xi.23, 171; ibid. 100, 1:241r–43v, 1416.ii.17; ibid. 101, 2:36r–7v, dated 1396.vi.27 but given a sentence in 1421.ii.7.

143. Ibid. 100, 1:241r–3v, 1416.ii.17. In addition, all their property was to be confiscated.

144. See Neumann *Behemoth;* Chomsky, *World Orders*, 120–29; Townshend, *Making the Peace,* chap. 2.

145. Rocke, *Friendly Affections;* Zorzi, "Judicial System"; Dean, "Criminal Justice."

146. Although the vicariate of the Valdarno inferiore reached and even crossed the banks of the Arno, including Figline, Castro San Giovanni, and Montevarchi, its cases came predominantly from its more mountainous zones on the eastern slopes of the Pratomagno, from the strongholds of the Battifolle north of Romena to those of the Ubertini south of Montevarchi and into the Val d'Ambra. As far as sex and political crimes are concerned, Figline hardly appears in the records of this vicariate, 1398–1434. Another vicariate called the Valdarno inferiore was created immediately after the conquest of Pisa in 1406, when the former *contado* of Pisa was divided into three vicariates. The Valdarno inferiore of Pisa was contiguous with that of the Valdarno inferiore of San Miniato and included the northernmost zones of the *contado* of Pisa, extending through the Val di Serchio; see Salviati, *Cronica,* 261.

One objection to these geographical comparisons might be that different vicariates were being created over the first fifteen years of the fifteenth century. But as indicated earlier, these *extrinseci* records contain records from the *podestà* of places in the Mugello and the Chianti before they formally were called vicariates. More important, three-quarters of the sex crimes from 1398 through 1434 were adjudicated in 1415 or afterward (193 of 255 cases). If only sex crimes brought to trial after 1414 are considered, the rank order of the three vicariates most highly implicated in sex crimes does not change at all; the Valdarno superiore towers over the rest even more than when the entire series is considered. But these statistics can be questioned as well for the absence of a common denominator, whether it be the total number of cases adjudicated or the populations of these vicariates. I have tallied the cases for vol. 76, which covers 1427 and part of 1426 and 1428. The distribution of total cases for these years does not match the distribution of sex crimes over the long duration. First, the vicariates of Pisa and the maritime zone of Livorno lead the list, with 189 cases, followed by the Valdarno inferiore (San Miniato) with 183. In the third position, three vicariates cluster closely together: the Valdarno superiore (152 cases), the Mugello (144), and the Valdelsa and Pesa (143). Far out of proportion with its sex crimes, the sparsely populated mountains within the vicariate of Anghiari adjudicated the least number of cases of any vicariate in the period 1426–28 (17 cases). Of course, a more rigorous treatment of these data would require the painstaking and time-consuming task of tallying all the cases found in these records, which include approximately eight thousand cases.

147. Less than 2 percent of the sex crimes found in my survey were adjudicated in these districts. For the first years, many such cases were still adjudicated in the traditional tribunals of the Florentine *contado*—the *podestà* and the *capitano del popolo*—as can be witnessed by the numbers of political insurrections from these mountainous zones preserved in these records. But after 1405 the *filze* from the Alpi fiorentine were filled with mundane matters of robbery and assault, largely the sort of crime that would never earn a glance from the microhistorian, and crime from these districts consequently disappears from the records of the *podestà* and the *capitano*.

148. ASF, Giudice 99, 3:337v–39v, 1416.v.16.

149. See Becker, "Problemi della finanza pubblica"; Molho, "Fisco e società," and *Florentine Public Finances;* Herlihy, "Direct and Indirect Taxes"; la Roncière, "Indirect Taxes." See esp. the work of Conti, "Catasti agrari," "L'imposta diretta," and "Ricordi fiscali"; Cammarosano, "Il sistema fiscale"; but also the works of younger scholars such as Ciappelli, "Il Cittadino fiorentino."

150. This argument forms a part of a book I am now researching on peasant revolts and the Florentine territorial state in the early Renaissance.

151. ASF, Provv. reg. 93, 92v–93r, 1404.ix.18.

152. Chittolini, "Ricerche sull'ordinamento territoriale"; Zorzi, *L'amminis-trazione,* 29–30; Zorzi, "Lo stato territoriale."

153. Fabbri, "La sottomissione di Volterra," chap. 5; Connell, "Clientelismo e stato territoriale."

154. See Ninci, *Le "Consulte e pratiche" (1404),* 18, 25, 27, 29, sessions of 8–10 January 1404–5.

155. On the different fortunes of various regions within the Apennines according to the *catasto* of 1427, see Cherubini, "La società dell'Appennino," 130–31; Cherubini, "Qualche considerazione."

156. For the Florentine repression of the Aretine tax revolt of 1431, see Pasqui, "Una congiura per liberare Arezzo"; for the harsh penalties meted out against the revolts in Volterra of 1430; see ASF, Giudice 102, 2:93r–95r, 1430.x.9; ibid., 2:95v–98v, 1430.ix.19; and ibid., 2:99r–100v, 1430.x.25.

157. As best can be determined from the sentences, most of the cases adjudicated by the vicariate courts came from the vicar's own inquisition, as opposed to being denounced by the victims. Moreover, as Dean, "Criminal Justice," 17, finds for Bologna, denunciations by local parish rectors and subordinate *podestà* also declined in the Florentine territory during the early fifteenth century.

158. ASF, Provv. reg. 117, 28.iv.1427, 72r–3v.

159. Chittolini, "Ricerche sull'ordinamento territoriale," 326: "ma è innegabile l'impressione che in questi decenni si instauri una organizzazione di governo che dimostrerà capacità di durare—in confronto con altri stati regionali—una singolare compattezza."

7. Prosperity in the Countryside

1. See Hatcher, "England in the Aftermath of the Black Death," which considers the well-being of the English peasantry through the fourteenth century.

2. Most important, see Le Roy Ladurie, *Les paysans de Languedoc;* Postan, *Essays on Medieval Agriculture,* esp. 41–48.

3. See Bois, *Crise du féodalisme;* Hatcher, *Plague, Population, and the English Economy;* Herlihy, *Medieval and Renaissance Pistoia,* and *Black Death.* Bois's work is Marxist, whereas Herlihy's and Hatcher's demographic interpretations are highly critical of both Marxist and Malthusian models. On the less optimistic side are Poos, *Rural Society,* esp. 30–31; Ginatempo, *Crisi di un territorio;* Raveggio and Mazzi, *Gli uomini e le cose;* Epstein, "Cities, Regions, and the Late Medieval Crisis"; and Brucker, "Economic Foundations."

4. Genicot, "Crisis." Also see Aston and Philpin, *Brenner Debate;* Epstein, *Island for Itself.*

5. See Muir, "Introduction: Observing Trifles"; Ginzburg and Poni, "Name and the Game"; Ginzburg, "Spie."

6. Cohn, "Inventing Braudel's Mountains."

7. The weight of these determinants were calculated by regression analysis; see ibid.

8. The rate declined both in terms of the relationship between the estimate of property value and the final tax assessment in the final report, called the *lira,* as well as according to the coefficients assigned to that assessment. For instance, throughout the 1380s, Florence charged peasants only between ten and twelve soldi per lira assessed; by 1400, the rate had reached one and half florins, or twelve times the earlier rate.

9. These population figures are based on six villages: S. Martino a Campi, S. Maria in Padule, Villa di S. Giusto, S. Maria a Morello, Montecuccolo, and Montecarelli. These were the only villages for which I found complete records in the *estimi* and *catasti* from 1371 through 1460.

10. I derived the index for constant lire by calculating twenty-five-year averages from the grain prices in Goldthwate, "I prezzi."

11. The records of the vicariate courts are peppered with such corruption cases; see chap. 6.

12. The increase was for households with able-bodied men between the ages of fourteen and seventy. Before the *catasto* of 1427, even widows without property were usually charged a tax of six to ten soldi.

13. Klapisch-Zuber, "Mezzadria e insediamenti," 154.

14. See ibid. and the notarial books of the Mazzetti family, who worked the villages from the city walls of Florence west through the Arno Valley parishes of Quarto, Quinto, Sesto, and into the hills of Calenzano; ASF, Not. antecos. M 352–53, M 355–59; their records survive from 1348 to 1426, with only a few lacunae.

15. Genicot, "Crisis"; Hatcher, "England in the Aftermath of the Black Death,"

and *Plague, Population*, 34: "within a decade of the plague many towns were showing signs of strong recovery."

16. I made these calculations from more than five thousand land transactions in the *gabelle dei contratti* of Siena from 1294 to 1460; see Cohn, "Movement of Landed Property."

17. Herlihy and Klapisch-Zuber, *Les Toscans*, chap. 2.

18. See Le Roy Ladurie, *Les paysans de Languedoc*, 1:167–68; Epstein, *Island for Itself*, 220; Hatcher, *Plague, Population, and the English Economy*, 50: Slicher van Bath, *Agrarian History*, 173–89.

19. See Molho, "Tre città-stato"; Wickham, *Mountains*, chap. 12; Braudel, *Mediterranean*, 1:41.

20. These paragraphs are a brief summary of research I am now pursuing on taxation, peasant revolts, and the growth of the Florentine territorial state.

21. Herlihy, *Medieval and Renaissance Pistoia;* also see Le Roy Ladurie, *Les paysans de Languedoc*, 1:142–43; Herlihy and Klapisch-Zuber, *Les Toscans*, 439–42.

22. Herlihy and Klapisch-Zuber, *Les Toscans*, 439–42. Klapisch-Zuber, "Le dernier enfant," reconstructs the families of Florentine merchants mainly from the fifteenth century through *ricordanze*, finding that families did limit their births in wedlock—and well before menopause, if a sufficient number of male children survived to ensure the passage of patrimonies into male hands. Also see Klapisch-Zuber, "La fécondité des Florentines."

23. See Klapisch-Zuber's review of the literature, "Hidden Power of Women"; Langer, "Infanticide," and "Further Notes"; Kellum, "Infanticide in England"; Helmholz, "Infanticide in the Province of Canterbury."

24. Coleman, "L'infanticide dans le haut Moyen Age."

25. Braudel, *Mediterranean*, 1:44, 47; McNeill, *Mountains of the Mediterranean World*. See also the remarks of Viazzo, *Upland Communities*, 13–15 143–52, who argues that outmigration has been overstated as a homeostatic mechanism for regulating mountain populations.

26. Herlihy, *Medieval Households*, 67.

27. Klapisch-Zuber, "Hidden Power of Women," 166. See Toubert's quick dismissal of Coleman's argument in "Le moment carolingien." Similarly, Molho, while accepting as puzzling the sex ratios for 1427 and 1480, rejects out of hand the suggestion that they may have resulted from infanticide: *Marriage Alliance*, 215.

28. Cherubino da Siena, *Regole delle vita matrimoniale*, cited in Herlihy and Klapisch-Zuber, *Les Toscans*, 441. On Fra Cherubino's sermons on sexual practices, also see King, *Women of the Renaissance*, 10–11; and Heißler, *Frauen der italienischen Renaissance*, 102–4, and 108–9.

29. Herlihy and Klapisch-Zuber, *Les Toscans*, 328, 338–39. Their claim about the plague, however, runs counter to the reports of contemporary chroniclers and what researchers find for plagues in the early modern period as well as for today: women are more resistant than men. See Hatcher, *Plague, Population, and the English Economy*, 60; Hollingsworth, "Plague Mortality Rates"; and for recent

plagues, Butler, "Black Death." The English chroniclers of the plague of 1361—
Thomas Walsingham, Ralph Higden, the chronicler of Louth Park Abbey, and
John of Reading (see Horrox, *Black Death,* 85–87)—report that the plague killed
off men but largely spared women. I wish to thank Jim Bolton for this information.

30. Molho, *Marriage Alliance,* 214–15.

31. Sermini, *Novelle di Gentile Sermini,* story 12, "L'autore e ser Cecco da Perugia," 169–78. In 1348, however, the mountains were not spared from the plague's
ravages. The Florentine *provvisioni* of that year single out the mountain community of Mangona, in the Alpi fiorentine, for special assistance in paying off its
debts due to its high mortalities. ASF, Provv. reg., 36, 8v–10v, 1348.ix.12.

32. McNeill, *Mountains of the Mediterranean World,* 274ff.

33. Herlihy and Klapisch-Zuber, *Les Toscans,* 332–36.

34. Of household heads, 572 of 1,419 did not list their age; 612 of 1,125 wives of
household heads did not.

35. With the *estimo* of 1371, the surveys divided the population into *stanti* (those
who had remained in the village since the last tax survey), *tornanti* and *venuti*
(those who had settled in the village since the last survey), *usciti* (those who had
left), and *morti* (household heads who had died). Only rarely did the village syndics in 1371 or afterward list the household members or any ages of those enumerated as *usciti.*

36. For children (those less than twenty years old), the age rounding was not as
severe; nor did it change over time but, instead, varied between 21 and 28 percent
of this age group.

37. This ratio appears to have remained constant from the earliest reliable birth
records to the present and across cultures. Indeed, some of the earliest records for
establishing sex ratios come from the Quattrocento Florentine baptismal records;
see Lastri, *Ricerche.*

38. Herlihy and Klapisch-Zuber, *Les Toscans,* 339, n. 50.

39. See Sermini, *Novelle,* story 12, 169. See Cohn, "Inventing Braudel's Mountains."

40. The age rounding from Prato in the *estimi* was more extreme than that from
the countryside: 68.6 percent of city dwellers twenty years of age and older
rounded their ages (a total of 1,593 with specified ages).

41. Herlihy and Klapisch-Zuber, *Les Toscans,* 340; they even call abandonment
"un infanticide larvé." For a more optimistic view of medieval abandonment, see
Boswell, *Kindness of Strangers.* This view has been sharply criticized, however, by
Kertzer and White, "Cheating the Angelmakers."

42. Such are the conclusions of Coleman's analysis of the polyptych of Saint
Germain de Prés, "L'infanticide dans le haut Moyen Age." She finds a high inverse
correlation between sex ratios and property holdings. These conclusions, and not
the general conclusion of whether or not these ninth-century French peasants
were guilty of infanticide as Toubert and others assume, are criticized by Zerner,
"La population de Villeneuve-Saint-Georges," esp. table 3. For Renaissance Flor-

ence, Trexler argues similarly that abandonment was the result of impoverishment; see "Foundlings of Florence," 266–68, 274.

43. For the *miserabili,* 256 boy infants, 206 girls; for those with taxable property, 360 boys, 294 girls.

44. This decile had 135 male infants aged two or under and 104 girl infants that age.

45. Herlihy and Klapsich-Zuber, *Les Toscans,* fig. 13, and table 48; Herlihy, *Medieval Households,* table 6.5. In his last published essay, "Biology and History," 577, Herlihy argues that in societies "anxious to propagate their genotypes" rich families "are better advised to invest in sons. They are also more likely than the poor to practice female infanticide."

46. See ASF, Provv. reg. 61, 64r–66r.

47. In 1371 the population of Mangona was 709, in 1383, 459. In the tax survey of 1365 (which enumerates only household heads), Mangona had been larger still, comprising 203 families as opposed to 176 in 1371. With the wars against the Ubaldini, Montecarelli's population declined even more drastically, from 535 in 1371 to 225 in 1383. In 1980 the population of Mangona was 112 and that of Montecarelli 203.

48. The population was 278 in 1393, 134 in 1402.

49. On the prevalence of daughters to inherit, at least in elite families when no sons survived, see Kuehn, *Law, Family, and Women,* 238–57. In the crisis years of 1430–39, when war followed by famine raged through the mountains of the Casentino, the sex ratios of entrants to the hospital of San Gallo from the countryside declined; see Herlihy and Klapisch-Zuber, *Les Toscans,* 339.

50. See Trexler, "Foundlings of Florence," 266.

51. For the merchant class, see Fabbri, *Alleanza matrimoniale;* Klapisch-Zuber, "Le dernier enfant," 283: "L'épouse est alors choisie avant tout en fonction des aptitudes reproductrices qu'elles laisse deviner, et la réussite d'un couple se mesurera au nombre des héritiers mâles qu'il laissera."

52. These battlefields can be mapped by, among other sources, peasant pleas for tax concessions because of warfare and its destruction to crops and villagers.

53. Trexler, "Foundlings of Florence," 263.

54. Ibid., 266–68; Herlihy and Klapisch-Zuber, *Les Toscans,* 338.

55. On the history of this hospital and of abandonment in Florence, see Gavitt, *Charity and Children.*

56. Takahashi, "I bambini e i genitori," 48: "Secondo i dati dello Spedale di San Gallo, durante il periodo dal 1395 al 1419, 11 dei 39 esposti non originari di Firenze venivano dal Mugello ed anche nei successivi quarant'anni dal 1420 al 1459, i bambini continuavano a giungere dall'area."

57. Klapisch-Zuber, "Blood Parents and Milk Parents," 141; Sandri, *L'ospedale di S. Maria della Scala,* chap. 5; Sandri, "Baliatico mercenario."

58. Klapisch-Zuber, "Women Servants," 65–66; Pinto, "Il personale."

59. Gavitt, *Charity and Children.*

60. McNeill, *Mountains of the Mediterranean World,* 274.

61. On variations in the wealth of the mountains, see Cherubini, "La società dell'Appennino," 130–31. Also see Herlihy and Klapisch-Zuber, *Les Toscans*, 346–47.

62. Braudel, *Mediterranean*, 1:51–53.

63. Klapisch-Zuber and Demonet, "A uno pane e uno vino"; Klapisch-Zuber, "Déclin démographique," 266.

64. By the *catasto* of 1460, this extraordinary regularity of blocking married sons from directing the family regardless of the age or health of the father appears to have been easing. In that survey seven sons out of 906 families had replaced their fathers as household heads.

65. Again, in 1460 this practice seems to have been changing as more mothers with even adolescent sons appear as household heads.

66. Klapisch-Zuber, "Blood Parents and Milk Parents," "Female Celibacy and Service," and "Women Servants in Florence," 56–80.

67. Klapisch-Zuber, "Women Servants in Florence," 63.

68. Trexler, "Widow's Asylum," 143.

69. See, for instance, Thomas, *Religion and the Decline of Magic,* chaps. 14–18.

70. In the vicariate criminal records for the territory of Florence, in which thousands of cases have survived from 1398 through 1434, I spotted only three cases involving magical incantation or that smack of witchcraft; ASF, Giudice, intrinseci 98, 79r–80v; ibid. 100, 91r–v; 190r–191r. But even in these cases, witchcraft (*stregoneria*) is not charged by the courts; instead, their deeds are called *maleficam matematicam,* and the women defendants (and all are women in these cases) are called by terms such as *feminam incantatricem.* From Ruggiero's *Binding Passions,* it appears that such cases were more prevalent in the Veneto.

71. Klapisch-Zuber, "Cruel Mother," 120.

Bibliography

Archives

AREZZO

ASA: Archivio di stato, Arezzo
    Antichi notari: Protocollo d'antichi notari aretini Perg.: Pergamene e carte
      varie
Arch. dei laici: L'Archivio della fraternità dei laici di Arezzo
    Testamenti
Arch. capitolare, Arezzo: Archivio capitolare di Arezzo

ASSISI

Sacro convento: Sacro convento di Assisi; Fondo antico di San Francesco
    Instrumenta I–X
    Archive amministrativi
    Buste Z: Testamenti, 1363–1543
Bibl. com.: Biblioteca comunale
    Notarile
Archivio capitolare, Assisi: Archivio capitolare di Assisi
    Archivium assisium ecclesie S. Rufini
    Co. S. Francesco: Compagnia di San Francesco
    Co. S. Stefano: Compagnia di Santo Stefano

FLORENCE

ASF: Archivio di stato, Firenze
    Not. antecos.: Notarile antecosimiano (including notarial protocols from
      Florence, Arezzo, and Pisa)
    Dipl.: Diplomatico
      Arch. gen.: Archivio generale, Florence
      Domenicani d'Arezzo
      Misericordia d'Arezzo
      Olivetani d'Arezzo
      Olivetani di Firenze
      Santa Maria in gradibus, Arezzo
      S. M. Nuova: Santa Maria Nuova
      S. M. Novella: Santa Maria Novella

S. Croce: Santa Croce
Santa Felicità
Santissima Annuziata
Santa Maria di Badia
Cistercensi (Florence)
Archivi delle Compagnie Soppresse
Catasto
Estimi
Statuti della repubblica fiorentina
AP: Atti del podestà
CP: Capitano del popolo
Esecutore degli ordinamenti di giustizia
Giudice: Giudice degli appelli e nullita: intrinseci and extrinseci
Otto di guardia della repubblica
Ufficiali di notte
Provv. reg.: Provvisioni registri
Statuti delle comunità
Compagnie Soppresse, San Frediano
Consulte e Pratiche
Archivio Arcivescovile, Firenze
Visite
Arch S. Lorenzo: Biblioteca Medicea Laurenziana, Archivio di San Lorenzo

PERUGIA

ASPr: Archivio di stato, Perugia
Not. bast.: Notarile bastardelli
Not. prot.: Notarile protocolli
Perg.: Pergamene
San Domenico
San Francesco al Prato
San Maria di Monte Luce
Monte Morcino
Misericordia
Ospedale di Santa Maria della Misericordia, Contratti
Archivio di San Pietro
Liber contractuum

PISA

ASPi: Archivio di stato, Pisa
Osp. di S. Chiara: Ospedale di Santa Chiara
Protocolli
Contratti e testamenti

Dipl.: Diplomatico
    Acquisto cappelli
    Misericordia
    Olivetani di Pisa
    Opera di primaziale
    Sant'Anna
    San Benedetto
    San Domenico
    San Lorenzo alle rivolte
    Santo Marto
    San Martino
    San Michele in Borgo
    San Paolo all'Orto

SIENA

ASS: Archivio di stato, Siena
    Not. antecos.: Notarile antecosimiano
    Not. postcos.: Notarile postcosimiano
    Dipl.: Diplomatico
        Arch. gen.: Archivio generale
AA: Archivio arcivescovile di Siena (AA)
    Sinodi
    Visite
Biblioteca comunale, Siena

Printed Sources

Alberti, Leon Battista. *I libri della famiglia.* Translated by Renée Neu Watkins. Columbia, S.C., 1969.

Azzi, Giustiniano Degli, ed. *Statuti di Perugia dell'anno MCCCXLII.* In *Corpus statutorum italicarum* 4, 9. Rome, 1913–16.

Balletto, Laura, ed. *Statuta Antiquissima Saone (1345).* 2 vols. Vols. 8 and 9 of *Collana storica di fonti e studi.* Genoa, 1971.

Boccaccio, Giovanni. *Il corbaccio.* Edited by Giulia Natali. Milan, 1992.

———. *Decameron.* Vol. 4 of *Tutte le opere di Giovanni Boccaccio.* Edited by Vittore Branca. Milan, 1976.

Bonaini, Francesco, ed. *Constituta legis et usus MCCXXIIII.* Vol. 2 of *Statuti inediti della città di Pisa dal XII al XIV secolo.* Florence, 1854.

Bongi, S., and L. Del Prete. *Statutum Lucani communis an. MCCCVIII.* Luca, 1990 (1867).

Borromeo, Carlo. *Ammaestramenti.* Edited by P. Pio Mauri. 2d ed. Milan, 1902.

Caggesse, Romolo, ed. *Statuti della repubblica fiorentina.* 2 vols. Florence, 1910–21.

Camerani, Giulia Marri, ed. *Statuto di Arezzo (1327).* Florence, 1946.

Cantini, Lorenzo, ed. *Legislazione toscana raccolta ed illustrata.* 30 vols. Florence, 1747–1800.

Casini, Bruno, ed. *Statuto del comune di S. Maria a Monte (1391).* Vol. 2 of *Fonti sui comuni rurali toscani.* Florence, 1963.

Catherine of Siena. *I, Catherine: Selected Writings of Saint Catherine of Siena.* Edited and translated by Kenelm Foster and Mary Ronayne. London, 1980.

da Certaldo, Paolo. *Libro di buoni costumi.* In *Mercanti scrittori: ricordi nella Firenze tra Medioevo e Rinascimento,* edited by Vittore Branca. Milan, 1986.

Cherubino da Siena. *Regole delle vita matrimoniale.* In *Scelta di curiosità lettere inedite o rare dal secolo 13. al 17,* no. 228, edited by F. Ambrini and C. Negroni. Bologna, 1888.

Conti, Elio. ed. *Le "Consulte e Pratiche" della repubblica fnel Quattrocento (1401).* Pisa, 1981.

Firenzuola, Angelo. *I ragionamenti.* In *Opere di Angelo Firenzuola,* edited by Delmo Maestri. Turin, 1977.

Gianfranceschi, Ida, ed. *Gli statuti di Sarzana del 1330.* In *Collana storica della Liguria orientale* 3. Bordighera, 1965.

Guasti, Cesare, ed. *I capitoli del comue di Firenze.* 2 vols. Florence, 1865.

Lamboglia, Nino, ed. *Gli antichi statuti di Apricale (1267–1430).* In *Collana storico archeologica della Liguria occidentale* 24. Bordighera, 1986.

Machiavelli, Niccol. *Mandragola, Clizia.* Edited by Ezio Raimondi and Gian Mario Anselmi. Milan, 1984.

Messini, Angelo, and Feliciano Baldaccini, eds. *Statuta communis Fulginei.* In *Deputazione di storia patria per l'Umbria* 6. Perugia, 1969.

Molho, Anthony, and Franek Sznura, eds. *Alle bocche della piazza: diario d'annonimo Fiorentino (1382–1401).* Florence, 1986.

Ninci, Renzo, ed. *Le "Consulte e Pratiche" della repubblica fiorentina (1404).* Rome, 1991.

Orlandi, Stefano, ed. *"Necrologio" di S. Maria Novella: testo integrale dall'inizio al MDIV corredato di note biografiche tratte da documenti coevi.* 2 vols. Florence, 1955.

Pitti, Buonaccorso. *Ricordi.* In *Mercanti scrittori: ricordi nella Firenze tra medioevo e rinascimento,* edited by Vittore Branca. Milan, 1986.

Sacchetti, Franco. *Il Trecentonovelle.* Edited by Antonio Lanza. Florence, 1984.

Salviati, Iacopo. *Cronica, o memorie di Iacopo Salviati dall'anno 1398 al 1411.* In *Delizie degli eruditi toscani* 18, edited by Fr. Ildefonso di San Luigi. Florence, 1784.

Savio, Pietro, ed. *Statuta comunali di Villanova d'Asti.* In *Studi e testi* 61. Vatican City, 1934.

Schiaffini, Alfredo, ed. *Testi fiorentini del Dugento e dei primi del trecento.* Florence, 1954.

Sercambi, Giovanni. *Novelle.* Edited by Giovanni Sinicropi. In *Scrittori D'Italia* 250. Bari, 1972.

Sermini, Gentile. *Le novelle di Gentile Sermini da Siena.* Livorno, 1874.

Singleton, Charles, ed. *Canti carnascialeschi del Rinascimento.* Bari, 1936.

Statuta populi et communis Florentiae (1415). 3 vols. Freiberg, 1778–82.

Stefani, Marchionne di Coppo. *Cronaca fiorentina.* Edited by Niccolò Rodolico. In *Rerum Italicarum scriptores,* new series 30, pt. 1. Castello, 1903.

Villani, Giovanni. *Nuova cronica.* 3 vols. Edited by Giuseppe Porta. Parma, 1990.

Vito, A. F. *De B. aemiliana seu humiliana, vidua tertii ordinis S. Francisci.* In *Acta sanctorum,* May 17. Antwerp, 1685.

Zdekauer Lodovico, ed. *Il constituto del comune di Siena dell'anno 1262.* Milan, 1897.

Secondary Sources

Alberigo, Giuseppe. "Carlo Borromeo come modello di vescovo nella chiesa post-Tridentina." *Rivista storica italiana,* 79 (1967): 1031–52.

Antonelli, Giovanni. "La magistratura degli Otto di guardia a Firenze." *Archivio Storico Italiano* (hereafter, *ASI*) 92 (1954): 3–40.

Ariès, Philippe. *The Hour of Our Death.* Translated by H. Weaver. New York, 1981.

———. *Western Attitudes toward Death: From the Middle Ages to the Present.* Translated by P. Ranum. Baltimore, 1974.

Aston, T. H., and C. H. E. Philpin, eds. *The Brenner Debate: Agrarian Class Structure and Economic Development in Pre industrial Europe.* Cambridge, 1985.

Bailey, Victor. "Reato, giustizia penale e autorità in Inghilterra: un decennio di studi storici, 1969–1979." *Quaderni Storici* (hereafter, *QS*) 44 (1980): 581–602.

Banker, James. *Death in the Community: Memorialization and Confraternities in an Italian Commune in the Late Middle Ages.* Athens, Ga., 1988.

Baron, Hans. *The Crisis of the Early Italian Renaissance: Civic Humanism and Republican Liberty in an Age of Classicism and Tyranny.* 2 vols. Princeton, N.J., 1955.

Becker, Marvin. "Problemi della finanza pubblica fiorentina della seconda metà del Trecento e dei primi del Quattrocento." *ASI* 123 (1965): 433–66.

Bellomo, Manilo. *La condizione giuridica della donna in Italia: vicende antiche e moderne.* Turin, 1970.

———. *Ricerche sui rapporti patrimoniali tra coniugi: contributo alla storia della famiglia medievale.* Milan, 1961.

Bendiscoli, Mario. *Dalla riforma alla controriforma.* Bologna, 1974.

Benson, Pamela Joseph. *The Invention of the Renaissance Woman: The Challenge of Female Independence in the Literature and Thought of Italy and England.* University Park, Pa., 1992.

Binion, Rudolph. "Fiction as Social Fantasy: Europe's Domestic Crisis of 1879–1914." *Journal of Social History* 27 (1994): 679–99.

Bizzocchi, Roberto. *Chiesa e potere nella toscana del Quattrocento.* Bologna, 1987.

Bois, Guy. *Crise du féodalisme: économie rurale et démographie en Normandie orientale du début du 14e siècle au milieu du 16e siècle.* Paris, 1976.

Boswell, John. *The Kindness of Strangers: Abandonment of Children in Western Europe from Late Antiquity to the Renaissance.* New York, 1988.

Brackett, John. *Criminal Justice and Crime in Late Renaissance Florence.* Cambridge, 1992.

——. "The Florentine Onestà and the Control of Prostitution, 1403–1680." *Sixteenth Century Journal* 24 (1993): 273–300.

Braudel, Fernand. *The Mediterranean and the Mediterranean World in the Age of Philip II.* 2 vols. Translated by Siân Reynolds. New York, 1966.

Braverman, Harry. *Labor and Monoploy Capital: The Degradation of Work in the Twentieth Century.* New York, 1974.

Brentano, Robert. "Il movimento religioso femminile a Rieti nei secoli XIII–XIV." In Rusconi, *Il movimento religioso femminile.*

——. *A New World in a Small Place: Church and Religion in the Diocese of Rieti, 1188–1378.* Berkeley, Calif., 1994.

Brown, Judith C. *Immodest Act: The Life of a Lesbian Nun in Renaissance Italy.* New York, 1986.

——. "Monache a Firenze all'inizio dell'età moderna: un'analisi demografica." *QS* 29 (1994): 117–152.

——. "A Woman's Place Was in the Home: Women's Work in Renaissance Tuscany." In Ferguson, Quilligan, and Vickers, *Rewriting the Renaissance.*

Brown, Judith C., and Jordan Goodman. "Women and Industry in Florence." *Journal of Economic History* 40 (1980): 73–80.

Brown, Peter. *The Cult of the Saints: Its Rise and Function in Latin Christianity.* Chicago, 1981.

Brownmiller, Susan. *Against Our Will: Men, Women and Rape.* New York, 1975.

Brucker, Gene. *The Civic World of Early Renaissance Florence.* Princeton, N.J., 1977.

——. "The Economic Foundations of Laurentian Florence." In *Lorenzo il Magnifico e il suo mondo: Convegno Internazionale di studi (Firenze, 9–13 giugno 1992),* edited by Gian Carlo Garfagnini. Florence, 1994.

——. *Florentine Politics and Society, 1343–1378.* Princeton, N.J., 1962.

——. *Giovanni and Lusanna: Love and Marriage in Renaissance Florence.* Berkeley, Calif., 1986.

——. *The Society of Renaissance Florence.* New York, 1971.

Burckhardt, Jacob. *The Civilization of the Renaissance in Italy.* Translated by S. G. C. Middlemore. London, 1929 (1860).

Butler, T. "The Black Death, Past and Present: The Plague in the 1980s." *Transactions of the Royal Society of Tropical Medicine* 83 (1984): 458–60.

Calvi, Giulia. *Il contratto morale: madri e figli nella toscana moderna.* Bari, 1994.

——. "Diritti e legami: madri, figli, stato in toscana (XVI–XVIII secolo)." *QS* 86 (1994): 487–510.

Cammarosano, Paolo. "Il sistema fiscale delle città toscane." In *La toscana nel secolo XIV: caratteri di una civiltà regionale,* vol. 2, edited by Sergio Gensini. Pisa, 1988.

Carmichael, Ann. *Plague and the Poor in Renaissance Florence*. Cambridge, 1986.

Casagrande, Carla. "The Protected Woman." In Klapisch-Zuber, *Silences of the Middle Ages*.

Casagrande, Giovanna, "Il fenomeno della reclusione volontaria nei secoli del basso medioevo." *Benedictina* 35 (1988): 475–507.

———. Forme di vita religiosa femminile nell'area di Città di Castello nel sec. XIII." In Rusconi, *Il movimento religioso femminile*.

———. "Penitenti e disciplinati a Perugia e loro rapporti con gli mendicanti." *Mélanges de l'école française de Rome, Moyen Age-Temps Modernes* (hereafter, *MEFR*) 89 (1977): 711–21.

Castellini, A. "Il Cardinale Francesco Maria Tarugi." *Bollettino Siense Storia Patria* (hereafter, *BSSP*) 2–7 (1943–48): 88–109.

Catoni, Giuliano. "Interni di conventi senesi del Cinquecento." *Ricerche Storiche* 10 (1980): 171–203.

Cavaciocchi, Simonetta, ed. *La donna nell'economia secc. XIII–XVIII*. Florence, 1990.

Chabod, Federico. *Per la storia religiosa dello stato di Milano durante il dominio di Carlo V: note e documenti*. 2d ed. Turin, 1971.

Chabot, Isabelle. "La reconnaissance du travail des femmes dans la Florence du bas Moyen Age: contexte idéologique et réalité." In Cavaciocchi, *La donna nell'economia*.

———. "'Sola, donna, non gir mai': le solitudini femminili nel Tre-Quattrocento." *Memoria: Rivista di Storia delle Donne* 18 (1986): 7–24.

———. "'La sposa in nero': la ritualizzazione del lutto delle vedove fiorentine (secoli XIV–XV)." *QS* 86 (1994): 421–62.

Chambers, David S., and Trevor Dean. "Clean Hands and Rough Justice in Renaissance Italy: An Investigating Magistrate in Mantua and Ferrara." Unpublished manuscript.

Chaunu, Pierrre. *La mort à Paris: 16, 17 et 18e siècles*. Paris, 1978.

Cherubini, Giovanni. "La società dell'Appennino settentrionale (secoli XIII–XV)." In *Signori, contadini, borghesi: ricerche sulla società italiana del basso medioevo*. Florence, 1974.

———. "Qualche considerazione sulle campagne dell'Italia centro-settentrionale tra l'XI e il XV secolo." In *Signori, contadini, borghesi*.

Chiffoleau, Jacques. *La comptabilité de l'au-dela: les hommes, la mort et la religion dans la région d'Avignon à la fin du Moyen Age, vers 1320–vers 1480*. Paris, 1978.

———. "Perchè cambia la morte nella region di Avignon alla fine del Medioevo." *QS* 17 (1982): 449–65.

Chittolini, Giorgio. "Ricerche sull'ordinamento territoriale del dominio fiorentino agli inizi del secolo XV." In *La formazione dello stato regionale e le istituzioni del contado: secoli XIV e XV*. Turin, 1978.

Chittolini, Giorgio, and Giovanni Miccoli. *Storia d'Italia: Annali 9, la chiesa e il potere politico del medioevo all'età contemporanea*. Turin, 1986.

Chojnacki, Stanley. "Dowries and Kinsmen in Early Renaissance Venice." *Journal of Interdisciplinary History* 4 (1975): 571–600.

———. "Kinship Ties and Young Patricians in Fifteenth-Century Venice. *Renaissance Quarterly* 38 (1985): 240–70.

———. "Marriage Legislation and Patrician Society in Fifteenth-Century Venice." In *Law, Custom, and the Social Fabric in Medieval Europe: Essays in Honor of Bryce Lyon,* edited by Bernard S. Bachrach and David Nicholas. Kalamazoo, Mich., 1990.

———. "'The Most Serious Duty': Motherhood, Gender, and Patrician Culture in Renaissance Venice." In *Refiguring Woman: Perspectives on Gender and Italian Renaissance,* edited by Marilyn Migiel and Juliana Schiesari. Ithaca, N.Y., 1991.

———. "Patrician Women in Early Renaissance Venice." *Studies in the Renaissance* 21 (1974): 176–203.

———. "The Power of Love: Wives and Husbands in Late Medieval Venice." In *Women and Power in the Middle Ages,* edited by Mary Erler and Maryanne Kowaleski. Athens, Ga., 1988.

Chomsky, Noam. *World Orders, Old and New.* London, 1994.

Ciappelli, Giovanni. "Il Cittadino fiorentino e il fisco alla fine del Trecento e nel corso del Quattrocento: uno studio di due casi." *Società e Storia* 12 (1989): 823–72.

Cipolla, Carlo M. *Cristofano and the Plague: A Study in the History of Public Health in the Age of Galileo.* London, 1973.

Civiltà ed economia agricola in toscana nei secc. XIII–XV: problemi della vita delle campagne nel tardo medioevo (Pistoia, 21–24 aprile 1977). Pistoia, 1981.

Cockburn, J. S. "The Nature and Incidence of Crime in England, 1559–1625: A Preliminary Survey." In *Crime in England, 1550–1800,* edited by J. S. Cockburn. Princeton, N.J., 1977.

Cohen, Elizabeth S. "Camilla the Go-Between: The Politics of Gender in a Roman Household (1559)." *Continuity and Change* 4 (1989): 53–77.

———. "Honor and Gender in the Streets of Early Modern Rome." *Journal of Interdisciplinary History* 22 (1992): 597–625.

Cohen, Elizabeth S., and Thomas V. Cohen. *Words and Deeds in Renaissance Rome: Trials before the Papal Magistrates.* Toronto, 1993.

Cohen, Sherrill. *The Evolution of Women's Asylums since 1500: From Refuges for Ex-Prostitutes to Shelters for Battered Women.* New York, 1992.

Cohn, Jr., Samuel K. "Burckhardt Revisited from Social History." In *The Renaissance: Cultural Definition,* edited by Alison Brown. Oxford, 1995.

———. *The Cult of Remembrance and the Black Death: Six Renaissance Cities in Central Italy.* Baltimore, 1992.

———. *Death and Property in Siena, 1205–1800: Strategies for the Afterlife.* Baltimore, 1988.

———. "Inventing Braudel's Mountains: The Florentine Alps after the Black

Death." In *Portraits of Medieval and Renaissance Living*, edited by Samuel K. Cohn Jr. and Steven Epstein. Ann Arbor, Mich., 1996.

———. *The Laboring Classes in Renaissance Florence*. New York, 1980.

———. "The Movement of Landed Property in Siena before and after the Black Death." Unpublished manuscript.

———. Review of Pastore, *Crimine e giustizia*. In *Journal of Modern History* 65 (1993): 875–76.

Cohn, Samuel K., Jr., and Oscar Di Simplicio. "Alcuni aspetti della politica matrimoniale della nobiltà senese, 1560–1700 circa." In *Forme e techniche del potere nella città (secoli XIV–XVII)*. edited by S. Bertelli. Perugia, 1979–80.

Coleman, Emily. "L'infanticide dans le haut Moyen Age." *Annales: E.S.C.* 29 (1974): 315–35.

Comba, Rinaldo. "'Apetitus libidinis cohercateur': strutture demografiche, reati sessuali e disciplina dei comportamenti nel Piemonte tardomedievale." *Studi Storici* 27 (1986): 529–77.

Connell, William. "Clientelismo e stato territoriale: il potere fiorentino a Pistoia nel XV secolo." *Società e Storia* 53 (1991): 523–43.

Conti, Elio. *I Catasti agrari della repubblica fiorentina e il Catasto particellare toscano* (secoli XIV–XIX). Rome, 1966

———. *L'imposta diretta à Firenze nel Quattrocento (1427–1494)*. Rome, 1984.

———. *Ricordi fiscali di Matteo Palmieri (1427–1474)*. Rome, 1983.

Cooper, J. P. "Patterns of Inheritance and Settlement by Great Landowners from the Fifteenth to the Eighteenth Centuries." In Goody, Thirsk, and Thompson, *Family and Inheritance*.

Cortese, Ennio. "Per la storia del munio in Italia." *Rivista Italiana per le Scienze Giuridiche* 8 (1955–56): 323–474.

Crabb, Ann Morton. "How Typical Was Alessandra Macinghi Strozzi of Fifteenth-Century Florentine Widows?" In *Upon My Husband's Death: Widows in the Literature and Histories of Medieval Europe*, edited by Louise Mirrer. Ann Arbor, Mich., 1992.

Croix, Alain. *La Bretagne aux 16e et 17e siècles: la vie, la mort, la foi*. Paris, 1981.

Cropper, Elizabeth. "The Beauty of Women: Problems in the Rhetoric of Renaissance Portraiture." In Ferguson, Quilligan, and Vickers, *Rewriting the Renaissance*.

Darnton, Robert. *The Great Cat Massacre and Other Episodes in French Cultural History*. New York, 1985.

Davidsohn, Robert. *Storia di Firenze*. Translated by Eugenio Dupré-Theseider and G. B. Klein. 8 vols. Florence, 1972 (1896–1927).

Davis, Natalie Z. *Fiction in the Archives: Pardon Tales and Their Tellers in Sixteenth-Century France*. Stanford, Calif., 1987.

———. *The Return of Martin Guerre*. Cambridge, Mass., 1983.

———. "City Women and Religious Change." In *Society and Culture in Early Modern France*. Stanford, Calif., 1975.

Davis, Natalie A., and Arlette Farge. "The Horizons of Everyday Life." In Davis and Farge, *Renaissance and Enlightenment Paradoxes*.

———, eds. *Renaissance and Enlightenment Paradoxes*. Vol. 3 of *A History of Women in the West*, edited by Georges Duby and Michelle Perrot. Cambridge, 1993.

Dean, Trevor. "Criminal Justice in Mid-Fifteenth-Century Bologna." In Dean and Lowe, *Crime, Society, and the Law*.

Dean, Trevor, and K. J. P. Lowe. "Writing the History of Crime in the Italian Renaissance." In Dean and Lowe, *Crime, Society, and the Law*.

Dean, Trevor, and K. J. P. Lowe, eds. *Crime, Society, and the Law in Renaissance Italy*. Cambridge, 1994.

Delumeau, Jean. *Le péché et la peur: la culpabilisation en Occident (XIIIe–XVIIIe siècles)*. Paris, 1983.

———. *La peur en Occident (XIVe–XVIIIe siècles): une cité assiégée*. Paris, 1978.

del Lungo, Isidoro. *La donna fiorentina del buon tempo antico*. Florence, 1906.

Diefendorf, Barbara D. "Family Culture, Renaissance Culture." *Renaissance Quarterly* 40 (1987): 661–81.

Di Simplicio, Oscar. "La criminalità a Siena 1561–1808: problemi di ricerca." *QS* 49 (1982): 242–64.

———. *Peccato penitenza perdono Siena, 1575–1800: la formazione della coscienza nell'Italia moderna*. Milan, 1994.

———. "Perpetuas: The Women Who Kept Priests, Siena 1600–1800." In Muir and Ruggiero, *History from Crime*.

Dorini, Umberto. *Il diritto penale e la delinquenza in Firenze nel XIV secolo*. Lucca, 1923.

Dubuis, Pierre. "Comportamenti sessuali nelle Alpi del basso medioevo: L'esempio della castellania di Susa." *Studi Storici* 27(1986): 577–607.

Duby, Georges. "The Courtly Model." In Klapisch-Zuber, *Silences of the Middle Ages*.

Duby, Georges, and Michelle Perrot. "Writing the History of Women." In Klapisch-Zuber, *Silences of the Middle Ages*.

Du Cange, Charles Du Fresne Sieur. *Glossarium Mediae et Infimae Latinitatis*. 7 vols. Paris, 1845.

Edgerton, Samuel Y., Jr. *Pictures and Punishment: Art and Criminal Prosecution during the Florentine Renaissance*. Ithaca, N.Y., 1985.

Elias, Norbert. "On Transformation of Aggressiveness." *Theory and Society* 5 (1978): 229–42.

Enfance abandonnée et société en Europe: XIVe–XXes: actes du colloque international, Rome, 30–1 janvier, 1987. Rome, 1991.

Epstein, Stephan. "Cities, Regions and the Late Medieval Crisis: Sicily and Tuscany Compared." *Past & Present* 130 (1991): 3–50.

———. *An Island for Itself: Economic Development and Social Change in Late Medieval Sicily*. Cambridge, 1993.

Ercole, Francesco. "L'istituto dotale nella pratica e nella legislazione statutaria dell'Italia superiore." *Rivista Italiana per le Sienze Giuridiche* 46 (1910): 197–211.

Fabbri, Lorenzo. *Alleanza matrimoniale e patriziato nella Firenze del'400: studio sulla famiglia Strozzi.* Florence, 1991.

——. "La sottomissione di Volterra allo stato fiorentino: controllo istituzionale e strategia di governo (1361–1435)." Ph.D. thesis, Università degli studi di Firenze, 1994.

Ferguson, Margaret W., Maureen Quilligan, and Nancy J. Vickers, eds. *Rewriting the Renaissance: The Discourses of Sexual Difference in Early Modern Europe.* Chicago, 1986.

Finucci, Valeria. *The Lady Vanishes: Subjectivity and Representation in Castiglione and Ariosto.* Stanford, Calif., 1992.

Foucault, Michel. *Folie et déraison: histoire de la folie à l'age classique.* Paris, 1961.

Frugoni, Chiara. "The Imagined Woman." In Klapisch-Zuber, *Silences of the Middle Ages.*

Franceschi, Franco. *Oltre il "Tumulto": i fiorentini dell'arte della lana fra Tre- e Quattrocento.* Florence, 1993.

Fustel de Coulanges, N. D. *La cité antique: étude sur le culte, le droit, les institutions de la Grèce et de Rome.* Paris, 1864.

Galetti, Paola. "La donna contadina: figure femminili nei contratti agrari italiani dell'alto medioevo." In Muzzarelli, Galetti, and Andreolli, *Donne e lavoro nell'Italia medievale.*

Gatrell, V. A. C. "The Decline of Theft and Violence in Victorian and Edwardian England." In Gatrell, Lenman, and Parker, *Crime and the Law.*

Gatrell, V. A. C., Bruce Lenman, and Geoffrey Parker, eds. *Crime and the Law: The Social History of Crime in Western Europe since 1500.* London, 1980.

Gauvard, Claude. *"De Grace especial": crime, état et société en France à la fin du Moyen Age.* Paris, 1991.

Gavitt, Philip. *Charity and Children in Renaissance Florence: The Ospedale degli Innocenti, 1410–1536.* Ann Arbor, Mich., 1990.

Genicot, Léopold. "Crisis: From the Middle Ages to Modern Times." In *The Cambridge Economic History of Europe: I,* 2d ed., edited by M. M. Postan. Cambridge, 1966.

Giardina, Camillo. "'Advocatus' e 'mundualdus' nel Lazio e nell'Italia meridionale." *Rivista di Storia del Diritto Italiano* 9 (1936): 291–310.

Gill, Katherine. "Open Monasteries for Women in Late Medieval and Early Modern Italy: Two Roman Examples." In Monson, *Crannied Wall.*

——. "Women and the Production of Religious Literature in the Vernacular, 1300–1500." In Matter and Coakley, *Creative Women in Medieval and Early Modern Italy.*

Ginatempo, Maria. *Crisi di un territorio: il popolamento della toscana senese alla fine del medioevo.* Florence, 1988.

Ginzburg, Carlo. *I Benandanti: stregoneria e culti agrari tra Cinquecento e Seicento.* Turin, 1966.

―――. *Il formaggio e i vermi: il cosmo di un mugnaio del '500.* Turin, 1976.

―――. "Microstoria: due o tre cose che so di lei." *QS* 29 (1994): 511–39.

―――. "Spie: radici di un paradigma indiziario." In *Crisi della ragione,* edited by A. Gargani. Turin, 1979.

Ginzburg, Carlo, and Carlo Poni. "The Name and the Game: Unequal Exchange and the Historiographic Marketplace." In Muir and Ruggiero, *Microhistory and the Lost Peoples of Europe.*

Goldberg, P. J. P. *Women, Work, and Life Cycle in a Medieval Economy: Women in York and Yorkshire c. 1300–1520.* Oxford, 1992.

Goldthwaite, Richard. "The Florentine Palace as Domestic Architecture." *American Historical Review* 77 (1972): 977–1012.

―――. "I Prezzi del grano a Firenze dal XIV al XVI secolo." *QS* 28 (1975): 5–36.

―――. *Private Wealth in Renaissance Florence: A Study of Four Families.* Princeton, N.J., 1968.

Goody, Jack. *Death, Property, and the Ancestors: A Study of the Mortuary Customs of the Lodagaa of West Africa.* Stanford, Calif., 1962.

―――. "Inheritance, Property, and Women: Some Comparative Considerations." In Goody, Thirsk, and Thompson, *Family and Inheritance.*

Goody, Jack, Joan Thirsk, and E. P. Thompson, eds. *Family and Inheritance: Rural Society in Western Europe, 1200–1800.* Cambridge, 1976.

Greenblatt, Stephen J. *Renaissance Self-Fashioning from More to Shakespeare.* Chicago, 1980.

Gregory, Heather. "Daughters, Dowries, and the Family in Fifteenth-Century Florence." *Rinascimento.* 2d ser. 27 (1987): 215–37.

Grendi, Edoardo. "Micro-analisi e storia sociale." *QS* 35 (1977): 506–20.

―――. "'Premessa' to *Fonti criminali e storia sociale.*" *QS* 66 (1987): 695–700.

―――. "Sulla 'storia criminale': risposta a Mario Sbriccoli." *QS* 73 (1990): 269–75.

Grieco, Sara F. Mathews. *Ange ou diablesse: la représentation de la femme au XVIᵉ siècle.* Paris, 1991.

―――. "The Body, Appearance, and Sexuality." In Davis and Farge, *Renaissance and Enlightment Paradoxes.*

Guichard, Pierre. *Structures sociales "orientales" et "occidentales" dans l'Espagne musulmane.* Paris, 1977.

Guidi, Guidubaldo. *Il governo della città-repubblica di Firenze del primo Quattrocento.* Florence, 1981.

Gurr, T. R. "Historical Trends in Violent Crime: A Critical Review of the Evidence." *Crime and Justice: An Annual Review of Research* 3 (1981): 295–353.

Gutkind, Kurt S. *Fraunbriefe aus der italienische Renaissance: Gesammelt und Ubertragen.* Heidelberg, 1928.

Hajnal, J. "European Marriage Patterns in Perspective." In *Population and History,* edited by D. V. Glass and D. E. C. Eversley. London, 1965.

Hammer, Carl I., Jr. "Patterns of Homicide in a Medieval University Town: Fourteenth Century Oxford." *Past & Present* 78 (1978): 3–23.

Hanawalt (Westman), Barbara. "The Female Felon in Fourteenth-Century England." *Viator* 5 (1974): 253–68.

———. "The Peasant Family and Crime in Fourteenth Century England." *Comparative Studies in Society and History* 18 (1976): 297–320.

Hatcher, John. "England in the Aftermath of the Black Death." *Past & Present* 144 (1994): 3–35.

———. *Plague, Population, and the English Economy, 1348–1530.* London, 1977.

Heißler, Sabine. *Frauen der italienischen Renaissance: Heilige, Kriegerinnen, Opfer.* Pfaffenweiler, 1990.

Helmholz, R. H. "Infanticide in the Province of Canterbury during the Fifteenth Century." *History of Childhood Quarterly* (1975): 379–90.

Henderson, John. *Piety and Charity in Late Medieval Florence.* Oxford, 1994.

Herlihy, David. "Biology and History: The Triumph of Monogamy." *Journal of Interdisciplinary History* 25 (1995): 571–83.

———. *The Black Death and the Transformation of the West.* Edited by Samuel Cohn Jr. Cambridge, Mass., 1997.

———. "Deaths, Marriages, Births, and the Tuscan Economy (ca. 1300–1550)." In *Population Patterns in the Past,* edited by Ronald Lee. New York, 1977.

———. "Did Women Have a Renaissance? A Reconsideration." *Medievalia et Humanistica,* new ser. 13 (1985): 1–22.

———. "Direct and Indirect Taxes." In *Finances et comptabilités urbaines du XIIIe au XVIe siècle.* Brussels, 1964.

———. "Family Solidarity in Medieval Italian History." In *Economy, Society, and Government in Medieval Italy,* edited by David Herlihy, Robert S. Lopez, and Vsevolod Slessarev. Kent, Oh., 1969.

———. Foreword to Klapisch-Zuber, *Women, Family, and Ritual in Renaissance Italy.*

———. "Growing Old in the Quattrocento." In *Old Age in Preindustrial Society,* edited by Peter Stearns. New York, 1982.

———. "Mapping Households in Medieval Italy." *Catholic Historical Review* 58 (1972): 1–21.

———. *Medieval Households.* Cambridge, Mass., 1985.

———. *Medieval and Renaissance Pistoia: The Social History of an Italian Town, 1200–1430.* New Haven, Conn., 1967.

———. *Opera Muliebria: Women and Work in Medieval Europe.* New York, 1990.

———. "Santa Caterina and San Bernardino: Their Teachings on the Family." In *Atti del Simposio internazionale Cateriniano-Bernardiniano,* edited by Domenico Maffei and Paolo Nardi. Siena, 1982.

———. "Some Psychological and Social Roots of Violence in Tuscan Cities." In *Violence and Civil Disorder in Italian Cities, 1200–1500,* edited by Lauro Martines. Berkeley, Calif., 1972.

———. "Women's Work in the Towns of Traditional Europe." In Cavaciocchi, *La donna nell'economia.*

Herlihy, David, and Christiane Klapisch-Zuber. *Les Toscans et leurs familles: une étude du catasto florentin de 1427.* Paris, 1978.

Hobsbawn, Eric. "The Revival of Narrative: Some Comments." *Past & Present* 86 (1980): 3–8.

Hoffman, Philip T. *Church and Community in the Diocese of Lyon, 1500–1789.* New Haven, Conn., 1984.

———. "Wills and Statistics: Tobit Analysis and the Counter-Reformation in Lyon." *Journal of Interdisciplinary History* 14 (1984): 813–34.

Hollingsworth, Mary and T. H. "Plague Mortality Rates by Age and Sex in the Parish of St. Botolph's without Bishopsgate, London, 1603." *Population Studies* 25 (1971): 131–46.

Horrox, Rosemary, ed. *The Black Death.* Manchester Medieval Source Series. Manchester, 1994.

Hughes, Diane O. "Distinguishing Signs: Ear-Rings, Jews, and Franciscan Rhetoric in the Italian Renaissance City." *Past & Present* 112 (1986): 3–59.

———. "Domestic Ideals and Social Behavior: Evidence from Medieval Genoa." In *The Family in History,* edited by Charles E. Rosenberg. Philadelphia, 1975.

———. "From Brideprice to Dowry in Mediterranean Europe." *Journal of Family History* 3 (1978): 262–96.

———. "Regulating Women's Fashion." In Klapisch-Zuber, *Silences of the Middle Ages.*

———. "Representing the Family: Portraits and Purposes in Early Modern Italy." *Journal of Interdisciplinary History* 17 (1986): 7–38.

———. "Struttura familiare e sistemi di successione ereditaria nei testamenti dell'Europa medievale." *QS* 33 (1976): 929–53.

———. "Urban Growth and Family Structure in Medieval Genoa." *Past & Present* 66 (1975): 3–28.

Hunecke, Volker. "Intensità e fluttuazioni degli abbandonni dal XV al XIX secolo." In *Enfance abandonée.* Rome, 1991.

Hunniset, R. F. *The Medieval Coroner.* Cambridge, 1961.

Johnson, Geraldine. "The Lion on the Piazza: Patrician Politics and Public Statuary in Central Florence." In *Secular Sculpture, 1350–1550,* edited by Thomas Frangenberg and Phillip Lindley. Stanford, U.K., 1995.

Kellum, Barbara A. "Infanticide in England in the Later Middle Ages." *History of Childhood Quarterly* (1974): 367–88.

Kelly, Joan (Gadol). "Did Women Have a Renaissance?" In *Women, History, and Theory: The Essays of Joan Kelly.* Chicago, 1984.

———. *Leon Battista Alberti: Universal Man of the Early Renaissance.* Chicago, 1973.

Kent, D. V. *The Rise of the Medici: Faction in Florence, 1426–1434.* Oxford, 1978.

Kent, F. W. *Household and Lineage in Renaissance Florence: The Family Life of the Capponi, Ginori, and Rucellai.* Princeton, N.J., 1977.

Kent, F. W., and D. V. Kent. *Neighbours and Neighbourhood in Renaissance Florence: The District of the Red Lion in the Fifteenth Century.* Locust Valley, N.Y., 1982.

Kertzer, David I., and Michael J. White. "Cheating the Angelmakers: Surviving Infant Abandonment in Nineteenth-Century Italy." *Continuity and Change* 9 (1994): 451–80.

King, Margaret L. "Booklined Cells: Women and Humanism in the Italian Renaissance." In Labalme, *Beyond Their Sex*.

———. *Women of the Renaissance*. Chicago, 1991.

Kirshner, Julius. "Maritus Lucretur Dotem Uxoris Sue Premortue in Late Medieval Florence." Zeitschrift der Savigny-Stiftung für Rechtsgeschichte 121. *Kanonistische Abteilung 77* (1991): 111–55.

———. "Materials for a Gilded Cage: Non-Dotal Assets in Florence (1300–1500)." In *The Family in Italy from Antiquity to the Present*, edited by Richard Saller and David Kertzer. New Haven, 1991.

———. "Wives' Claims against Insolvent Husbands in Late Medieval Italy." In *Women of the Medieval World: Essays in Honor of John H. Mundy,* edited by Julius Kirshner and Suzanne F. Wemple. Oxford, 1985.

Kirshner, Julius, and Jacques Pluss. "Two Fourteenth-Century Opinions on Dowries, Paraphernalia, and Non-Dotal Goods." *Bulletin of Medieval Canon Law* 9 (1979): 65–77.

Klapisch-Zuber, Christiane. "Blood Parents and Milk Parents: Wet Nursing in Florence, 1300–1530." In *Women, Family, and Ritual*.

———. "The 'Cruel Mother': Maternity, Widowhood, and Dowry in Florence in the Fourteenth and Fifteenth Centuries." In *Women, Family, and Ritual*. First in *Annales: E.S.C.* 38 (1983): 1097–109.

———. "Déclin démographique et structure du ménage: l'exemple de Prato, fin XIVe–fin XVe siècle." In *Famille et parenté dans l'occident médiéval: actes du colloque de Paris (6–8 Juin 1974),* edited by Georges Duby and Jacques Le Goff. Rome, 1977.

———. "Le dernier enfant: fécondité et vieillissement chez les Florentines XIVe–XVe siècles." In *Mélanges offerts à Jacques Dupàquier*, edited by Jean-Pierre Bardet, François Lebrun, and René Le Mée. Paris, 1993.

———. "An Ethnology of Marriage in the Age of Humanism." In *Women, Family, and Ritual*. First in *Annales: E.S.C.* 36 (1981): 1016–27.

———. "La fécondité des Florentines (XIV–XVIe siècles)." *Annales de Démographie Historique* (1988): 41–57.

———. "Female Celibacy and Service in Florence in the Fifteenth Century." In *Women, Family, and Ritual*. First in *Annales de Démographie Historique* (1981): 289–302.

———. "La femme et le lignage florentin (xive–xvie siècles)." In *Persons in Groups: Social Behavior as Identity Formation in Medieval and Renaissance Europe*, edited by Richard Trexler. Binghamton, N.Y., 1985.

———. "Les femmes dans les rituels de l'alliance et de la naissance à Florence." In *Riti e rituali nelle società medievali,* edited by Jacques Chiffoleau, Lauro Martines, and Agostino Paravicini Bagliani. Spoleto, 1994.

———. "The Griselda Complex: Dowry and Marriage Gifts in the Quattrocento." In *Women, Family, and Ritual.* First in *MEFR* 94 (1982): 7–43.

———. "The Hidden Power of Women." In Klapisch-Zuber, *Silences of the Middle Ages.*

———. "Holy Dolls: Play and Piety in Florence in the Quattrocento." In *Women, Family, and Ritual.* First in *Les jeux à la Renaissance,* edited by J.-C. Margolin and P. Ariès. Paris, 1983.

———. "Including Women." In Klapisch-Zuber, *Silences of the Middle Ages.*

———. *La maison et le nom: stratégies et rituels dans l'Italie de la Renaissance.* Paris, 1990.

———. "Mezzadria e insediamenti rurali alla fine del medio evo." In *Civiltà ed economia agricola in Toscana nei secc. XIII–XV.*

———. "The Name 'Remade': Given Names in Florence in the Fourteenth and Fifteenth Centuries." In Klapisch-Zuber, *Women, Family, and Ritual.* First in *L'Homme* 20 (1980): 77–104.

———. "Il pubblico, il privato, l'intimità: una introduzione." *Ricerche Storiche* 16 (1986): 451–58.

———. "Women Servants in Florence during the Fourteenth and Fifteenth Centuries." In *Women and Work in Preindustrial Europe,* edited by Barbara A. Hanawalt. Bloomington, Ind., 1986.

———. "Zacharias; or, the Ousted Father: Nuptial Rites in Tuscany between Giotto and the Council of Trent." In *Women, Family, and Ritual.* First in *Annales: E.S.C.* 34 (1979): 1216–43.

———. "Le 'zane' della sposa: la donna fiorentina e il suo corredo nel rinascimento." In *La famiglia e le donne nel rinascimento a Firenze.* Bari, 1988. First in *Mémorie* 11–12 (1984): 12–23.

———. *Women, Family, and Ritual in Renaissance Italy.* Translated by Lydia Cochrane. Chicago, 1985.

———, ed. *Silences of the Middle Ages.* Vol. 2 of *A History of Women in the West,* edited by Georges Duby and Michelle Perrot. Cambridge, 1992.

Klapisch-Zuber, Christiane, and Michel Demonet. "'A uno pane e uno vino': The Rural Tuscan Family at the Beginning of the Fifteenth Century." In *Women, Family, and Ritual.* First in *Annales: E.S.C.* 27 (1972): 873–901.

Kohler, J., and G. degli Azzi. *Das Florentiner Strafrecht des XIV Jahrhunderts.* Mannheim-Leipzig, 1909.

Kristeller, Paul O. "Learned Women of Early Modern Italy: Humanists and University Scholars." In Labalme, *Beyond Their Sex.*

Kuehn, Thomas. "'Cum consensu mundualdi': Legal Guardianship of Women in Quattrocento Florence." *Viator* 13 (1980): 309–33.

———. *Emancipation in Late Medieval Florence.* New Brunswick, N.J., 1982.

———. "Law, Death, and Heirs in the Renaissance: Repudiation of Inheritance in Florence." *Renaissance Quarterly* 45 (1992): 484–516.

———. *Law, Family, and Women: Toward a Legal Anthropology of Renaissance Italy.* Chicago, 1991.

————. Review of Cohn, *Death and Property. Journal of Modern History* 62 (1990): 624–26.

Labalme, Patricia M., ed. *Beyond Their Sex: Learned Women of the European Past.* New York, 1980.

Langer, William L. "Further Notes on the History of Infanticide." *History of Childhood Quarterly* (1974): 129–34.

————. "Infanticide: A Historical Survey." *History of Childhood Quarterly* (1974): 353–65.

Lansing, Carol. *The Florentine Magnates: Lineage and Faction in a Medieval Commune.* Princeton, N.J., 1991.

la Roncière, Charles-M. de. "Indirect Taxes, or 'Gabelles,' at Florence in the Fourteenth Century: The Evolution of Tariffs and Problems of Collection." In *Florentine Studies,* edited by Nicolai Rubinstein. London, 1968.

————. *Prix et salaires à Florence au XIVe siècle (1280–1380).* Rome, 1982.

————. "Regards sur la femme dans la Florence du Trecento." In *Histoire et société: mélanges offerts à Georges Duby.* Aix-en-Provence, 1992.

Lastri, Marco. *Ricerche sull'antica e moderna popolaziione della città di Firenze.* Florence, 1775.

Lazzareschi, E. "Una mistica senese: Passitea Crogi, 1564–1615." *BSSP* 22 (1915): 419–433.

Lenman, Bruce, and Geoffrey Parker. "The State, the Community, and Criminal Law in Early Modern Europe." In Gatrell, Lenman, and Parker, *Crime and the Law.*

Le Roy Ladurie, Emmanuel. "Chaunu, Lebrun, Vovelle: The New History of Death." In *The Territory of the Historian,* vol.1, translated by Ben Reynolds and Siân Reynolds. Chicago, 1979.

————. *Les paysans de Languedoc.* 2 vols. Paris, 1966.

————. *Montaillou: village occitan, de 1294 à 1324.* Paris, 1974.

Lesnick, Daniel R. "Insults and Threats in Medieval Todi." *Journal of Medieval History* 17 (1991): 71–91.

Letteratura italiana: gli autori, dizionario bio-bibliografico e indici. 2 vols. Turin, 1991.

Levi, Giovanni. *L'eredità immateriale. carriera di un esorcista nel Piemonte del Seicento.* Turin, 1985.

Litchfield, R. Burr. *Emergence of a Bureaucracy: The Florentine Patricians, 1530–1790.* Princeton, N.J., 1986.

Livi-Bacci, Massimo. *Population and Nutrition: An Essay on European Demographic History.* Cambridge, 1991.

Lombardi, Daniela, and Flores Reggiani. "Da assistita a serva: circuiti di reclutamento delle serve attraverso le istituzioni assistenziali (Firenze-Milano, XVII–XVIII secoli)." In Cavaciocchi, *La donna nell'economia.*

Lowe, K. J. P. "Female Strategies for Success in a Male-Ordered World: The Benedictine Convent of le Murate in Florence in the Fifteenth and Early Sixteenth Centuries." In *Women in the Church*. Studies in Church History 27. Oxford, 1990.

Lundsgaarde, Henry P. *Murder in Space City: A Cultural Analysis of Houston Homicide Patterns*. New York, 1977.

Maclean, Ian. *The Renaissance Notion of Woman: A Study in the Fortunes of Scholasticism and Medical Science in European Intellectual Life*. Cambridge, 1980.

McNeill, J. R. *The Mountains of the Mediterranean World: An Environmental History*. Cambridge, 1992.

Madero, Marta. *Manos violentas, palabras vedadas: la injuria en Castile y Leon, siglos XIII–XV*. Madrid, 1992.

Maine, Sir Henry. *Dissertations on Early Law and Custom*. London, 1883.

Manikowska, Halina. "'Accorr'uomo': il 'Popolo' nell'ammistrazione della giustizia a Firenze durante il XIV secolo." *Ricerche Storiche* 18 (1988): 523–49.

Marrara, Danilo. *Riseduti e nobilità: profilo storico-instituzionale di un'oligarchia toscana nei secoli XVI–XVII*. In *Biblioteca del "Bollettiino Storico Pisano."* No. 16. Pisa, 1976.

Martin, John. "Out of the Shadow: Heretical and Catholic Women in Renaissance Venice." *Journal of Family History* 5 (1985): 21–34.

Martines, Lauro. *An Italian Renaissance Sextet: Six Tales in Historical Context*. Translated by Murtha Baca. New York, 1994.

———. "A Way of Looking at Women in Renaissance Florence." *Journal of Medieval and Renaissance Studies* 4 (1974): 15–28.

Matter, E. Ann, and John Coakley, eds. *Creative Women in Medieval and Early Modern Italy: A Religious and Artistic Renaissance*. Philadelphia, 1994.

Mazzi, Maria Serena. "Cronache di periferia dello stato fiorentino: reati contro la morale nel primo quattrocento." *Studi Storici* 27 (1987): 609–35.

———. "Incanti amorosi e seduzioni nel Decameron: un'immagine della sensualità medievale." In *Studi storici: cultura e società nell'Italia medievale, studi per Paolo Brezzi*. Rome, 1988.

———. "Il mondo della prostituzione nella Firenze tardo medievale." *Ricerche Storiche* 14 (1984): 337–63.

———. *Prostitute e lenoni nella Firenze del Quattrocento*. Milan, 1991.

Molho, Anthony. "Fisco e società a Firenze nel quattrocento (a proposito di una ricerca di Elio Conti)." *Società e Storia* 8 (1985): 929–36.

———. "The Florentine Oligarchy and the Balìa of the Late Trecento." *Speculum* 43 (1968): 23–51.

———. *Florentine Public Finances in the Early Renaissance, 1400–1433*. Cambridge, 1971.

———. *Marriage Alliance in Late Medieval Florence*. Cambridge, 1994.

———. "Politics and the Ruling Class in Early Renaissance Florence." *Nuova Rivista Storica* 52 (1968): 401–20.

———. "*Tamquam vere mortua*: Le professioni religiose femminili nella Firenze del tardo medioevo." *Società e Storia* 43 (1989): 1–44.

———. "Tre città-stato e i loro debiti pubblici: quesiti e ipotesi sulla storia di

Firenze, Genova, e Venezia." In *Italia 1350–1450: tra crisi, trasformazione, sviluppo: atti del tredicesimo Convegno Internazionale di studio (Pistoia 10–13 maggio 1991)*. Florence, 1993.

Molho, Anthony, and Julius Kirshner. "The Dowry Fund and the Marriage Market in Early Quattrocento Florence." *Journal of Modern History* 50 (1978): 403–38.

Mols, Roger. "Saint Charles Borromée, pionnier de la pastorale moderna." *Novelle revue théologique* 79 (1957): 600–21, 715–47.

Monson, Craig, ed. *The Crannied Wall: Women, Religion, and the Arts in Early Modern Europe*. Ann Arbor, Mich., 1992.

Muir, Edward. "Introduction: Observing Trifles." In Muir and Ruggiero, *Microhistory and the Lost Peoples of Europe*.

———. *Mad Blood Stirring: Vendetta and Factions in Friuli during the Renaissance*. Baltimore, 1993.

Muir, Edward, and Giudo Ruggiero, eds. *History from Crime: Selections from Quaderni Storici*. Baltimore, 1994.

———. *Microhistory and the Lost Peoples of Europe*. Translated by Eren Branch. Baltimore, 1991.

Muzzarelli, Maria Giuseppina, Paola Galetti, and Bruno Andreolli, eds. *Donne e lavoro nell'Italia medievale*. Turin, 1991.

Nardi, Franco. "Aspetti della vita dei religiosi a Siena nell'età della Controriforma (1600–1650)." *BSSP* 93 (1986): 194–240.

———. "Matteo Guerra e la Congregazione dei Sacri Chiodi (secc. XVI–XVII): aspetti della religiosità senese nell'età della controriforma." *BSSP* 91 (1984): 12–148.

Neumann, Franz. *Behemoth: The Structure and Practice of National Socialism, 1933–1944*. 2d ed. London, 1967.

Norberg, Kathryn. *Rich and Poor in Grenoble, 1600–1814*. Berkeley, Calif., 1985.

Oblelkevich, James, ed. *Religion and the People, 800–1700*. Chapel Hill, N.C., 1979.

Oliger, L. "Regula Reclusorum Angliae et questiones tres de vita solitaria saec. XIII–XIV." *Antonianum* 34 (1934): 265–66.

Opitz, Claudia. "Life in the Late Middle Ages." In Klapisch-Zuber, *Silences of the Middle Ages*.

Padgett, John F. "Marriage and Elite Structure in Renaissance Florence, 1282–1500." Paper prepared for the Social Science History Association, 14 October 1994.

Papi, Anna Benvenuti. "Le forme comunitarie della penitenza femminile francescana: schede per un censimento toscano." In Pazzelli and Temperini, *Prime manifestazioni*.

———. "Umiliana dei Cerchi: nascita di un culto nella Firenze del Dugento." *Studi Francescani* 77 (1980): 87–117.

Parenti, Giuseppe. *Prezzi e mercato del grano a Siena (1546–1765)*. Florence, 1942.

Pasqui, Ubaldo. "Una congiura per liberare Arezzo dalla dipendenza dei fiorentini (1431)." *ASI*, 5th ser. 5 (1890): 1–19.

Pastore, Alessandro. *Crimine e giustizia in tempo di peste nell'Europa moderna.* Rome, 1991.

———. "Testamenti in tempo di peste: la pratica notarile a Bologna nel 1630." *Societa et Storia* 5 (1982): 263–97.

Pazzelli, R., and L. Temperini, eds. *Prime manifestazioni di vita comunitaria maschile e femminile nel movimento Francescano della penitenza (1215–1447): atti del Convegno di Studi Francescani, Assisi, 30 giugno–2 luglio 1981.* Rome, 1982.

Pertile, Antonio. *Storia del diritto privato.* Vol. 3 of *Storia del diritto Italiano.* Padua, 1871.

Pinto, Giuliano. "Controllo politico e ordine pubblico nei primi vicariati fiorentini: gli 'atti criminali degli ufficiali forensi.'" *QS* 49 (1982): 226–41.

———. "Il personale, le balie e i salariati dell'ospedale di San Gallo di Firenze negli anni 1395–1406: note per la storia del salariato nelle città medievale." *Ricerche Storiche* 4 (1974): 113–68.

Pitkin, Hanna Fenichel. *Fortune Is a Woman: Gender and Politics in the Thought of Niccolò Macchiavelli.* Berkeley, Calif., 1984.

Pocock, John. *The Machiavellian Moment: Florentine Political Thought and the Atlantic Republican Tradition.* Princeton, N.J., 1975.

Poos, Lawrence R. *A Rural Society after the Black Death: Essex 1350–1525.* Cambridge, 1991.

———. "Sex, Lies, and the Church Courts of Pre-Reformation England." *Journal of Interdisciplinary History* 25 (1995): 585–607.

Postan, M. M. *Essays on Medieval Agriculture and General Problems of the Medieval Economy.* Cambridge, 1973.

Power, Eileen. *English Medieval Nunneries.* New York, 1964.

Prevenier, Walter. "Violence against Women in a Medieval Metropolis: Paris around 1400." In *Law, Custom, and the Social Fabric in Medieval Europe: Essays in Honor of Bryce Lyon,* edited by Bernard S. Bachrach and David Nicholas. Kalamazoo, Mich., 1990.

Prosperi, Adriano. "La figura del Vescovo fra '400 e '500." In Chittolini and Miccoli, *Storia d'Italia.*

Raggio, Osvaldo. *Faide e parentele: lo stato genovese visto della Fontanabuona.* Turin, 1990.

Raveggi, Sergio, and Maria Serena Mazzi. *Gli uomini e le cose nelle campagne fiorentine del Quattrocento.* Florence, 1983.

Revel, Jacques. "Microanalisi e costruzione del sociale." *QS* 86 (1994): 549–75.

Riemer, Eleanor S. "Women, Dowries, and Capital Investment in Thirteenth-Century Siena." In *The Marriage Bargain: Women and Dowries in European History,* edited by Marion A. Kaplan. New York, 1985.

———. "Women in the Medieval City: Sources and Uses of Wealth by Sienese Women in the Thirteenth Century." Ph.D. diss., New York University, 1975.

Rigon, Antonio. "I laici nella chiesa padovana del Duecento. Conversi, oblati penitenti." In *Contributi alla storia della chiesa padovana nell'età medioevale,* vol. 1. Padua, 1979.

Rocke, Michele. "Il controllo dell'omosessualità a Firenze nel XV secolo: gli 'Ufficiali di Notte.'" *QS* 66 (1987): 701–24.

———. *Friendly Affections, Nefarious Vices: Homosexuality, Male Culture, and the Policing of Sex in Renaissance Florence.* New York, 1996.

———. "Sodomites in Fifteenth-Century Tuscany: The Views of Bernardino of Siena." In *The Pursuit of Sodomy: Male Homosexuality in Renaissance and Enlightenment Europe,* edited by K. Gerard and G. Hekma. New York, 1989.

Romano, Dennis. "The Regulation of Domestic Service in Renaissance Venice." *Sixteenth Century Journal* 22 (1991): 661–77.

Ronzani, M. "Penitenti e ordini mendicanti a Pisa sino all'inizio del Trecento." *MEFR* 89 (1977): 733–41.

Rosenthal, Elaine G. "The Position of Women in Renaissance Florence: Neither Autonomy nor Subjection." In *Florence and Italy: Renaissance Studies in Honour of Nicolai Rubinstein,* edited by Peter Denley and Caroline Elam. London, 1988.

Ross, James Bruce. "The Middle-Class Child in Urban Italy, Fourteenth to Early Sixteenth Century." In *The History of Childhood: The Untold Story of Child Abuse,* edited by Lloyd deMause. New York, 1974.

Rubin, Patricia. *Giorgio Vasari: Art and History.* New Haven, 1995.

Ruggiero, Guido. "The Abbot's Concubine." Lecture at the Villa I Tatti, 1993.

———. *Binding Passions: Tales of Magic, Marriage, and Power at the End of the Renaissance.* New York, 1993.

———. *The Boundaries of Eros: Sex Crime and Sexuality in Renaissance Venice.* New York, 1985.

Rusconi, Roberto. "Confraternite, compagnie e devozioni." In Chittolini and Miccoli, *Storia d'Italia.*

———. "Discorso conclusivo." In *Prime manifestazioni di vita comunitaria maschile e femminile,* edited by R. Pazzelli and L. Temperini. Rome, 1982.

———, ed. *Il movimento religioso femminile in Umbria nei secoli XIII–XIV: atti del convegno internazionale di studio nell'ambito delle celebrazioni per l'VIII centenario della nascita di S. Francesco d'Assisi.* Florence, 1984.

Sandri, Lucia. "Baliatico mercenario e abbandonno dei bambini alle istituzioni assistenziali: Un medesimo disagio sociale?" In *Donne e lavoro nell'Italia medievale,* edited by Maria Guiseppina Muzzarelli, Paola Galetti, and Bruno Andreolli. Turin, 1991.

———. "Modalità dell'abbandono dei fanciulli in area urbana: gli esposti dell'ospedale di San Gallo di Firenze nella prima metà del XV secolo." In *Enfance abandonée.* Rome, 1991.

———. *L'ospedale di S. Maria della Scala di S. Gimignano nel Quattrocento: contributo alla storia dell'infanzia abbandonata.* Florence, 1982.

Sbriccoli, Mario. "Fonti giudiziarie e fonti giuridiche: reflessioni sulla fase attuale degli studi di storia del crimine e della giustizia." *Studi Storici* 29 (1988): 491–501.

Scaraffia, Lucetta, and Gabriella Zarri, eds. *Donne e fede: santità e vita religiosa in Italia.* Bari, 1994.

Schen, Claire. "Charity in London, 1500–1620: From the 'Wealth of Souls' to the 'Most Need.'" Ph.D. diss., Brandeis University, 1994.

Sebastiani, Lucia. "Monasteri femminili milanesi tra medioevo e età moderna." In *Florence and Milan, Comparisons and Relations: Acts of Two Conferences at Villa I Tatti 1982–1984*, vol. 2, edited by C. Smyth and G. Garfagnini. Florence, 1989.

Sensi, Mario. "Incarcerate e recluse in Umbria nei secoli XIII e XIV: un Bizzocaggio centro-italiano." In *Il movimento religioso femminile,* edited by Roberto Rusconi. Florence, 1984.

———. "La monacazione delle recluse nelle Valle Spoletina." In *S. Chiara da Montefalco e il suo tempo: atti del quarto convegno di studi storici ecclesiastici dell'arcidiocesi di Spoleto,* edited by C. Leonardi and E. Menestò. Perugia-Florence, 1985.

Servadio, Gaia. *La donna nel Rinascimento.* Milan, 1986.

Sharpe, J. A. *Crime in Early Modern England, 1550–1750.* London, 1984.

Skinner, Quentin. *The Renaissance.* Vol. 1 of *The Foundations of Modern Political Thought.* Cambridge, 1978.

Slicher van Bath, B. H. *The Agrarian History of Western Europe, A.D. 500–1850.* Translated by Olive Ordith. London, 1963.

Spierenburg, Peter. "Faces of Violence: Homicide Trends and Cultural Meanings, Amsterdam, 1431–1816." *Journal of Social History* 27 (1994): 701–16.

Stella, Alessandro. *La révolte des Ciompi: les hommes, les lieux, le travail.* Paris, 1993.

Stern, Laura Ikins. *The Criminal Law System of Medieval and Renaissance Florence.* Baltimore, 1994.

———. "Inquisition Procedure and Crime in Early Fifteenth-Century Florence." *Law and History Review* 8 (1990): 297–308.

Stone, Lawrence. *The Crisis of the Aristocracy, 1558–1641.* Oxford, 1965.

———. *The Family, Sex, and Marriage in England, 1500–1800.* New York, 1978.

———. "Interpersonal Violence in English Society." *Past & Present* 101 (1983): 22–33.

———. "The Revival of Narrative: Reflections on a New Old History." *Past & Present* 85 (1979): 3–24.

Stone, Lawrence, and J. C. Fawtier Stone. *An Open Elite? England, 1540–1880.* Oxford, 1984.

Strocchia, Sharon T. "Remembering the Family: Women, Kin, and Commemorative Masses in Renaissance Florence." *Renaissance Quarterly* 42 (1989): 635–54.

Stuard, Susan Mosher. Introduction to *Women in Medieval Society,* edited by Susan Mosher Stuart. Philadephia, 1976.

Takahashi, Tomoko. "I bambini abbandonati presso lo spedale di Santa Maria a San Gallo di Firenze nel tardo medioevo (1395–1463)." *Annuario: Istituto Giapponese di Cultura* 24 (1990–91): 59–81.

———. "I bambini e i genitori 'Espositori' dello spedale di santa Maria degli Innocenti di Firenze nel XV secolo." *Annuario: Istituto Giapponese di Cultura* 25 (1991–92): 35–75.

Tamassia, Nino. *La famiglia italiana nei secoli decimoquinto e decimosesto.* Milan, 1910.

Thomas, Keith. *Religion and the Decline of Magic.* Oxford, 1971.

Thomasset, Claude. "The Nature of Woman." In Klapisch-Zuber, *Silences of the Middle Ages.*

Tomas, Natalie. *'A Positive Novelty': Women and Public Life in Renaissance Florence.* Victoria, Australia.

Toubert, Pierre. "Le moment carolingien (VIIIe–Xe siècle)." In *Histoire de la famille,* vol. I, edited by André Burguière, Christiane Klapisch-Zuber, Martine Segalen, and Françoise Zonabend. Paris, 1986.

Townshend, Charles. *Making the Peace: Public Order and Public Security in Modern Britain.* Oxford, 1993.

Trexler, Richard C. "Le célibat à la fin du Moyen Age: les religieuses de Florence." *Annales: E.S.C.* 27 (1972): 1329–50.

———. "Death and Testament in the Episcopal Constitutions of Florence (1327)." In *Renaissance Studies in Honor of Hans Baron,* edited by Anthony Molho and John Tedeschi. Dekalb, Ill., 1971.

———. *Dependence in Context in Renaissance Florence.* Binghamton, N.Y., 1994.

———. "The Foundlings of Florence, 1395–1455." *History of Childhood Quarterly* (1973): 259–84.

———. "Infanticide in Florence: New Sources and First Results." *History of Childhood Quarterly* (1973): 98–116.

———. "La prostitution florentine aux XVe siècle: patronages et clientèles." *Annales: E.S.C.* 36 (1981): 983–1015.

———. *Public Life in Renaissance Florence.* New York, 1980.

———. "Ritual in Florence: Adolescence and Salvation in the Renaissance." In *Pursuit of Holiness,* edited by C. Trinkhaus and H. Oberman. Leiden, 1972.

———. "A Widow's Asylum of the Renaissance: The Orbatello of Florence." In *Old Age in Preindustrial Society,* edited by Peter Stearns. New York, 1982.

Turchini, Angelo. *Clero e fedeli a Rimini in eta post-Tridentina. Italia Sacra: studi e documenti di storia ecclesiastica* 27. Rome, 1978.

Vasari, Giorgio. *Le vite de' più eccellenti pittori scultori e architettori.* Turin, 1986.

Viazzo, Pier Paolo. *Upland Communities: Environment, Population, and Social Structure in the Alps since the Sixteenth Century.* Cambridge, 1989.

Vovelle, Michele. *La mort et l'occident, de 1300 à nos jours.* Paris, 1983.

———. *Piété baroque et la déchristianisation en Provence au XVIIIe siècle: les attitudes devant la mort d'après les clauses des testaments.* Paris, 1973.

Waley, Daniel. *Italian City-Republics.* 3d ed. London, 1988.

Walter, Ingeborg. "Infanticidio a Ponte Bocci, 2 Marzo 1406: Elementi di un processo." *Studi Storici* 27 (1986): 637–48.

Walzer, Michael. *The Revolution of the Saints: A Study in the Origins of Radical Politics.* New York, 1976.

Weaver, Elissa B. "The Convent Wall in Tuscan Convent Drama." In Monson, *Crannied Wall.*

————. "Le muse in convento: la scrittura profana delle monache italiane (1450–1650)." In Scaraffia and Zarri, *Donne e fede.*

————. "Suor Maria Clemente Ruoti, Playwright and Academician." In Matter and Coakley, *Creative Women in Medieval and Early Modern Italy.*

Weissman, Ronald. *Ritual Brotherhood in Renaissance Florence.* New York, 1982.

Wickham, C. J. *The Mountains and the City: The Tuscan Appennines in the Early Middle Ages.* Oxford, 1988.

Wiesner, Mary. "Spinsters and Seamstresses: Women in Cloth and Clothing Production." In Fergason, Quilligan and Vickers, *Rewriting the Renaissance.*

Wright, A. D. *The Counter-Reformation: Catholic Europe and the Non-Christian World.* New York, 1982.

Zancan, Marina. "La donna." In *Letteratura italiana: le questioni,* edited by R. Antonelli and A. Cicchetti. Turin, 1986.

Zarri, Gabriella, ed. *Finizione e santità tra medioevo ed età moderna.* Turin, 1991.

————. "Le istituzioni dell'educazione femminile." In *Le sedi della cultura nell'Emilia Romagna: I secoli moderni.* Bologna, 1984.

————. "I monasteri femminili a Bologna tra il XIII e il XVII secolo." *Atti e memorie: Deputazione di storia patria per le province di Romagna,* new ser. 24 (1973): 133–224.

————. "I monasteri femminili benedettini nella diocesi di Bologna (XIII–XVII)." *Ravennatensia* 9 (1980): 333–71.

————. "Monasteri femminili e città (secoli XV–XVIII)." In Chittolini and Miccoli, *Storia d'Italia.*

————. "Les prophètes de cour dans l'Italie de la Renaissance." *MEFR* 102 (1990): 649–75.

————. *Le sante vive: profezie di corte e devozione femminile tra '400 e '500.* Turin, 1990.

Zerner, Monique. "La population de Villeneuve-Saint-Georges et de Nogent-sur-Marne au XIe siècle d'après le polyptyque de Saint-Germain-des-Prés." *Annales de la Faculté des Lettres et Sciences Humaines de Nice* 37 (1979): 17–24.

Zorzi, Andrea. *L'amministrazione della giustizia penale nella repubblica fiorentina: aspetti e problemi.* Florence, 1988. Also in *ASI* 533 (1987): 391–453; *ASI* 534 (1987): 527–78.

————. "Giusdicenti e operatori di giustizia nello stato territoriale fiorentino del XV secolo." *Ricerche Storiche* 19 (1989): 517–52.

————. "I fiorentini e gli uffici pubblici nel primo Quattrocento: concorrenza, abusi, illegalità." *Quaderni Storici* 22 (1987): 725–51.

————. "The Judicial System in Florence in the Fourteenth and Fifteenth Centuries." In Dean and Lowe, *Crime, Society, and the Law.*

————. "Lo stato territoriale fiorentino (secoli XIV–XV): aspetti giurisdizionali." *Società e Storia* 50 (1990): 799–825.

Index

abandonment, 2, 14, 106, 158-60, 163, 172 n. 74, 199 n. 16, 214 nn. 41, 42, 215 nn. 55, 56

Abbati family, 180 n. 9

abbess of Lombardy, 107

abortion, 149

absolutism, 74

adoption, 150

adultery, 16–17, 33–34, 100, 106, 115–17, 129, 205 n. 86, 208 n. 127, 208 n. 132

Africa, 17, 52

age rounding, 152, 156, 214 nn. 36, 40

ages, 214 n. 35

Agliana, 107, 119

Alberti family: Giannozzo, 18–19, 32–33; Leon Battista, 4–5, 18–19, 31, 33, 38

Albizzi family, 93; government of, 38

Alexander V (pope), 113

Alpi fiorentine, 122, 132–33, 135, 142, 147, 149, 162, 211 n. 147, 214 n. 31

Alps, 205 n. 84; Greziani, 132–33

altars, altarpieces, 40, 112

Altopascio, 112

American Indians, 51

ancestors, 55, 97; worship of, 1–2

Anghiari, 103, 116, 124, 131, 134–36, 206 n. 110, 210 n. 146

anthropology, 11

Appalachia, 132

Appenines, 121, 211 n. 155, 216 n. 61. *See also* Alpi fiorentine; Bologna; Casentino; Firenzuola; mountains; Romagna

Apricale, 206 n. 109

Arezzo, 39–40, 45–49, 55, 83, 94, 129, 134, 195 n. 32; *contado*, 131, 135, 183 n. 57, 183 n. 61, 208 n. 132; rebellion, 123–25, 211 n. 156

Ariès, Phillipe, 39

Ariosto, Lodovico, 98

aristocracy, 10–11, 17, 19, 49, 56, 77, 96, 207 n. 111. *See also* feudatories

Arno river, 132

artisans, 3, 10. *See also* Ciompi; wages; workers

Asia, Asiatic societies, 106, 149

Assisi, 39–40, 55, 83–84, 94

Avignon, 43

Bailey, Victor, 125, 208 n. 125

Banker, James, 86, 192 n. 13

baptismal registers, 7, 214 n. 37

Barbialle, 113

Baron, Hans, 1, 207 n. 123

Battifolle, 117

Becker, Marvin, 134

Bellomo, Manilo, 8

Benson, Pamela, 168 n. 16, 169 n. 26

Bernardino da Siena, Saint, 15, 38, 89, 115, 120, 148, 150, 195 n. 36

bestiality, 101

Bibbiena (Arezzo), 115

Binion, Rudolf, 197 n. 65

Bisenzio, 138, 146

Black Death. *See* plague

blasphemy, 3, 16, 29, 198 n. 8

Boccaccio, Giovanni: *Corbaccio*, 115, 204 n. 82; *Decameron*, 13, 16–17, 35, 107–8, 110–11, 115, 173 n. 3, 191 n. 6, 200 n. 30, 203 n. 57, 203 n. 70, 204 nn. 71, 73, 79, 205 n. 86

Bologna, 84–85, 87, 121, 131, 192 n. 13, 209 n. 140, 211 n. 157; alps, 141; border with Florence, 134

Bolton, Jim, 214 n. 29

Borgo San Lorenzo, 132

Borgo San Sepolcro, 84, 87, 116, 124, 192 n. 13

Borromeo, Carlo, 59–60, 185 nn. 5, 10, 186 n. 12

Borromeo, Federigo, 185 n. 10

Bossi, Francesco, 58–59, 61, 72, 94, 186 n. 12

Boswell, John, 214 n. 41
Brackett, John, 175 n. 26
Braudel, Fernand, 150, 156, 161
Brown, Judith, 6, 95, 170 n. 37, 193 n. 15
Brucker, Gene, 21, 99
Bruni, Leonardo, 31
Bücher, Karl, 167 n. 10
Buco di Morello, 30
Burckhardt, Jacob, 1, 4–6, 10, 17–19, 56, 96, 103, 168 nn. 10–11.
burial, 58, 63–64, 187 n. 23

Calenzano, 212 n. 14
Calvana mountains, 138
Calvi, Giulia, 13
Calvinism, 57, 184 n. 2
Campi, 104, 198 n. 6
Campogialli, 207 n. 118
Cancellieri, Ricciardo, 121, 125, 207 n. 111
capi di famiglia. See *estimi*
capitano del popolo, 21, 23, 36–37, 99, 105, 121–22, 135, 174 n. 18, 211 n. 147
Caprona, 110
carcerate. See nuns
Carmichael, Ann, 191 n. 6
carnival, 178 n. 67, 199 n. 26; songs, 93
Casaboccaccio, 101
Casagrande, Carla, 197 n. 63
Casagrande, Giovanna, 86–87
Casassi, Messer Mariano, 112–13
Casentino, 130, 134–35, 159–61, 195 n. 32, 215 n. 49
Castel Bonizi, 100
Castel Fiorentino, 107, 109, 205 n. 85
Castel Focognano, 124
Castelfranco (Valdarno inferiore), 112
Castel Ranchi, 124
Castiglione, Baldessare, 5
Castiglione Aretino, 117
castration, 102, 105, 204 n. 74, 206 n. 110
catasti (taxes), 7, 14, 85–86, 121, 134, 137–38, 141–42, 146–48, 150–52, 155–56, 159–60, 162, 193 nn. 15, 16, 212 n. 12
Cathars, 95
Cathedral of Siena, 64
Catherine of Siena, Saint, 72, 95, 169 n. 28, 195 n. 36, 197 n. 63
cattle, livestock, 148

Cecchetti, Bartolomeo, 168 n. 10
Cerchi family: Consillius f.q. Ser Olivieri, 41, 180 n. 8; Umiliana, 95, 171 n. 64, 180 n. 8
Certaldo, 205 n. 86
Cévennes, 147
Chabot, Isabelle, 7, 118, 192 n. 15, 206 n. 98
chanson de geste, 5, 168 n. 16
chapels, 88
charity, 76, 93, 186 n. 18, 187 n. 23. See also confraternities; dowry; hospitals; monasteries; piety
Chaunu, Pierre, 39
Cherubini, Giovanni, 156, 216 n. 61
Cherubino da Siena, Fra, 150, 213 n. 28
Chianti, 99, 119, 159, 161, 198 n. 1, 210 n. 146
Chiffoleau, Jacques, 39
Chittolini, Giorgio, 134, 136, 211 n. 159
Chiusi (della Verna), 134
Chojnacki, Stanley, 9–10, 12–13, 85, 168 nn. 10, 12; 171 n. 56, 193 n. 19, 195 n. 44
Ciompi, revolt of, 20–23, 28, 30, 32–33, 37–38, 142, 172 n. 1
Cipolla, Carlo, 167 n. 5
Città di Castello, 87
Ciuto Brandini, 22
class (social), 61, 77, 96, 175 n. 36, 185 n. 8, 186 n. 13, 191 n. 6, 197 n. 71
clergy. See crime; friars; monks; priests
climate, 146
Clizia, 115, 178 n. 64. See also Machiavelli
cloth industry, 7–8, 22, 170 n. 37
Cohen, Elizabeth, 177 n. 58, 199 n. 12, 206 n. 104
Cohen, Sherrill, 186 n. 20, 191 n. 2
Cohen, Thomas, 199 n. 12
Cohn, Samuel K., 39, 169 n. 28, 176 n. 40, 179 n. 3, 184 n. 63, 195 n. 36, 200 n. 38, 208 n. 131
coitus interruptus, 148
Coleman, Emily, 149, 213 n. 27, 214 n. 42
Comba, Rinaldo, 205 n. 84
comparative history, 11–12, 14–15, 55, 134
condottieri (mercenaries), 19, 161–62
confession booths, 59
confraternities, 36, 60, 64, 86, 178 n. 66, 185 n. 8, 186 n. 19, 196 n. 46; new congregations, 62–65, 72, 186 n. 20

Connell, William, 134
conservatori dell'onestà di monasteri, 175 n. 26
conservatori delle leggi, 175 n. 26, 198 n. 5
consiglio maggiore, 123
consilia, 8
Consulte e Pratiche, 125, 134–36, 207 n. 121
contado (countryside of Florence), 22, 122, 132, 137, 145, 156, 208 n. 131, 211 n. 147; welfare of 121, 134
Cordigliano (Perugia), 51
Corneto (Pisa), 205 n. 86
corody, 93
corruption, abuse of office, 112–14, 204 n. 70, 212 n. 11
Corsica, 17
Cortona, 99, 134
Council of Trent, 35, 58, 61, 69, 72–73, 96. *See also* Counter Reformation
Counter Reformation, 2, 7–8, 15, 57–76, 92, 94–95, 184 n. 2, 186 n. 11; visitations, 1–2, 58–61, 84–85, 94, 185 nn. 5, 10, 186 n. 19, 187 n. 27
courtly love, 5
courts, princely, 169 n. 19
crime, 16; assault and battery, 25, 29, 32–33, 35–37, 176 nn. 38–39, 177 n. 61; burglary, 27, 208 n. 131; of clergy, 112; homicide (murder), 28–29, 35, 37, 112, 176 nn. 46–47, 208 n. 131; indebtedness, 25; inquisitions, 177 n. 50, 178 n. 65, 200 n. 34, 201 n. 42, 211 n. 157; patterns, 176 n. 38; rural, 27–28, 32–33; sex, 105, 127–28, 130–32, 136, 186 n. 12, 200 n. 36, 201 n. 38, 202 n. 52; theft, 27. *See also* adultery; blasphemy; gambling; incest; infanticide; pederastry; poisoning; rape; rebellion; sodomy
criminal statistics, 120–21, 125–26, 200 n. 38, 208 nn. 126, 131, 210 n. 146
Crogi, Passitea, 72
Croix, Alain, 179 n. 2

Dante Alighieri, 19
daughters, 52; as universal heirs, 182 n. 51, 215 n. 49
Davis, Natalie Z., 186 n. 15
Dean, Trevor, 131, 173 n. 6, 177 n. 59, 209 n. 140, 211 n. 157

death, 74
death penalties, 209 n. 141; beheading, 112, 133; cremation, 100–101; hanging, 131; live burial, 131, 210 n. 142. *See also* punishments
del Lungo, Isidoro, 19
Delumeau, Jean, 186 n. 11
democracy, 131
demography. *See* population
deschi da parto, 14
Diefendorf, Barbara, 172 n. 65, 197 n. 56
Di Simplicio, Oscar, 191 n. 54
disinheritance, 49–50
districtus, 134, 207 n. 116
dolls, 14
Dominicans, 108. *See also* friars; Santa Maria Novella
Dominici, Giovanni, 38
Don Giovanni, 116, 119
Donoratico, Count, 191 n. 3
dowry, 8, 12, 14, 30, 41, 50, 55, 73, 200 n. 30; *corredo*, 11; funds, 2, 42, 66, 77, 86, 88–93, 96, 194 nn. 31, 32; inflation, 11, 192 n. 13, 193 nn. 18, 19; law, 189 n. 38; *morgengabe* (countergifts, *antefacta*), 9, 13; mothers', 69; prices, 130; Roman, 10
drugs, 128
drunkenness, 116
Dubuis, Pierre, 205 n. 84
Duby, Georges, 15, 168 n. 16
Durkheim, Emile, 209 n. 140

ecclesiastical courts, 110, 112, 202 n. 55, 203 n. 64
education, 47, 68–69, 169 n. 25; catechism, 185 n. 10; Latin examinations, 59
Edward III, 85
elderly, 149, 162–64
Eleanor of Aquitaine, 5
England, 7, 57, 85, 105, 173 n. 4, 200 n. 37, 208 n. 125, 212 n. 1, 214 n. 29
Ercole, Francesco, 54, 183 n. 60
esecutore degli ordinamenti di giustizia, 21, 105, 174 n. 18
estimi (tax registers), 7, 22, 121, 137–38, 148, 151–52, 155, 160, 162–63, 165, 214 n. 35; *capi di famiglia*, 138, 152, 162
Europe, 201 n. 43

Fabbri, Lorenzo, 134
family, 38, 50, 68, 90; clans, 56, 128; coat of
 arms, 42, 46, 70, 197 n. 69; ideology, 41,
 52, 97, 197 n. 71; kinship, 118–19, 195
 n. 44; limitation, 138, 148–51, 157–65, 213
 n. 22; lineage, 10, 41, 51–52, 54–56, 64,
 70–71, 75, 77, 97; 190 n. 52, 197 n. 68
 (see also inheritance); names, 13, 28, 70,
 73, 176 n. 40; structure, 4
famine, 90, 195 n. 39, 215 n. 49
feminism, 15, 72–73
feudatories, 102, 122–25. See also
 aristocracy
Ficino, Marsilio, 30
fideicommissarii, 68
Field, Arthur, 207 n. 122
Figline, 210 n. 146
Firenzuola, 120, 206 n. 108
Firenzuola, Angelo, 204 n. 70
flags, 124
flattery, 104, 113, 116, 129
Florence, 39–45, 53–55, 83, 88, 95; coats
 of arms, 124; dominion, 122–36; finances, 133; government of the Minor
 Guilds, 37; historiography, 138. See also
 Albizzi; baptismal registers; capitano del
 popolo; contado; crime; districtus; esecu-
 tore degli ordinamenti; hospitals; law;
 Medici family; otto di guardia; podestà;
 vicariate courts
Foiano, 208 n. 127
Foligno, 203 n. 59
football hooliganism, 128
foreigners, 89
Forlì, 121
Foucault, Michel, 187 n. 24
foundling homes. See hospitals
France, 178 n. 72; historiography, 186 n. 16
Franceschi, Franco, 7
Francesco II (duke of Tuscany), 184 n. 3
Franciscans, 58; Observants, 86
Frassino, 132
friars, 111–12, 151. See also Dominicans;
 Santa Croce; Santa Maria Novella
Friuli, 102, 199 n. 26
Fucecchio, 108–9
funerals, 9
Fustel de Coulanges, N.D., 182 n. 47

gabelle dei contratti, 213 n. 16
gabelles, 123, 133, 141. See also taxation
gambling, 29, 198 n. 8
gangs, 177 n. 60
Garfagnana, 98
Gatrell, V.A.C., 200 n. 38
Gavitt, Philip, 215 n. 55
gender, 177 n. 58, 196 n. 46
Genicot, Léopold, 137
genitalia, 199 n. 22
Genoa, 9–12, 112, 178 n. 72, 193 n. 18, 197
 n. 71
geography, 133, 152
Germany, 7
ghettos, blacks, 128
Ghizzano, 109
Gill, Katherine, 94, 196 n. 55
Ginzburg, Carlo, 167 n. 6, 186 n. 11
Giordano da Pisa, Fra, 115, 120
Giotto, 43
Giovanna, Monna, 197 n. 63
Giudici degli Appelli e nullità, 98, 208 n. 127
godparents, 114
Goldberg, P.J.P., 7
Goldthwaite, Richard, 4, 10, 19, 22, 173
 n. 13, 175 n. 25
Gonzaga, Isabella, 19
Goodman, Jordan, 170 n. 37
Goody, Jack, 52
graves. See burial
Greek history, 131
Gregory XIII (pope), 58
Gregory, Heather, 192 n. 15, 193 n. 18
Grendi, Edoardo, 3, 105–6, 125
Guerra, Matteo, 185 n. 8
Guicciardini family, Niccolò, 44
Guidalotti family, 181 n. 15

Hajnal, J., 189 n. 37
Hanawalt, Barbara, 177 n. 61, 200 n. 37
Hatcher, John, 201 n. 44, 212 nn. 1, 3, 213
 n. 15
Heißler, Sabine, 173 n. 3, 202 n. 44
Henderson, John, 86
Herlihy, David, 4, 6–7, 14, 52, 134, 148–50,
 158, 161, 169 n. 28, 171 nn. 48, 56, 59; 178
 nn. 68, 72, 212 n. 3, 213 n. 29, 214 n. 41,
 215 n. 45

Hoffman, Philip, 179 n. 2, 186 n. 13, 15
homosexuality, 29–31, 111–12, 200 n. 32. *See also* rape; sodomy
honor, 37
hospitals, 40, 86–87; administration, 112–13; foundling homes, 106; Innocenti, 160, 215 n. 55; Misericordia of Prato, 156–57; San Gallo, 159–60, 215 n. 49; Santa Maria della Scala (Florence), 159
househeads. 162, 216 nn. 64, 65
households. *See* population
Hughes, Diane Owen, 4, 6, 9–10, 170 n. 48, 195 n. 44, 197 nn. 68, 71
humanism, 6, 125, 131
husbands, 58; gratitude of, 64–65, 67–69; as universal heirs, 182 n. 53

ideology, 125
illegitimacy, 46, 51
incest, 100, 102–3, 114–15, 129–30, 132–33, 199 n. 17, 204 n. 73
individualism, 56, 58, 96
infanticide, 2, 100–101, 105–6, 149–51, 157–58, 163, 199 n. 16, 200 n. 37, 201 n. 43, 208 n. 131, 214 n. 41, 215 n. 45
inflation, 130. *See also* dowry
inheritance: heirs, 44, 66; patrilineal descent, 1, 9–11, 91, 95, 170 n. 46, 181 n. 15, 182 nn. 47–48; patterns of, 39, 52; primogeniture, 182 n. 48; succession, 188 n. 33. *See also* family; property
Irmion, abbot, 150
Ischia, 119
Iuochis family, 180 n. 16
ius patronatus, 41

jewelry, 55
Joan of Arc, 169 n. 28
John XXII (pope), 86
John XXIII (pope; Baldassarre Cossa), 113
Johnson, Géraldine, 207 n. 116

Kelly, Joan Gadol, 4–6, 168 nn. 16, 19, 169 n. 28
Kent, Dale V., 4
Kent, Francis W., 4
kidnapping, 117
kin, kinship. *See* family

King, Margaret, 167 n. 5
Kirshner, Julius, 8, 54, 96, 170 n. 41
Klapisch-Zuber, Christiane, 4, 6, 9, 12–14, 118, 148–50, 158, 160–62, 164, 167 n. 4, 171 nn. 56, 59, 172 n. 66, 178 n. 72, 182 n. 56, 183 n. 60, 196 n. 56, 213 nn. 22, 29, 214 n. 41, 215 n. 51
Kuehn, Thomas, 8, 38, 170 n. 46, 179 n. 3, 182 n. 56

labor shortages, 7
Ladislao of Naples, 208 n. 127
Lamporecchio, 108
landlords, 146; women, 27
Languedoc, 17
Lansing, Carol, 95, 171 n. 64
la Roncière, Charles-M. de, 134, 175 n. 25
law, 17, 173 n. 3; agriculture, 175 n. 37; canon, 110, 115; enforcement, 198 n. 4 (*see also* lay chaplains); English, 200 n. 37; intestate, 52; Lombard, 9–10, 28, 54, 56, 183 n. 56, 184 n. 63; Roman, 8, 28, 54, 56, 184 n. 63. *See also* statutes
lay chaplains, 24, 175 nn. 29–30
Le Murate, 93
Lenman, Bruce, 106, 200 n. 38, 208 n. 126, 209 n. 140
Leonardo da Vinci, 30
Le Roy Ladurie, Emmanuel, 179 n. 2
lèse-majesté, 112
Lesnick, Daniel, 173 n. 4
letters, 20, 36, 173 n. 13
life cycle, 162
Livi-Bacci, Massimo, 191 n. 6
Livorno, 99, 134, 210 n. 146
Lombardi, Daniela, 8, 170 n. 39
London, 195 nn. 41, 44
low countries, 7
Lowe, K.J.P., 95, 173 n. 6, 177 n. 59, 203 n. 58
Lucca, 110–11, 117, 129, 177 n. 48, 209 n. 132
Lucignano, 119
Lundsgaarde, Henry, 176 n. 47
Lyon, 186 n. 13, 18

Machiavelli, Niccolò, 31, 35, 103, 105, 115
Maine, Sir Henry, 182 n. 47
Malthus, malthusian, 137, 148–49, 212 n. 3

Mammi, 117
Mangona, 115, 140, 158, 214 n. 31, 215 n. 47
manners, 29, 31, 35, 129, 199 n. 26
Mantua, 6
Maremma senese, 119
marriage, 9, 31, 90; age at, 189 n. 37; com-
 panionate, 65, 184 n. 2, 188 n. 32; — ties,
 11; remarriage, 65. *See also* adultery
married women, 35, 53; rights of, 47; sex
 with, 117, 205 n. 84. *See also* adultery
Marti, 114
Martin, John, 186 n. 15
Martines, Lauro, 4, 19, 90, 167 n. 4, 173
 n. 14, 202 n. 45, 204 n. 83
Marxist, 212 n. 3
marzocco, 124–25, 207 n. 116
Masetto da Lamporecchio, 107, 111, 202
 n. 44
Mazzetti family, 212 n. 14
Mazzi, Maria Serena, 100, 103, 105, 115, 169
 n. 19, 199 n. 12, 202 n. 44
McNeill, J. R., 150, 161
Medici family, rule of the, 20, 37–38, 99,
 126, 174 n. 20; Cosimo (il Vecchio), 21,
 28; Cosimo II, 188 n. 33; Giovenco di
 Giuliano, 13
memory, 45–46
mezzadria, mezzadri (sharecropping, share-
 croppers), 25, 68, 103, 146
Michelangelo (Buonarroti), 30
microhistory (new narrative history, microstoria), 3, 5–6, 106, 115, 120, 122, 138, 167
 nn. 5–6, 199 n. 9
migration, 2, 7, 142, 148, 151, 159–60,
 163–65, 213 n. 25
Milan, 84–85, 87, 112, 186 n. 12; war with,
 121, 123–26, 134, 140, 142–43, 158–59, 192
 n. 13, 207 n. 118
miserabili, 145, 157, 215 n. 43. *See also* poor
Modena, 121
Molho, Anthony, 8–9, 89, 134, 151, 170
 n. 47, 171 n. 59, 174 n. 14; 176 n. 40, 193
 nn. 16, 18, 200 n. 33, 208 n. 127
monasteries, monastic life, 51; 64, 151;
 monks in sex scandals, 111–12. *See also*
 Dominicans; Franciscans; friars; nuns
Montagna Pistoiese, 125, 142, 207 n. 121
Montaillou, 115

monte, 208 n. 127
Montecarelli, 158, 215 n. 47
Montecatini, 131
monte delle doti, 9, 90, 193 n. 16
Montegutolo, 117
Montespertoli, 112
Montetopoli, 205 n. 86
Montevarchi, 210 n. 146
Morelli, Giovanni di Pagolo, 12, 115
mothers, motherhood, 40, 52
mountains, mountaineers, 125, 131–33, 135–
 36, 137, 214 n. 31
Mugello, 44, 99, 129, 133, 138, 140, 158–60,
 162, 198 n. 1, 210 n. 146
Muir, Edward, 102, 167 n. 6, 199 n. 26
mundualdus, 9, 28, 34, 54, 170 n. 44, 176
 n. 42, 182 n. 56
mutilation. *See* punishments

Naples, 108
Nardi, Franco, 185 n. 10, 191 n. 55
neighborhood, 22, 172 n. 1, 191 n. 6
nobility. *See* aristocracy
Norberg, Kathryn, 179 n. 2, 186 n. 15, 187
 n. 24
notaries, 110, 113–14, 179 n. 3, 182 n. 56, 184
 n. 3, 196 n. 49, 204 n. 70, 212 n. 14; formula, 187 n. 29; as rebels, 203 n. 63
nuns, nunneries; 78–89, 92, 150–51, 186
 n. 21, 192 n. 15, 202 n. 53; Benedictines,
 192 n. 13; pious women, penitent
 women, *carcerate, romite*, 86–87, 94, 194
 n. 27; poor Clares, 108–10; regulations
 of, 194 n. 26; sex with, 107–11, 202 nn.
 44, 45, 203 n. 59

Oblelkvich, James, 186 n. 11
onestà, 175 n. 26, 178 n. 65, 209 n. 134
Orbatello, 164
otto di guardia, 21, 23–25, 35, 37, 105, 174
 n. 20, 178 n. 65, 209 n. 134

Padgett, John, 170 n. 47
Padua, 87
Palazzuolo, 123, 206 n. 108
Paolo da Certaldo, 14, 115, 119–20
Papi, Anna Benvenuti, 86, 196 n. 56
paraphernalia, 54

parental authority, 43, 180 n. 16

Paris, 44, 181 n. 16

parish (*popolo*), 24, 211 n. 157; records, 149

Parker, Geoffrey, 106, 200 n. 38, 208 n. 126, 209 n. 140

Parte Guelfa, 124, 131, 205 n. 91

Pastore, Alessandro, 125

patria potestà, 38

patronage, 112, 203 n. 66

peasants, peasantry, 47, 70, 137, 174 n. 19; communes, 122. See also *contado*; crime; mountains; population; rebellion; taxes

pederasty, 29–30, 177 n. 53

Perrot, Michelle, 15

Perugia, 39–40, 49–51, 54–55, 78, 83, 87, 94, 182 nn. 51, 53, 183 n. 57, 183 n. 61, 184 n. 63, 192 n. 11

Pescia, 114

Petrarch, Francesco, 77

Piccolomini family, 58, 74

Pietramala (Arezzo), 124

piety, 39, 52, 179 nn. 2, 5, 180 n. 8, 186 nn. 13, 15, 187 n. 28

pilgrimage, 107

pinzochere. See tertiaries

Pisa, 39–41, 49, 52–55, 87, 99–100, 107–8, 110, 132–34; 182 n. 55, 183 n. 56, 187 n. 57; *contado*, 210 n. 146; rebellion, 123; war with, 126, 159

Pistoia, 104–5, 134–35, 141, 148, 162

Pitti, Buonaccorso, 98, 112–13

pitture infamanti, 101, 199 n. 19

plague (pestilence), 41, 138, 147, 151, 158, 165, 187 n. 28, 191 n. 6, 213 n. 29, 214 n. 31; Black Death of 1348, 22, 24–25, 32, 53–54, 76–78, 84, 87, 88, 90, 134, 137; plague of 1362–63, 2, 39, 45, 47–48, 52, 76–77, 89–90, 92, 96

Pocock, John, 207 n. 123

Podere Fiorentino, 120, 122–23

podestà, 16–17, 21, 35–37, 99, 105, 115, 121–23, 129, 134, 141, 174 n. 18, 199 n. 16, 204 n. 77, 208 n. 131; 210 n. 146, 211 n. 147

Podio di Lucca, 53

Poggibonsi, 120

poisoning, 117, 205 n. 86

political crimes. *See* rebellion

polyptych of Saint-Germain-des-Prés, 149–50, 214 n. 42

Poni, Carlo, 167 n. 6

Ponsacco, 119

Ponte Bocci, 100

Pontenano, 123–25, 136

poor, poverty, 63, 146, 160, 191 n. 6; of Christ, 88, 96; girls, 66

poor Clares. *See* nuns

Poos, Lawrence, 173 n. 4, 208 n. 130

Poppi, 117

population, 31, 87, 89–90, 134, 137, 143–45, 152, 165, 178 n. 68, 188 n. 37, 212 n. 9; decline, 21–22, 25, 121–22, 158–59; 215 n. 47

Portico di Romagna, 115

Power, Eileen, 85

Prato, 16–17, 138, 146, 163, 214 n. 40

Pratomagno, 123, 132, 135–36, 210 n. 146

prices, grain, and other commodities, 90, 145, 175 n. 25, 212 n. 10

priests: absentee, 60; as rebels, 112, 124, 203 n. 63; in sex scandals, 108, 111, 114–15, 203 n. 70, 204 n. 74

primitive rebels, 34, 177 n. 59

primogeniture. *See* inheritance

prison, jail, 111, 113, 116. *See also* punishment

private spheres, 2, 167 n. 4

processions, 59, 186 n. 14

property: entail, 41, 52; rights, 47, 182 n. 47, 188 n. 33; values, 146, 192 n. 8, 196 n. 56

prostitution, 20, 29, 124, 175 n. 26, 202 n. 52, 209 n. 134

Provence, 186 n. 16

provvisioni, 121–22, 135–36, 147, 195 n. 35, 214 n. 31

punishments, 107; fines, 130, 176 n. 37, 200 n. 30, 202 n. 52; mutilation, 104, 130–31, 200 n. 28, 209 nn. 140–41 (*see also* castration); prison, 105, 111, 199 n. 25; torture, 130, 209 n. 140; whipping, 105, 114, 130–31, 200 n. 30. *See also* death penalties

Quaderni Storici, 5, 125

quantitative methods (history), 5, 14, 125

Quarto, 212 n. 14

Quinto, 212 n. 14

rape: heterosexual, 29–31, 37, 103, 107, 109, 115, 118, 120, 127, 129, 177 n. 51, 202 n. 52, 203 n. 59, 205 n. 91, 206 nn. 108–10, 209 nn. 133, 136–37, 209 n. 141; homosexual, 29

Rassina, 103

rebellion, peasant, 122–25, 127–31, 133–35, 142, 147, 198 n. 8, 203 n. 63, 207 n. 111, 208 n. 127, 211 n. 156. See also Ciompi

Reggiani, Flores, 8, 170 n. 39

regression analysis, 212 n. 7

Renaissance civility. See manners

Renaissance state, 3; state building, 125

representation, of women, 169 n. 23

Republican thought, 207 n. 123

Revel, Jacques, 167 n. 6

Ricasoli, 119

ricordanze (diaries), 12–14, 20, 149, 160, 164, 213 n. 22

Riemer, Eleanor, 52, 182 n. 52

ritual, 14

Rocca di San Casciano, 122, 124

Rocke, Michael, 131, 177 n. 52

Romagna, 119, 122–23, 132–35, 142, 158

Romano, Denis, 172 n. 74

romantic love, 130

Rome, 13, 87, 177 n. 58, 206 n. 104

romite. See nuns

Rosenthal, Elaine, 9, 170 n. 44, 182 n. 56

Rucellai family, 181 n. 15

Ruggiero, Guido, 120, 177 n. 51, 201 n. 38

rural bourgeoisie, 122

Sacchetti, Franco, 35, 43, 98, 111, 114–15, 177 n. 62, 198 nn. 4, 5, 199 n. 22, 202 n. 46, 204 nn. 73, 74, 77, 79, 205 n. 86

saints, 5, 169 nn. 19, 28; "santi vivi," 185 n. 10

salvation, 15, 75

Salviati, Jacopo, 98, 103, 200 n. 28

Sambuca (Pistoiese), 121, 123. See also Montagna Pistoiese

samples, sampling, 175 n. 34, 179 n. 4, 184 n. 3, 187 n. 26, 198 n. 8, 199 n. 15

San Casciano, 101

Sandri, Lucia, 160, 172 n. 74

San Giovanni day (festa di), 36, 141

San Gueninello, 101

San Miniato al Tedesco, 98, 100–102, 107, 113, 115, 129, 132, 198 n. 1, 199 n. 25

San Severino, 116

Santa Chiara, 87

Santa Croce (Florence), 30, 180 n. 8. See also Franciscans

Santa Maria a Monte, 129, 206 n. 108, 209 n. 133

Santa Maria della Scala (Siena), 87. See also hospitals

Santa Maria Novella: church of, 43; friars at, 180 n. 14

Santa Maria Novella, quarter of, 159

Santa Maria Nuova, 87, 179 n. 4

Sant'Ambrogio, parish of, 16, 172 n. 1

Saone, 206 n. 109

Sarzana, 112, 206 n. 109

Scarperia, 133, 199 n. 16

Schen, Claire, 195 nn. 41, 44

secret meetings, 123

Sesto, 212 n. 14

Senni, 199 n. 16

Sensi, Mario, 86

Sercambi, Giovanni, 35, 111, 115, 117, 199 nn. 17, 22, 202 n. 45, 203 n. 70

Sermini, Gentile, 111, 151, 156, 214 n. 31

servants, domestic servitude, 8, 14, 163, 165, 172 n. 74; male, 111. See also wet nurses

sex ratios, 106, 149–59, 161–64, 213 n. 27, 215 n. 49

sexual mores, 135

sexual violence, 191 nn. 54–55. See also crime; incest; rape; wife beating

Sharpe, J. A., 106, 201 nn. 38, 39

Shearman, John, 208 n. 128

shepherdesses, 119–20

Siena, 39–41, 50, 52, 55, 57–76, 85, 88, 90, 117, 179 n. 3; war with, 126, 187 nn. 23, 28

Skinner, Quentin, 207 n. 123

slander, 16, 173 n. 4

slavery, 164

sodomy, 29, 104, 112, 116, 205 n. 88; heterosexual, 119, 149. See also homosexuality; rape

soldiers, 204 n. 70

sons, 40, 215 n. 45. See also inheritance

Spain, 51

Spierenburg, Peter, 176 n. 46

Statutes, 9; Apricale, 206 n. 109; Arezzo, 183 n. 57, 208 n. 132; Firenzuola, 206 n. 108; Florence, of 1322–25, 175 n. 37, 176 n. 44, 206 n. 108; Florence, of 1415, 28, 120, 175 n. 37, 176 n. 44, 203 n. 64, 206 nn. 108–9; Foligno, 203 n. 59; Lucca, 177 n. 48, 209 n. 132; Palazzuola, 206 n. 108; Perugia, 183 n. 57; Pisa, 182 n. 55, 183 n. 56, 187 n. 57; Santa Maria a Monte, 206 n. 108, 209 n. 133; Saone, 206 n. 109; Sarzana, 206 n. 109; Siena, 65, 67, 183 n. 56, 189 n. 38; Tuscany, 188 n. 33; Villanuova d'Asti, 205 n. 86

Stefani, Marchionne di Coppo, 22

Stern, Laura, 174 n. 20, 203 n. 64

Steward, George R., 167 n. 6

Stone, Lawrence, 5, 57, 65, 184 n. 2

street theater, 125

Strocchia, Sharon, 9, 170 n. 46

Strozzi family, 117; Alessandra, 19, 37, 173 n. 13, 174 n. 14; Alexio, 43, 180 n. 14; Antonio, 193 n. 18

Subbiano, 134–35

synods (Siena), 58

Takahashi, Tomoko, 160, 215 n. 56

Tarlati, Tarlatus, 195 n. 32

Tarugi, Francesco Maria, 59, 185 n. 10, 186 n. 19

taverns, 30

taxes, taxation, 121, 134, 137, 145, 158–60; assessments, 212 n. 8; collectors, collecting, 122, 148, 162; concessions, incentives, 122, 136, 151, 195 n. 35, 207 n. 113; fraud, 113, 203 n. 69; inequality, 143, 146; law, 160; petitions, 207 n. 118, 215 n. 52; policy, 124, 134, 147; rates, 138–43, 212 n. 8; records, 137; underregistration, 150–51. See also *catasti*; *estimi*; gabelles

technology, 8

Terranuova, 116

tertiaries, 46, 71, 94, 196 n. 55–56

testaments, 2, 39, 58–59, 179 n. 3, 191 n. 3; demographic contingencies, 70; language of, 50; mutual, 67; nonpious bequests, 61; pious bequests, 90–93; restrictive clauses, 40, 43–50, 96, 179 n. 6

Thomas Aquinas, Saint, 181 n. 14

Toubert, Pierre, 214 n. 42

transhumance, 119–20

Trappola, 117

Treggiaia, 116

Tre Maggiori, 121–22, 195 n. 35

Trexler, Richard, 6, 30–31, 36, 84–85, 159–60, 164, 169 n. 28; 178 n. 67, 192 n. 15, 193 n. 16, 215 n. 42

tyranny, 123–25

Ubaldini, lords, 122, 158; wars with, 215 n. 47

Ubertini, lords, 122, 158, 210 n. 146

ufficiali di notte, 30, 175 n. 26, 178 n. 65

unmarried women (*puellae*), sex with, 119–20, 204 n. 70, 206 n. 99

vagabonds, 109, 116, 119

Valdarno inferiore, 107–9, 112, 119, 132–33, 138, 198 n. 4, 205 n. 91, 210 n. 146

Valdarno superiore, 116–17, 119, 131, 134, 136, 160, 204 n. 70, 209 n. 134

Valdelsa, 99, 112, 198 n. 1, 210 n. 146

Val Demone (Sicily), 147

Val di Chiana, 159

Valdinievole, 114, 129, 131, 159

Valle fiorentine, 135

Vasari, Giorgio, 1

Venice, 9–13, 85, 94, 120, 168 n. 10, 171 n. 56, 172 n. 74, 177 n. 51, 193 n. 19, 201 n. 38, 209 n. 137

Verghereto, 119

Verona, 178 n. 68

Viazza, Pier Paolo, 213 n. 25

vicariate courts, 36, 98, 107, 110, 122, 128, 134, 147, 164, 178 n. 65, 198 n. 1, 201 n. 42, 210 n. 146, 211 n. 157, 212 n. 11, 216 n. 70

Vignale, 119

Villa Marsane, 132

Villani, Giovanni, 84, 86

Villanuova d'Asti, 205 n. 86

Vinci, 42

violence, 103. *See also* death penalties; punishment; rape; rebellion; war

Volterra, 123, 134, 136; rebellion, 211 n. 156

Vovelle, Michel, 39, 186 n. 16

wages, 8, 146, 164–65, 176 n. 37, 201 n. 44
Walzer, Michael, 184 n. 2
war, warfare, 121, 135, 137, 147, 158, 165, 189
    n. 37, 208 n. 127, 215 n. 52. *See also*
    Milan; Pisa; Siena; Ubaldini
wealth, 138, 140, 142, 146–47, 159, 162, 196
    nn. 49, 50, 216 n. 61
Weaver, Elissa, 202 n. 53, 203 n. 58
wedding, 13
Weissman, Ronald, 36
wet nurses, 14, 160. *See also* servants
Wiesner, Mary, 170 n. 30
widowers, 162, 170 n. 41
widows, widowhood, 10, 12–13, 35, 138, 162,
    164, 177 n. 62, 204 nn. 82, 83, 206 n. 98,

212 n. 12; settlements for, 44, 53, 55, 65,
    67, 183 nn. 57–58, 60, 61; sex with, 115,
    117–19; as universal heirs, 188 n. 37
wife beating, 35, 116, 191 n. 54, 205 n. 86
witchcraft, 105, 164, 216 n. 70
wives, 58; gratitude of, 67; newlyweds,
    115–16. *See also* adultery; married women
workers, work, women, 6–8, 171 n. 48;
    German, 7
Wright, A. D., 185 n. 10

Zarri, Gabriella, 6, 12, 84, 86, 94, 168 n. 19,
    192 n. 13
Zerner, Monique, 214 n. 42
Zorzi, Andrea, 131, 134, 175 n. 30, 209 n. 140

Library of Congress Cataloging-in-Publication Data

Cohn, Samuel Kline.
Women in the streets : essays on sex and power in Renaissance Italy /
Samuel K. Cohn Jr.
p.   cm.
Includes bibliographical references and index.
ISBN 0-8018-5308-7 (hc : alk. paper). — ISBN 0-8018-5309-5 (pbk. : alk. paper)
1. Women—Italy—Social conditions.   2. Women—History—Renaissance, 1450–1600.
3. Renaissance—Italy.   4. Italy—Social life and customs.   I. Title.
HQ1149.I8C64   1996
305.42′0945—dc20   96-11611